John Wesley and the Education of Children

Scholars have historically associated John Wesley's educational endeavours with the boarding school he established at Kingswood, near Bristol, in 1746, primarily because of the importance he himself placed on it. Nevertheless, his educational endeavors extended well beyond this single institution, since they were based not just on a desire for academic advancement, but were motivated by individualistic, familial and evangelical considerations. By examining all aspects of his work, this book sets out Wesley's thinking and practice concerning child-rearing and education, particularly in relation to gender and class, in its broader eighteenth-century social and cultural context.

Drawing on writings from Churchmen, Dissenters, economists, philosophers and reformers as well as educationalists, this study demonstrates that the political, religious and ideological backdrop to Wesley's work was neither static nor consistent. It also highlights Wesley's eighteenth-century fellow Evangelicals including Lady Huntingdon, John Fletcher, Hannah More and Robert Raikes to demonstrate whether Wesley's thinking and practice around schooling was in any way unique.

This study sheds light on the attitude of Wesley and his contemporaries to children, child-rearing, piety and education and demonstrates how Wesley's attitude to education was influencing and influenced by the society in which he lived and worked. As such, it will not only be useful to academics with an interest in Methodism, but to those interested in broader aspects of eighteenth-century education and schooling, as well as those concerned with attitudes towards children, gender, class and religiosity.

Linda A. Ryan is a mature researcher with an interest in early Methodism, and more specifically eighteenth-century attitudes to children, education and gender. She has previously published articles in *Wesley & Methodist Studies* and the *Journal of Religious History, Literature and Culture*.

Routledge Methodist Studies Series

Series Editor: William Gibson, Director of the Oxford Centre for Methodism and Church History, Oxford Brookes University, UK

Editorial Board:

Ted A. Campbell, Professor of Church History, Perkins School of Theology, Southern Methodist University, USA

David N. Hempton, Dean, Harvard Divinity School, Harvard University, USA

Priscilla Pope-Levison, Associate Dean, Perkins School of Theology, Southern Methodist University, USA

Martin Wellings, Superintendent Minister of Oxford Methodist Circuit and Past President of the World Methodist Historical Society, UK.

Karen B. Westerfield Tucker, Professor of Worship, Boston University, USA

Methodism remains one of the largest denominations in the USA and is growing in South America, Africa and Asia (especially in Korea and China). This series spans Methodist history and theology, exploring its success as a movement historically and in its global expansion. Books in the series will look particularly at features within Methodism which attract wide interest, including: the unique position of the Wesleys; the prominent role of women and minorities in Methodism; the interaction between Methodism and politics; the 'Methodist conscience' and its motivation for temperance and pacifist movements; the wide range of Pentecostal, holiness and evangelical movements; and the interaction of Methodism with different cultures.

Titles in the series:

Methodist Heritage and Identity
Brian E. Beck

John Wesley and the Education of Children
Gender, Class and Piety
Linda A. Ryan

John Wesley, Practical Divinity and the Defence of Literature
Emma Salgård Cunha

For more information on this series visit: https://www.routledge.com/religion/series/AMETHOD

John Wesley and the Education of Children
Gender, Class and Piety

Linda A. Ryan

LONDON AND NEW YORK

First published 2018
by Routledge

2 Park Square, Milton Park, Abingdon, Oxfordshire OX14 4RN
52 Vanderbilt Avenue, New York, NY 10017

Routledge is an imprint of the Taylor & Francis Group, an informa business

First issued in paperback 2019

Copyright © 2018 Linda A. Ryan

The right of Linda A. Ryan to be identified as author of this work has been asserted by her in accordance with sections 77 and 78 of the Copyright, Designs and Patents Act 1988.

All rights reserved. No part of this book may be reprinted or reproduced or utilised in any form or by any electronic, mechanical, or other means, now known or hereafter invented, including photocopying and recording, or in any information storage or retrieval system, without permission in writing from the publishers.

Notice:
Product or corporate names may be trademarks or registered trademarks, and are used only for identification and explanation without intent to infringe.

British Library Cataloguing in Publication Data
A catalogue record for this book is available from the British Library

Library of Congress Cataloging in Publication Data
Names: Ryan, Linda A., author.
Title: John Wesley and the education of children : gender, class, and piety / Linda A. Ryan.
Description: first [edition]. | New York : Routledge, 2017. | Series: Routledge Methodist studies series | Includes bibliographical references and index.
Identifiers: LCCN 2017023984 | ISBN 9781138092365 (hardback : alk. paper) | ISBN 9781315107516 (ebook)
Subjects: LCSH: Wesley, John, 1703-1791. | Education. | Christian education of children.
Classification: LCC BX8495.W5 R93 2017 | DDC 371.0092–dc23
LC record available at https://lccn.loc.gov/2017023984

ISBN: 978-1-138-09236-5 (hbk)
ISBN: 978-0-367-89036-0 (pbk)

Typeset in Bembo
by Taylor & Francis Books

Contents

Acknowledgements vii

Introduction 1
Historiography 1
John Wesley (1703–1791) 3
Historical context of John Wesley's work 5
Overview of chapters 8

1 **Child-rearing and education in eighteenth-century England** 13
  Concepts of childhood, gender and class 13
  Gendering education 18
  Pauper children – eighteenth-century philanthropy and education 24
  Conclusion 29

2 **Influences that helped shape John Wesley's educational thinking** 36
  Wesley's thinking on child-rearing and education 36
  Wesley's Anglican upbringing at Epworth 41
  Wesley at Charterhouse and Oxford 45
  Non-Anglican influences on Wesley's educational principles 48
  Conclusion 50

3 **The implementation of John Wesley's thinking on education** 58
  Education of girls and young women 59
  Tension between academic learning and piety 62
  Ascetic self-denial 67
  Religious revivals 68
  Wesley as author, editor and distributor of books 72
  Conclusion 76

4 Educating pauper children: 1723–1780 — 83

Children of the poor 'deserving' of an education 83
Evangelising the colliers at Kingswood 87
Wesley's preaching house schools 90
Wesleyan day schools for the poor 95
Conclusion 98

5 Kingswood boarding school: 1746–1780 — 105

Wesley's educational 'model' of piety, manliness and academic learning 105
Authority and management in the early years 108
Charles Wesley, Kingswood School and new concepts of childhood 111
Comparison with grammar schools, universities and Dissenting academies 114
Conclusion 120

6 Growing tension between education and Evangelism: 1760–1791 — 127

Importance of family 127
Drive to train preachers 132
Trevecka College 136
'Minutes Controversy' of 1770 139
Conclusion 141

7 Educating pauper children after 1780 — 148

Emergence of the Sunday school movement 149
John Wesley and Methodist Sunday schools 153
Female educators and role models 157
Sunday schools in a post-revolutionary age 163
Conclusion 165

Conclusion — 172

Bibliography — 181
Index — 197

Acknowledgements

My grateful thanks are warmly extended to Professor William Gibson, and Professor Joanne Brown of Oxford Brookes University, who have been unerringly generous in their support and encouragement for my work. Their level of expertise, which has significantly influenced my research, has been outstanding, and it has been a privilege and pleasure to work with them.

I am also indebted to Dr Peter Forsaith of the Oxford Centre for Methodism and Church History for allowing me access to archive material, and whose knowledge and guidance has been invaluable.

My grateful thanks go also to staff at the Methodist Archives and Research Centre, John Rylands University Library, University of Manchester for helping me track down valuable archive material, and to the archivist at Kingswood School, Bath, for her help and support during my research visits.

Linda Ryan
May 2017

Introduction

By taking account of the work of eighteenth-century educationalists, and of new forms of schooling, particularly that of the poor, this book develops a body of knowledge which for the first time accurately places John Wesley's educational programme in its broad social and cultural context. The focus of this study is not solely on one gender or social construct, but it examines the impact of Wesley's thinking and practice across social and gender divides. Only by doing so can its conclusions be said to have been fully tested. The originality of this book lies in the way it compares and contrasts Wesley's thinking and practice with that of his contemporaries working in the field of education. By taking account of recent scholarship on eighteenth-century attitudes to children, particularly children of the poor, the family and issues surrounding gender, new insights are offered into Wesley's attitude to the young, parenting, gender and class distinctions, as well as education and religiosity.

This book argues that although John Wesley took an interest in how children were raised and educated throughout his life, his thinking was complex and in some ways contradictory. In many respects, his views were grounded in Puritan traditions of the seventeenth century which emphasised original sin, and failed to acknowledge new concepts of the innocence of childhood which became more fashionable in the eighteenth century. Despite this, he advocated the thinking of Locke, and encouraged reading and learning. His Arminian philosophy championed self-improvement and gave his followers, particularly women and the poor, an invitation for self-advancement. Nevertheless, the evidence demonstrates that his educational practice was more strongly Evangelical than intellectual, more pious than academic.

Historiography

Over the last two decades Wesleyan scholarship has witnessed an increasing sophistication in the interpretation of Wesley's writings. There has been a growth in interdisciplinary and contextual studies, with scholarship becoming much more nuanced. Such an approach needs to be extended to John Wesley's educational work, which is currently fragmented and incomplete. Indeed, Alfred H. Body's *John Wesley and Education,* published in 1936, stands virtually alone in this field.

Influential scholarship of the 1950s and 1960s was unashamedly critical of Wesley's educational endeavours. J. H. Plumb claimed that Methodism 'was at its worst in its attitude to education'.[1] E. P. Thompson, who dominated scholarship for thirty to forty years, claimed in *The Making of the English Working Class*, first published in 1963, that 'Methodism was a strongly anti-intellectual influence, from which British popular culture has never wholly recovered'.[2] Drawing on an extensive range of eighteenth-century primary source material, both published and unpublished, including writings from Churchmen as well as Dissenters; economists, philosophers and reformers as well as educationalists, this study seeks to provide an accurate and balanced assessment both of Wesley's significance in the field of child-rearing and education, and his role in the development of educational initiatives.

Methodist scholars have historically placed great significance on Susanna Wesley's 'education letter' of 24 July 1732. Indeed, it has not only been seen as one of her most important pieces of writing, but is regarded as the model on which her son John based his education practice.[3] Although frequently criticised as austere and puritanical, by applying a more sophisticated approach to her writings, and building on the recent work of Elizabeth Lynch, Martha Bowden and Claire Potter, chapter two argues that not only did Susanna Wesley recognise the individuality of the child, but she regarded her children with affection and respect.

John Wesley's educational endeavours have predominantly been associated with the boarding school he established at Kingswood, near Bristol, in 1746, principally because of the importance he himself placed on it. Nevertheless, the school, even at its peak, educated no more than fifty pupils at any one time. Indeed, it is clear that Wesley's work extended well beyond the confines of the school that scholars have for many years used as a bench-mark by which to judge his educational practice. Arthur Ives, in his publication *Kingswood School in Wesley's Day and Since* comments of the adjoining colliers' school established at Kingswood in 1739: 'the story has an interest of its own, but to follow it here would take us off at a tangent'.[4] Research contained in this book suggests that to overlook Wesley's work with children of the poor at Kingswood, and elsewhere, is short-sighted, albeit perhaps understandable as source material is limited.

Equally important to this study is the recent work of non-Methodist scholars. Joanne Bailey's research highlights the importance of parental responsibility, and the significance of the parent–child relationship; it also draws attention to the importance of gender in discussions about child-rearing and education.[5] Rebecca Davis argues that eighteenth-century women commentators on education such as Hannah More and Sarah Trimmer carried an implicit authority in their writing, based on their accepted function as maternal educators.[6] Despite this, existing scholarship has frequently overlooked the provision of education for girls. This is primarily because, over the course of the eighteenth century, female education was largely overshadowed by an emphasis on the training of boys. This study seeks to redress this imbalance. Indeed, although

Porter argues that female education was primarily designed to equip young women for their primary role as wife and mother, research contained in this book suggests that the level of female education has been frequently underestimated.[7] Finally, of significance to how the work of Evangelicals is viewed, recent research argues that opinions of the eighteenth-century Church as hopelessly divided, and of clergy as being lazy and low in doctrine have, almost without exception, been redressed by modern scholarship.[8]

John Wesley (1703–1791)

John Wesley was one of the leading figures of his age. He was born in Epworth, Lincolnshire in 1703. Not only were both his parents, Samuel and Susanna Wesley, influential in his upbringing, but John Wesley grew up in an atmosphere of piety and learning. Educated at home until the age of ten, he attended Charterhouse School from January 1714, before going up to Christ Church, Oxford, in 1720. He was a Fellow of Lincoln College from 1726, and was ordained a priest of the Church of England in 1728. Throughout his life, Wesley maintained an allegiance to the Church of England, and espoused Christian values of virtue, morality and piety, alongside Puritan values of industriousness, sobriety, frugality and temperance.[9] He considered education not merely as a means of expanding intellect, but as an essential part of moral and spiritual development, arguing that the sole end of life, and consequently of education, was to prepare for eternity.[10]

Wesley was a prodigious reader. Although this enabled him to draw on a range of philosophies and practices in order to construct his own thinking, he nevertheless had firmly held views. By 1732, his growing interest in the upbringing and education of children prompted him to write to his mother asking her for an account of her Epworth system, which he later published in his *Journal* for 1749, and in *The Arminian Magazine* of 1784.[11] Wesley was also a prodigious writer. His *Journal*, published in twenty one instalments between 1740 and 1791, ran to over a million printed words.[12] He was the editor, author or publisher of more works than any other single figure in eighteenth-century Britain.[13] The very abundance of detail in Wesley's *Journals* and other writings provides a useful insight into the period.[14] Yet this is not unproblematic evidence. Rodell argues that 'a collection of quotations can be put together implying his support for all manner of often contradictory opinions, and shorn of their setting, these opinions can take on a wholly misleading significance'.[15] Furthermore, Gregory argues that Wesley's version of events can frequently be shown to have been highly partial.[16] His known propensity for editorial licence and close control of his projects and papers necessitates a degree of caution.[17]

Moral and spiritual development were essential elements of education because, for Wesley, salvation lay not in the Calvinist doctrine of the predestination of God, but an individual's pursuit of a life of holiness.[18] Although he upheld the Arminian doctrine of 'free will', Wesley argued that without the constraints of reason, this manifested itself in the young as 'self-will', something to be conquered if children were to be governed by the reason and piety of their parents. While the salvation of the child's soul depended on piety and virtue, learned in relationship with and by example of parents, this did not, in Wesley's view, necessitate the sort of deep emotional attachment brought about by parenthood. Wesley saw no place for a 'softening' in the relationship between parents and their offspring.[19] Indeed, he condemned 'good men' for being too 'easy' and for failing to 'restrain their children from evil'; 'a wise parent', he contended, 'should begin to break their child's will the first moment it appears'.[20] While this sentiment has been seen as austere, Wesley's methods were not based solely on punishment. Writing that 'the duty of educating children requires first encouragement, second correction', he stated:

> We should endeavour to make children in love with duty, by offering them rewards and invitations, and whenever they do well, encouraging them to go on… the second means is correction… when all fair means prevail not, then there is a necessity of using sharper, and let that be first tried in words, I mean not by railing and foul language, but in sober, yet sharp reproof, but if that fail too, then proceed to blows, 'He that spareth his rod hateth his son'.[21]

Indeed, despite being frequently condemned as unfeeling, Wesley's view was not unusual for the period; among those who held similar views was Quaker George Fox who claimed: 'Withhold not correction from thy child, for if thou beatest him with the rod he shall not die'.[22]

In regarding education as training for a life of holiness as well as academic attainment, Wesley's educational practice was frequently characterised by tension between piety and learning; that is, a desire to instruct children in Christian values of virtue, morality and piety, while at the same time providing academic learning conforming to these values. Although he demanded a rigorous standard of education, Wesley consistently employed Masters for their piety rather than their pedagogical credentials; pupils were commended for displays of religious fervour, rather than their intellectual achievement. Determined to challenge what he saw as the debauched and ruinous nature of eighteenth-century schools and universities, Wesley built a strong and rational foundation of religious instruction into the educational programme he instigated at the boarding school he established in Kingwood in 1746. While Wesley's decision to admit a small number of girls into the school in the early years, and his support of small boarding schools run by Methodists, might at first appear progressive, it is clear that he did not consider boys and girls as educational equals. Although he was a supporter of female education, Wesley's primary concern was to instil attitudes of piety and virtue, alongside such knowledge as was necessary to secure salvation. Nevertheless, such learning not only enabled girls to develop spiritually, but to expand their intellect.

A firm advocate of family religion, Wesley argued that it was the responsibility of parents to instruct their children from an early age in the family home.

He also acknowledged that this was not always possible. Particularly concerned for the plight of the poor, Wesley recognised the need to open day schools that their offspring might receive religious education. Although he 'determined to have them taught... to read, write and cast accounts', Wesley argued that children of the poor were to remain submissive, obedient and content, even though they had 'little or nothing in the world', for they had 'more than they deserve'.[23] In line with sentiments of the day, while boys in these schools were educated 'fit for any trade', all that was expected of girls was that their education 'fit them for the enjoyment of God in eternity'.[24] Religious instruction was designed to protect the poor against the dangerous influences of a non-Christian way of life, rather than ameliorate their condition, or give them aspirations above their station.

Evangelicals were concerned with reforming the character of the individual, not bringing about social change. In the closing decades of Wesley's life, there was a growing tension between a desire to 'form' the child, and a drive to 'reform' their parents. Family religion enabled faith to be enacted and reinforced outside the Church and school, and Wesley, like many of his fellow Evangelicals, did not confine himself to these institutions. Increasingly, he sought to strengthen family religion, built not only on the education of children, but the Evangelism of their parents. As a result, there was a growing need within the Methodist movement for men trained not only to preach, but to teach. Wesley's preachers, many of whom were from humble backgrounds, were encouraged by him to improve their education by reading and study. They were also encouraged to improve their learning by attending his boarding school at Kingswood. Towards the end of his life, Wesley's 'educational model' not only adapted to accommodate his preachers, but increasingly became a place where they might also send their sons.

Historical context of John Wesley's work

In order to accurately place John Wesley's educational programme in its broad social and cultural context, it is important to understand eighteenth-century perceptions of children, education, gender, piety and class. Underpinning an understanding of attitudes towards the young in the eighteenth century is the fact that historians have consistently identified the period as a watershed in thinking concerning children and childhood. Over the course of the century, philosophical works by John Locke and Jean-Jacques Rousseau provided a foundation for new concepts of childhood which not only acknowledged the individuality of the child, but by arguing that children were inherently innocent, recognised their potential for goodness.

Indeed, Locke's *Some Thoughts Concerning Education*, published in 1693, rapidly became a reference point for new ideas on education, and while it has historically been largely cited as a compendium for the fashioning of a gentleman, it was in fact written with both sons and daughters in mind.[25] Although Rousseau's *Emile*, published in 1762, reignited debate concerning child-rearing and education, his view that 'a woman's education must be planned in relation to man... She will always be in subjection to a man and she will never be free to set her own opinion above his', did little to change existing assumptions about female education.[26] These new concepts of childhood were not universally accepted and, with at least two hundred treatises on education published in England between 1762 and 1800, the debate they ignited was significant.

Among influential writers in the eighteenth century whose views on children and education were taken seriously were the political philosopher Bernard Mandeville and economist Adam Smith. As the oldest and largest sponsor of educational institutions, views expressed by leaders of the Church commanded attention; leading Anglican figures including White Kennett, Thomas Hayter and Francis Brokesby wrote and preached on the subject, as did prominent Dissenting figures, including Phillip Doddridge and Isaac Watts. The work of educational reformers such as Jonas Hanway and Sarah Trimmer was important, particularly as far as children of the poor were concerned.

Education was not solely confined to institutions. Parental responsibilities played an important part in the upbringing and early education of children. That children should attend Church and read the Bible was considered essential and printed catechisms providing questions and answers between parent and child were readily available. Parents were expected to read, pray, catechise and instruct their children in acceptable patterns of Christian behaviour.[27] High mortality rates in the eighteenth century meant that many children lost a parent in childhood. When possible, mothers generally had responsibility for the nurture of young children; once they had reached the age of seven, fathers made decisions concerning their offspring's discipline, training, education and future occupation.[28]

In a time pre-dating Locke, children had been largely regarded as the 'property' of their parents, or those *in loco parentis* at school or in the workplace.[29] Puritan thought regarded children as 'tarnished by original sin' and 'like a young colt, wanton and foolish, till he be broken by education and correction'[30] and Porter argues that this often led to child-rearing practices being stern and brutal.[31] New concepts of childhood not only softened attitudes, but raised questions among parents as to the degree of authority or liberty to be exercised in raising and educating children.

Those families that possessed the skills of reading and writing prized them and sought to pass them on to their offspring. Indeed, literacy became increasingly important to farmers and labourers in the face of economic change. Letter-writing aided and encouraged literacy by offering constant practice in writing; it was also an aid to piety. Not only could letters disseminate religious news, but they were a place where the correspondent could focus on God.[32] Over the course of the century a plethora of cheap reading materials became available, sufficient to stimulate many of the poor into gaining elements of literacy.[33] Children's books were predominantly designed for instruction, whether religious, moral or practical. To love books in youth was regarded as an indication of potential spirituality, and writers of memoirs and obituaries frequently noted with satisfaction that their subjects had been readers as children, isolated from the childish play of their fellows.[34]

While existing concepts of education were largely those inherited from the Tudors and Stuarts, the growing affluence and influence of the 'middling sort' brought about changes in educational institutions, which were reshaped to meet the needs of people anxious that their offspring acquire useful skills and social graces befitting their new-found genteel status.[35] The rise of prosperity resulting from the growth of mercantile capitalism, particularly during the 1750s and 1760s, meant that by the end of the century there was a powerful and extensive middle class whose enterprise, skill or circumstances had elevated them above the 'labouring poor'. This 'middling sort' had a wide range of incomes and a variety of professions and occupations, and included merchants and farmers who had transformed the faces of both urban and agrarian society.[36] In looking for an education for their sons that would fit them for a life in commerce, Dissenting academies offered parents an alternative curriculum to the grammar schools and universities of the day. Georgian society regarded effeminacy as the feminisation or weakening of men, and the risk to society of boys unable to mature into men of sterling character was regarded as profound.[37] Despite the anarchic and immoral nature of public schools and universities, not only did they offer a classical education, but supporters argued that they taught manly ideals of competition, endurance and self-reliance.

Piety and morality were essential elements in the assessment of 'character' in eighteenth-century society. Indeed, religion was central to people's lives, individually and collectively, in local communities and nationally. In the early part of the century nearly everyone was a member of the Church of England; less than six per cent of the population of England and Wales dissented from the Established Church; even in the 1790s, over 90% of the population at least nominally belonged.[38] The Bishop of Gloucester, William Warburton described the Establishment as a mutual contract between the State and the majority Church based upon common interests and utility.[39] Although there remained a general consensus that Church and State were interdependent, over the course of the century, religion increasingly became a matter of social status.[40] From the Toleration Act of 1689, legal relief afforded through annual Indemnity Acts gave Dissenters freedom to worship in their chapels, liberty to run schools and a good deal of practical power at the local level, despite theoretically being denied the full rights of citizenship by the operation of the Test Act of 1673 and the Corporation Act of 1661.[41]

Although Holmes describes the class structure in eighteenth-century Britain as a 'thing of infinite subtlety', there emerged from the mid-century onwards a growing class of people for whom poverty became a 'whole life' experience, and whose poverty was passed to their children.[42] There was a clear demarcation between those who paid poor-rates and those who were not only exempt from payment but who were all too likely to find themselves applying for relief.[43] Clergy asserted that poverty was the result not of sin, but of God's providential plan for the world; it was regarded as God's gracious method of allowing men to win salvation in the exercise of their mutual ties of obligation and gratitude.[44] The provision for the poor fell within the Poor Laws, which, although offering a 'safety net' to the poor, at no time gave them a personal 'right' to relief.[45] Matthew Decker claimed in *An Essay on the Causes of the Decline of Foreign Trade* of 1744: 'Not only did the regular care afforded by parish relief encourage sloth, but charity itself, given indiscriminately to beggars or through casual solicitation, contributed to the same evil'.[46]

Every child who died young, or who followed his or her parents into dependency and poverty, was a cumulative drain on society; children's potential needed to be harnessed though instruction both in the ways of the Church and in a work ethic.[47] In 1746, White Kennett declared in *The Christian Scholar*, 'Nothing has so much corrupted the latter age and debauched the morals of our present generation; nothing so much, as irreverence... to God, atheism, profaneness and all manner of irreligion'.[48] The inculcation of Christian values was designed to regulate and reform the poor and to teach the labouring classes to accept their lot and not to grieve for what they could not have.[49] Charity schools provided a form of inexpensive poor relief where, it was argued, instruction in the Bible and catechism would build up a God-fearing population, guard children against habits of sloth and debauchery and instil in them obedience to their superiors.[50] Educating the young to be virtuous and industrious was not only regarded by many as a prudent way of maintaining social order, it was also seen as a means by which these values might be passed on to their parents.[51] Despite this, Mandeville argued that educating the poor simply increased their desire for material things; and by bringing them into closer physical or intellectual proximity to their superiors, the nation would lose the sort of labourers it needed.[52]

During the 1780s and 1790s anxiety about the poor mounted among the ruling classes on several counts. While the economist Adam Smith argued that a growing population was a sign of an expanding economy, anxieties about the perceived fecklessness of the poor exposed fears about the problems arising from the increasing and unsustainable population.[53] That pauper children were more visible and audible than they had ever been raised calls for moral reform through education and fuelled a resurgence of evangelicalism from within the Church as well as among Dissenters.[54] The perceived threat of possible civil unrest following the French Revolution hardened attitudes towards the poor, and brought about attempts to exercise social control amid fears of political insurrection.[55] Indeed, over the course of the century, tensions between a drive for moral reform among the poor through religious instruction, and a desire that their children not be elevated 'above their station', but controlled through work, were never fully resolved.

Overview of chapters

Chapter one demonstrates that while the ideological backdrop to John Wesley's work was neither static nor consistent, questions of gender and class remained entrenched. The fashioning of a gentleman continued to largely define the education of boys of wealthy, or 'middling sort'. Although the level of female education is easy to underestimate, prevailing sentiments meant that instruction for girls was predominantly framed in a way that would enhance their future roles as wives and mothers. Among the poor, educating children of the lower orders was intended to make them good Christians, rather than elevate them above their peers.

John Wesley's upbringing at Epworth, discussed in chapter two, informed his belief in the importance of family in instructing children. His thinking on education favoured Locke, but did not compromise his strongly held Christian principles. The evidence presented in this chapter demonstrates that Susanna Wesley's educational thinking was more compassionate than has been argued and was in many ways governed by affection and respect for her children. John Wesley's time at Charterhouse and Oxford was influential in developing his thinking on education, gender, class and piety. Although he encouraged young women to improve themselves through learning, his primary concern was with their piety rather than their intellect.

Evidence suggests that Wesley's educational practice was governed by key themes, which are discussed in chapter three. Although he supported female education, Wesley did not consider boys and girls as educational equals. Tension in his thinking between piety and learning meant that his educational practice was frequently more strongly Evangelical than intellectual, more pious than academic. Wesley placed emphasis on ascetic self-denial, introspection and emotion, but overlooked their effects on the minds of adolescent boys. His thinking on what constituted suitable reading material was complex; although he wrote and published huge quantities of material, this was heavily edited to his own way of thinking. Nevertheless, it undoubtedly enhanced the religious and academic knowledge of his readers.

Education for children of the poor, discussed in chapter four, was frequently marked by tension between piety and a degree of learning that might give them aspirations 'above their station'. Wesley's Arminian doctrine ignited in Methodists a desire for self-improvement and self-advancement; nevertheless, his educational programme was not intended to break down existing social and gender boundaries. Although he opened day schools for the poor, Wesley kept tight control not only on what children were taught, but by whom they were instructed. He sought to protected children against the dangerous influences of a non-Christian way of life, rather than ameliorate their condition, arguing that the poor should be industrious, and deferential to their social superiors.

As chapter five demonstrates, Wesley's boarding school at Kingswood was gender and class defined. Although a few girls attended in the early years, his rules for the school echoed sentiments of the day regarding the fashioning of a gentleman. The eighteenth-century framework of household–family, which manifested itself in concepts of authority and possession, was central to Wesley's concept of Kingswood. Assuming every child would behave well and be as studious as he had been, Wesley showed little understanding of the effect his strict regime had on adolescent boys. Far from offering anything new at Kingswood, Wesley's boarding school in many ways conformed to eighteenth-century norms.

Chapter six covers the closing decades of Wesley's life, at a time which witnessed growing tension between education and Evangelism. Wesley increasingly looked to his preachers to promote family worship in the home. Lady Huntingdon's College at Trevecka held out the prospect of a training centre for the entire Methodist movement, but tension between Arminian and Calvinist factions saw Kingswood increasingly regarded as a place where Wesley's preachers might advance their learning, and where their sons might be educated. Not only were the 'parlour boarders' less than welcoming, but preachers' sons received a level of learning which led some to treat their parents with derision.

The emergence of the Sunday school movement, examined in chapter seven, had far-reaching consequences for the religious life of the poor. Instruction was basic and admission non-denominational. Wesley promoted Sunday schools among Methodist Societies, giving working class laymen and women opportunities for leadership roles.[56] Unpublished material provides an insight into John Fletcher's Sunday schools in Madeley. Through her series of *Cheap Repository Tracts*, Anglican Hannah More not only offered spiritual and moral guidance to unsophisticated readers, but provided girls with a female role model. Growing suspicion of the work of non-Anglican Evangelicals raised concerns over the education of the poor as attitudes hardened following the French Revolution of 1789.

The book concludes by setting out its key findings. It argues that John Wesley's views emphasised original sin and failed to acknowledge new concepts of innocent childhood; nevertheless, he advocated Locke and encouraged reading and learning. His female course of study was rooted in a restrictive religious perspective, but gave girls an opportunity to expand their intellect. He encouraged schooling for children of the poor, but this was designed to enhance piety, rather than offer learning that might give them aspirations 'above their station'. His Arminian philosophy championed self-improvement and gave his followers an invitation for self-advancement, but his educational practice was more strongly Evangelical than intellectual, more pious than academic.

Notes

1. Plumb, J. H. (1950) *England in the Eighteenth Century* Harmondsworth: Penguin Books p. 96
2. Thompson, E. P. (2013) *The Making of the English Working Class* London: Penguin Books p. 811
3. Lynch, Elizabeth (2003) 'John Wesley's Editorial Hand' in Gregory *John Wesley: Tercentenary Essays* Manchester: The John Rylands University Library p. 176
4. Ives, Arthur Glendinning (1970) *Kingswood School in Wesley's Day and Since* London: Epworth Press p. 3

5 Bailey, Joanne (2012) *Parenting in England c1760–1830* Oxford: Oxford University Press p. 52
6 Davis, Rebecca (2014) *Written Maternal Authority and Eighteenth-Century Education in Britain* Farnham: Ashgate p. 1–3
7 Training girls for their future role as wife or mother was important because if a daughter failed to trap a husband she faced living in impoverishment, or being a burden on her family. Porter, Roy (1998) *England in the Eighteenth Century* London: The Folio Society p. 28
8 Gibson, William (2001) *The Church of England 1688–1832* London: Routledge p. 1–6
9 Whitehead, John (1796) *The life of the Rev. John Wesley* vol. 2, London: Stephen Couchman p. 502
10 Baker, Frank (ed.-in-chief) (1984–) *Bi-centennial Edition: The Works of John Wesley* vol. 3 Nashville: Abingdon Press p. 25
11 Ibid. vol. 25 p. 330
12 Hindmarsh, Bruce D. (2005) *The Evangelical Conversion Narrative* Oxford: Oxford University Press p. 111
13 Rivers, Isabel (2010) 'John Wesley as Editor and Publisher' in Maddox, Randy L. & Vickers, Jason E. (eds.) *The Cambridge Companion to John Wesley* Cambridge: Cambridge University Press p. 145
14 Gregory, Jeremy (2010) 'The Long Eighteenth Century' in Ibid. p. 14
15 Rodell, Jonathan (2013) 'Methodism and Social Justice' in Gibson, William, Forsaith, Peter & Wellings, Martin (eds.) *The Ashgate Research Companion to World Methodism* Farnham: Ashgate p. 482
16 Gregory, Jeremy (2005) 'In the Church I will Live and Die' in Gibson, William & Ingram, Robert G. (eds.) *Religious Identities in Britain. 1660–1832* Aldershot: Ashgate p. 149–50
17 Forsaith, Peter S. (ed.) (2008) *Unexampled Labours* Peterborough: Epworth p. 3
18 Hindmarsh, Bruce D. (2005) *The Evangelical Conversion Narrative* Oxford: Oxford University Press p. 120
19 'The children of tender parents so called... are indeed offering up their sons and daughters unto the devil'. Wesley, John (1749b) *A Short Account of the School in Kingswood Near Bristol.* Bristol: Felix Farley p. 4
20 Baker (1984) *BCE* vol. 3 p. 348
21 Wesley, John (1749c) *The Manners of the Antient Christians* Bristol: Felix Farley p. 156
22 cited in Stewart, W. A. Campbell (1953) *Quakers and Education* London: The Epworth Press p. 58
23 Baker (1984) *BCE* vol. 9 p. 278; Wesley, John (1755) *Instructions for Children, Fourth Edition* London: Henry Cock p. 14
24 Baker (1984) *BCE* vol. 3 p. 335–7
25 Locke suggested that as far as young children in particular were concerned 'there will be some though not great difference' in the way they were to be raised. Rand, Benjamin (1927) (ed.) *The Correspondence of John Locke and Edward Clarke* London: Oxford University Press p. 121
26 Rousseau, Jean-Jacques (1762) *Emilius and Sophia* London: R. Griffiths, T. Becket and P. A. de Hondt p. 322–5
27 Hilton, Mary (2007) *Women and the Shaping of the Nation's Young* Aldershot: Ashgate Press p. 21

   The Church of England's publication of 1687 consisted of combinations of letters and Catechism, interleaved with blank pages for notes. Church of England (1687) *The ABC with Catechism* London: The Company of Stationers
28 Bailey, Joanne (2007) 'Reassessing Parenting' in Berry, Helen & Foyster, Elizabeth (eds.) *The Family in Early Modern England* Cambridge: Cambridge University Press p. 106, 219
29 Using scripture to argue that society had originated in one man, Adam, the political theorist Sir Robert Filmer, in *Patriarcha* published in 1680, claimed that

subordination of children to their father was 'by the ordination of God himself'. Tadmor, Naomi (2001) *Family and Friends in Eighteenth-Century England* Cambridge: Cambridge University Press p. 11
30 Fletcher, Anthony (2008) *Growing up in England* New Haven: Yale University Press p. 3
31 Porter, Roy (2000) *Enlightenment* London: Penguin Books p. 340
32 Whyman, Susan E. (2009) *The Pen and the People* Oxford: Oxford University Press p. 24–221
33 Hilton (2007) *Women and the Shaping of the Nation's Young* p. 21, 137
34 Rosman, Doreen (2010) *Evangelicals and Culture* Oregon: Pickwick Publications p. 161
35 Gibson (2001) *The Church of England 1688–1832* p. 5
36 Langford, Paul (1989) *A Polite and Commercial People* Oxford: Clarendon Press p. 59–68
37 Bailey (2012) *Parenting in England* p. 106
38 Jacob, William M. (2007) *The Clerical Profession in the Long Eighteenth Century* Oxford: Oxford University Press p. 7
39 Soloway, Richard A. (1969) *Prelates and People* London: Routledge p. 9
40 Langford (1989) *A Polite and Commercial People* p. 73
    The Test Act ensured that those who held public offices were members of the Church of England, with clergy, who were often justices of the peace, having responsibility for the administration of local government, managing charitable funds, organising poor relief and supervising local schools. Gregory (2010) 'The Long Eighteenth Century' p. 19
41 Mather, Frederick Clare (1992) *High Church Prophet* Oxford: Clarendon Press p. 64
42 Holmes, Geoffrey S. (1986) *Politics, Religion, and Society in England, 1672–1742* London: Hambledon Press p. 305
43 King, Steven (2000) *Poverty and Welfare in England 1700–1850* Manchester: Manchester University Press p. 22
44 Andrew, Donna T. (1989) *Philanthropy and Police* Princeton: Princeton University Press p. 17, 39
45 King (2000) *Poverty and Welfare in England 1700–1850* p. 50
34 cited in Andrew (1989) *Philanthropy and Police* p. 26
47 Levene, Alysa (2012) *The Childhood of the Poor* Basingstoke: Palgrave Macmillan p. 3–8
48 Kennett, White (1746) *The Christian Scholar, Ninth Edition* London: S. Birt p. 33
49 Andrew (1989) *Philanthropy and Police* p. 34–41
50 Jones, M. G. (1964) *The Charity School Movement* London: Frank Cass and Co. p. 4–14
51 Levene (2012) *The Childhood of the Poor* p. 6
52 Mandeville claimed 'a man who has had some education... will not make a good hireling and serve a farmer for a pitiful reward'. Mandeville, Bernard (1723) 'An Essay on Charity and Charity Schools' in *The Fable of the Bees* London: Edmund Parker p. 330
53 Andrew (1989) *Philanthropy and Police* p. 178; Bailey (2012) *Parenting in England c1760–1830* p. 108
54 Jacob (2007) *The Clerical Profession in the Long Eighteenth* p. 19
55 Shefrin, Jill (2009) 'Adapted for and Used in Infants' Schools' in Hilton, Mary & Shefrin, Jill (eds.) *Educating the Child in Enlightenment Britain* Farnham: Ashgate Press p. 166
56 Raikes, Robert (1785) 'An Account of the Sunday-Charity Schools, Lately Begun in Various Parts of England' published in *The Arminian Magazine: Consisting Chiefly of Extracts and Original Treatises on Universal Redemption* vols. 1–20, London: J. Paramore p. 43

1 Child-rearing and education in eighteenth-century England

By taking account of a broad spectrum of eighteenth-century source material, this chapter examines the context that underpinned John Wesley's thinking and practice concerning the way children should be raised and educated. Over the course of the eighteenth century new concepts of childhood, which stressed the potential goodness of children, became increasingly influential and resulted in an erosion of the Puritan emphasis on original sin, as well as a softening of Filmerian views on patriarchal authority. Nevertheless, the chapter demonstrates that religious and social sensitivities had a significant influence on how changing concepts of childhood were received, and religious affiliation continued to define child-rearing and educational practice.

While the ideological backdrop to Wesley's work was neither static nor consistent, questions of gender and class remained entrenched. Among the wealthy and 'middling sort' the fashioning of a gentleman continued to largely define education for boys. Although the level of female education is easy to underestimate, prevailing sentiments meant that instruction for girls was predominantly framed in a way that would enhance their future roles as wives and mothers. Among the poor, while the establishment of charity schools has been described as 'the greatest philanthropic passion of the day', educating children of the lower orders was intended to make them good Christians, rather than elevate them above their peers.[1]

Concepts of childhood, gender and class

In 1684 a Somerset landowner, Edward Clarke, asked his friend John Locke, a tutor to a gentlemen's son, for guidance on the education of his own son. In response, Locke produced the first of what became a series of letters, published under the title *Some Thoughts Concerning Education* in 1693. The letters were written for a young man from a specific social milieu, with advice on subjects including an education in the Classics, estate management and the continental tour. Indeed, Bygrave suggests that Locke intended from the outset that his treatise be designed for the 'gentleman' rather than for the 'scholar'.[2] While recognising that 'the qualifications requisite to trade and commerce and the business of the world are seldom or never to be had at grammar schools',

Locke contended that 'most to be taken care of is the gentleman's calling, for if those of that rank are, by their education, once set right, they will quickly bring all the rest into order'.[3]

In advising parents how to raise their children, Locke's treatise appears to deal primarily with the development of manliness. He asserted the male constitution was designed by nature to withstand hardships and fatigue, and argued that only by being exposed to them would boys become men of business, rather than beaus. To ensure that boys would be fit to bear arms and be soldiers, Locke contended that they needed to learn how to ride and to fence, since these were 'necessary parts of breeding that it would be thought a great omission to neglect'. While these sentiments appear to demonstrate a marked gender bias, Locke himself stated:

> I have said *he* here, because the principal aim of my discourse is how a young gentleman should be brought up from his infancy, which, in all things will not so perfectly suit the education of daughters, though where the difference of sex requires different treatment, it will be no hard matter to distinguish.[4]

There is clear evidence that Locke intended *Some Thoughts Concerning Education* for both sons and daughters, albeit that his writings were framed with specific echelons of society in mind. Indeed, Fletcher suggests that *Some Thoughts Concerning Education* was read widely among the 'middling sort' as well as the gentry.[5] In his letter to Edward Clarke, dated 1 January 1685, Locke suggested:

> There will be some though no great difference, for making a little allowance for beauty and some few other considerations of the sex, the manner of breeding of boys and girls, especially in their younger years, I imagine should be the same.[6]

In an earlier letter to Mary Clarke, Locke advised that 'meat, drink, lodging and clothing should be ordered after the same manner for the girls as for the boys'. While a dancing master would give boys 'graceful motions, manliness, and a becoming confidence', girls would learn 'fashion and easy comely motion'. He did concede one difference in the treatment of daughters, arguing that their governing and disciplining belonged to mothers; fathers ought 'to strike very seldom, if at all to chide his daughters', he wrote.[7] Indeed, Butler contends that far from advocating a special, separate and distinct form of education for girls, what Locke proposed for a girl's education closely resembled that of a young gentlemen. Both were to be home educated by a tutor, and learn modern languages through conversation, rather than by the rote memorisation method used in grammar schools.[8]

Locke believed that both boys and girls could be trained in the use of reason, and had intellectual potential which could be developed. His treatise argued that in terms of thought and reason children should be considered as a *tabula rasa*. He insisted that as no two children were alike, they would not be instructed by exactly the same method. Indeed, it was in Locke's recognition of the individuality of the child that his work was to have a profound effect on how children were raised and educated. They were to be treated as rational creatures, and great care was to be taken in forming their minds. Education, Locke stated, should above all 'fit a boy for daily life that he is able to deny himself his own desires, cross his own inclinations, and purely follow what reason directs as best'.[9]

Locke's aim, a significant feature of this new model of child-rearing, was to achieve happy, well-behaved and virtuous children in the present time, as opposed to preparing them for happiness in the next life.[10] Fletcher suggests that Locke's work was highly secular in tone.[11] Cunningham similarly argues that there was not the slightest inclination that the prime purpose of child-rearing was to produce a Christian.[12] The evidence appears to contradict this. Locke contended that:

> the child ought very early to have imprinted on his mind a true notion of God as the independent Supreme Being, author and maker of all things, from whom we receive all our good, that loves us, and gives us all things, and consequent to it a love and reverence of him.

While piety may not have been a principal aim of child-rearing, training of the moral, virtuous and social man was. Locke contended that children should be taught to pray and to read scripture–history, and to learn by heart the Lord's Prayer, Creed and Ten Commandments. The Bible, he suggested, provided children with easy and plain moral rules for reading and instruction in the whole conduct of life, and adherence to Christian moral principles contributed to the making of an English Gentleman.[13]

Locke was not concerned with the Puritan emphasis on 'breaking' a child's will, but sought from children a compliance and suppleness of their will, that they might submit to the reason of others.[14] He was by no means unique in proposing gentler methods of discipline and instruction without losing parental authority. During the later years of the seventeenth century, Ezell suggests, clergy had been promoting the tenderness of parents towards their children through sermons and pamphlets.[15]

Following the publication of *Some Thoughts Concerning Education* a gradual change in attitude led many parents to acknowledge that childhood was no longer solely a preparation for adulthood or heaven, but was to be valued in its own right. Parents were no longer bound by Puritan teaching on discipline and original sin. Parental authoritarianism increasingly gave way to a desire among parents to set a 'good example'.[16] While the importance of Christian principles of virtue, morality and piety continued to be stressed, conduct books increasingly encompassed a diverse range of courtesy and fashion advice for parents along with strictures on ethical behaviour.[17] Children were instructed in the benefits of working hard and being engaged in worthwhile activities. Industriousness, parents explained, would bring more time for self-improvement, and would make them happy.[18] There was a growing availability of toys and games as children were encouraged to play.[19] By the second half of the eighteenth century children's literature had become a well-established genre.[20]

Debate concerning the raising and educating of children was reignited in 1762 by the publication in France of Rousseau's *Emile; Or, On Education*. The book was translated into English in the same year, an indication of the interest it provoked. Although *Emile* ostensibly dealt with educational theory, when viewed together with Rousseau's *Social Contract* of 1762, Woodley argues, it appears to be rather a work of political philosophy.[21] Certainly, Rousseau began the book by suggesting that 'things are good as they came out of the hands of their Creator, but every thing degenerates in the hands of man'; and condemned what he regarded as 'those social institutions which stifle the emotions of nature'.[22]

Rousseau's celebration of a distinct phase of childhood, in which nature knew best, promoted a less interventionist form of parenting. Where Locke had instructed parents in their duty to train their children to become moral adults, Rousseau sought to abolish any such notion. Instead, he argued that 'they are always seeking the man in the child without reflecting what he is before he can be a man'. He condemned any idea that children should be taught or trained and argued that Locke's emphasis on developing the child's mind by practising reasoning should be abandoned, contending: 'If children were capable of reasoning, they would stand no need of education'. He claimed that the corrupting of a child's natural disposition arose when their memory was burdened with words without meaning, and things of no consequence; and that they were taught 'everything except the knowledge of themselves, the business of human life and the attainment of happiness'.[23]

Emile, Rousseau's fictional pupil, was to be educated exclusively by a single young tutor, who would be his companion for the twenty five years necessary to complete his education. He was to be given no verbal instructions, but was to learn from experience; away from the bondage of society, he was to grow up in accordance with nature, without the imposition of either moral rules or learning. Children, Rousseau asserted, were to be allowed freedom to play, and make whatever noise they pleased, and were to be indulged in everything which gave them pleasure. Referring to Locke's argument for reasoning with children as 'silly', he concluded that it was also contrary to nature, which 'would have them children before they are men'.[24]

Rousseau's book was not without its critics. Indeed it is difficult to envisage how a purely Rousseauian education could have been implemented, if only because of the difficulties in finding a suitable tutor. Woodley contends, however, that Rousseau, who left his five children in the care of an orphanage, always intended the work as a philosophical rather than practical guide to education. She suggests that Rousseau's philosophical opposition to exacting obedience from children may have come from the same root as his opposition to the imposition of authority in politics; certainly he wrote that 'civilised man is born, lives, and dies in slavery'.[25]

Rousseau's work was viewed with some suspicion in England. His programme of freedom raised fears of a potential threat to both religious and political stability even before the revolutionary changes of the late eighteenth century.[26] Nevertheless, *Emile* was widely read and discussed, and its claims about education taken seriously. Although Fletcher suggests that Rousseau's impact in England should not be exaggerated, education became a central concern, with at least two hundred treatises on education published in England between 1762 and 1800.[27] Levene claims that Rousseau had a significant influence on modes of parenting in elite circles, and his focus on child-rearing through indulgence and freedom was enhanced by the new consumer trappings of childhood.[28] Parental hopes for children began to be more openly configured in terms of worldly materialism, rather than everlasting salvation.[29]

Although forms of training advocated by Locke and Rousseau differed considerably, they both stressed malleability and potential for goodness in children, a perspective which rapidly became a new reference point for eighteenth-century thinking concerning children and childhood.[30] Indeed, the 'rational' or Lockean and the 'sentimental' or Rousseauian images of children were not regarded as opposing positions and many regarded the two views as compatible.[31] By the mid-eighteenth century the older patriarchal family authority was giving way to a new parental ideal characterised by a more affectionate and equalitarian relationship with children. Nevertheless, the role of both parents in the child's upbringing remained clearly defined.[32] James Buchanan declared in 1770:

> The father ought to lay out and superintend their education; the mother to execute and manage the detail of which she is capable. The father should direct the manly exertions of the intellectual and moral powers of his child: his imagination and the manner of these exertions are the peculiar province of the mother.[33]

New images of innocent and natural childhood were challenged on several fronts. Evangelicals continued to reiterate the Puritan emphasis on original sin. Hannah More declared in *Strictures on the Modern System of Female Education* of 1799 that it was:

> A fundamental error to consider children as innocent beings, whose little weaknesses may perhaps want some correction, rather than beings who bring into the world a corrupt nature and evil dispositions which it should be the great end of education to rectify.[34]

The *Evangelical Magazine* advised parents in 1799 to teach their children that 'they are sinful polluted creatures'; and although such thinking was not reflected in more popular advice books and was backward-looking in terms of popular belief, Cunningham suggests that there remained subcultures of child-rearing seemingly untouched by change. Even those who upheld Lockean values expressed concern about the excessive amount of money being spent by

18 *Child-rearing and education*

some parents, whose over-indulgence of children they deplored as morally corrupting.[35]

Gendering education

The thinking of Locke, and later of Rousseau, which argued against sending children to public schools raised for many the question of whether a child flourished under authority or liberty.[36] Adam Smith stated in his *The Theory of Moral Sentiments* that 'Domestic education is the institution of nature; public education the contrivance of man. It is surely unnecessary to say which is likely to be the wisest'.[37] Regarding the family as the main wellspring of national morality, virtue, in the view of religious authors like Sarah Trimmer, could only be nurtured within the home through the devoted vigilance of parents, who would supervise the early education and reading of their children with constant attention to the inculcation of religious principles.[38]

Despite the expansion of establishments for girls' education throughout the eighteenth century, the commonly held view was that the home was the most suitable place for girls to be educated. John Bennett declared in 1787: 'Whatever elegant or high-standing schools may be sought out for a girl, a mother seems the only governess intended by nature'.[39] Indeed, Gordon argues that among eighteenth-century philosophers Rousseau offered the most powerful articulation of the view that women were by nature destined for domestic duties.[40] This did little to change existing assumptions that girls belonged at home under the supervision of their mothers, where their virtue could be protected.

Girls were expected to be devout, to provide spiritual support in the household and to know how to conduct themselves in a moral fashion. Religious education was an important element in what they were taught.[41] Furthermore, Hannah More argued at the end of the eighteenth century that, far from detrimental, that girls were not taught Greek and Latin ensured that their education was free from pagan influences. Time occupied instead with Christian instruction, she believed, made women equal, if not superior, to men in matters of religion. While this suggests that her views on female education were anti-intellectual, she believed that there was value in 'masculine' subjects such as mathematics, since they forced girls to tackle hard work, which would not only expand their minds, but drive vanity out of them.[42] Indeed, More's father Jacob taught all five of his daughters at home and believed in serious study for women. At the age of 18, More and her sisters ran a girls' boarding school in Bristol that became an outstanding success.[43]

Mary Astell, a contemporary of Locke and a Greek scholar, argued that if all children were 'blank slates' at birth, with no innate ideas, and girls are taught embroidery, music and household management rather than mathematics and Greek, then it should not be surprising that women did not fully develop rationality.[44] Astell's *A Serious Proposal to the Ladies* published between 1694 and 1697 and *The Education of Girls* published in 1687 were both widely read and discussed in relation to the education of elite girls during the first half of the eightieth century.[45] Astell condemned those who taught young ladies to value themselves 'on nothing but their clothes', and advised girls that 'it will not be near so advantageous to consult with your dancing-master as with your own thoughts'. She encouraged them to use their own enquiry to search out the 'hidden beauties' of religion and advised them to become Christians by choice, rather than by conformity with those among whom they lived.[46]

Although the 'superficial' nature of female education among the elite generally may have failed to develop some girls' powers of reasoning, there were many women who possessed intellectual abilities, including a knowledge of mathematics or classical languages, having acquired these skills because they were either daughters of learned men who instructed them at home, or of wealthy men who employed tutors. By the end of the eighteenth century, Hester Chapone's *Letters on the Improvement of the Mind: Addressed to a Young Lady*, published in 1773 was widely read. Chapone believed that women had the same rational and moral nature as men; like Astell, she deplored the emphasis on mindless accomplishments for girls and sought to encourage their critical thought. Addressed to her fifteen-year-old niece, the *Letters* incorporated a course of self-education which included a systematic study of the Bible, training in accountancy and domestic management, translations of the Classics and a range of modern literature in French and English, as well as botany, geology, astrology, chronology, geography and ancient and modern history.[47]

Despite this, John Gregory's *A Father's Legacy to his Daughters*, published a year after Chapone's *Letters*, advised young women: 'But if you happen to have any learning, keep it a profound secret, especially from the men, who generally look with a jealous and malignant eye on a woman of great parts and a cultivated understanding'.[48] *A Father's Legacy* was the best-selling female conduct book of the late eighteenth century, selling 6,000 copies between 1774 and 1776 alone, and was frequently excerpted in periodicals and miscellanies.[49] The headmaster of Tonbridge School, Vicesimus Knox concluded:

> There are many prejudices entertained against the character of a learned lady; and perhaps if all ladies were profoundly learned, some inconveniences might arise from it; but I must own it does not appear to me, that a woman will be rendered less acceptable in the world, or worse qualified to perform any part of her duty in it, by having employed the time from six to sixteen, in the cultivation of her mind.[50]

Social conversation in domestic settings played an important educational role. Children were expected to participate actively in familial social gatherings and conversations.[51] Indeed, Cohen argues that social conversations fostered the development of much more sophisticated and rigorous intellectual training for girls than has hitherto been acknowledged.[52] Hannah More argued that dull learning by rote, an accepted method of the day, should be replaced by animated conversation and lively discussion between the teacher and pupil, making sensibilities of the pupil the first consideration.[53] Girls would record conversations they had participated in or listened to, as well as other aspects of their social life. 'Conversation' figured importantly in educational and conduct literature of the time, particularly literature aimed at females.[54] Because of women's key role in the maintenance of sociability, the social or 'familiar' conversation as instruction ensured that women's talk was not dismissed as mere chat; and written familiar conversation became a very successful mode of teaching.[55] Among Evangelical and Dissenting movements, girls were encouraged to write diaries and, Hindmarsh argues, the conversion narrative proved to be one of the most potent means of passing the piety of one generation on to another.[56]

Reading, which was often done aloud and discussed in the company of other girls, was considered very important; and an integral part of daily practice was to formulate critical comments about the reading or its authors.[57] In order for girls to develop the correct approach to life, they were encouraged to read edifying texts such as religious and moral treatises. Hannah More's answer to the trivial and superficial nature of female education was to encourage 'dry tough reading, [which] independent of the knowledge it conveys is useful as a habit and wholesome as an exercise'.[58] Although reading was generally approved of when associated with piety and chastity, girls were warned against reading that might have a pernicious effect on the female mind.[59] The reading of fiction, it was suggested, softened young women up for seduction.[60]

Over the course of the century a great number of schools for girls of all classes were established. Often falling into a gap between formal definitions of public and private education, these varied widely in their quality and scope. Small schools opened and closed as the need arose, or on the demise or retirement of the governess. Most schools combined writing and arithmetic with social 'accomplishments' designed to equip girls for marriage.[61] Mrs Masquerier's girls' boarding school in Kensington, London, advertised:

> Board, including French, English, writing, arithmetic, geography, needlework and dancing for twenty guineas a year and one guinea entrance. Parents or Guardians may depend on the utmost care taken of the young ladies morals and manners, and a particular tenderness shewn to their persons.
> NB The house is genteel and the situation remarkably healthful.
> To those who do not chuse to learn all the above branches, a reasonable deduction is made.[62]

In 1749, Sarah Fielding's *The Governess, or Little Female Academy*, was the first fictional narrative designed for, as Fielding herself put it, the 'Entertainment and Instruction of Young Ladies in their Education'. The story was set in a small boarding school for girls and Hilton suggests it quickly became a significant book. Unfortunately, most women teachers have remained largely invisible outside their fictional representations in contemporary novels.[63]

The question of the education of boys was rather more complex. Private education for wealthier families might, in addition to family support, include hiring a private tutor to teach children at home. In recognition of services rendered, and to compensate them for rather modest remuneration, some prosperous and influential families were able to help tutors to take holy orders and find a benefice.[64] Bernard de Mandeville, a philosopher and political economist, observed: 'Good sense ought to govern men in learning as well as in trade; no man ever bound his son apprentice to a goldsmith to make him a linen draper, then why should he have a divine for his tutor to become a lawyer or a physician?'.[65] Despite this, the post of tutor, particularly to families belonging to the nobility, was greatly sought after.[66] The disadvantages of a private education were outlined by Francis Brokesby, a Non-juring Leicestershire priest, who claimed that:

> They come from public schools more fitted for business, better qualified for employment and more safely to be trusted in the world; whereas my young master in his private education may perhaps have swallowed a great deal of Greek and Latin and run through divers good authors, but being broke loose from his tutor, guardian or relations, comes abroad so raw and unfledged as to the world that every flattering sycophant coaksweth him out of anything, and every designing knave over reacheth him.[67]

Many parish clergy taught, as boarders, sons of gentry and merchants; some were proprietors of considerable private educational establishments.[68] Private schools also found themselves having to counter claims that children's virtue would be threatened by the mixing of social classes, the multiplicity of pupils and the limited supervision in small schools. Proprietors of these establishments often advertised them as offering children in their care a 'moral education'.[69] Although out of the reach of many families, the level of fees charged made this form of education affordable to even the moderately comfortable middling ranks.[70]

Although parents were keen that their children attend school in order to learn to read and write, less well-off families needed to take account the fees charged and the possible loss of the child's earning capacity when attending school. At the beginning of the eighteenth century, Brokesby suggested that 'There are few country villages where some or other did not get a livelihood by teaching school, so that there are now not many but can write and read, unless it have been their own or their parents' fault'.[71] While there is no satisfactory means of estimating the number of children educated in private schools or even the number of schools themselves, the popularity of private education seems to have remained largely undiminished throughout the century, with schools being set up, or closed, depending on how individual enterprise and public interest dictated.[72]

There was no recognised method of becoming a teacher in these small schools and Neuburg suggests that teaching in them was regarded as a job that anyone could drift in to.[73] It was a frequent complaint that towards the lower and cheaper end of the schooling, men and women running schools had only a relatively basic education themselves; and in some cases the children were even subjected to abuse and neglect.[74] Attendance at these schools was also more likely to be intermittent or irregular, being dependent not only on the parents' continuing ability to pay the fees, but in rural areas possibly confined to winter months or less, according to opportunities for child labour.[75]

'Dame schools' were entirely independent enterprises, and required no standard of skill or experience on the part of those who taught in them. William Shenstone in his poem *The School-mistress*, published in 1742, wrote:

> In ev'ry village less reveal'd to fame,
> Dwells there dwells, in cottage known about a mile,
> A matron old, whom we school-mistress name,
> Who boasts unruly brats with birch to tame.[76]

Nonetheless, Hilton contends that small schools, which provided an education for children of tradesmen and the 'middling sort', and village 'dame schools' which taught children of labourers and artisans, helped ensure a steady stream of literate members in most communities.[77]

The acquisition of a classical education not only divided society along social and religious lines, but also by gender. Latin was regarded as the male elite's secret language that displayed not only a level of learning, but of superiority.[78] Even among those able to afford public schooling, boys were set on an entirely different path from girls both in the expectation and provision of their education, a disparity recognised at the time. White Kennett, later Bishop of Peterborough, writing concerning the defects of grammar schooling in 1706, concluded: 'The Masters of these schools set up for Greek and Latin only and so their dispensation excluded one sex altogether and was indeed too high for the meaner boys, born to the spade and the plough'.[79]

During the eighteenth century, children generally began elementary schooling between six and eight years of age and went on to grammar school between the ages of eight and eleven. Those proceeding to an apprenticeship attended grammar school up to age twelve to fourteen, while those destined for university left between the ages of fifteen to eighteen.[80] England had between one thousand and twelve hundred grammar schools in 1727; over the course of the century there were numerous grammar schools for boys offering boarding facilities, as well as education for day pupils.[81] Masters and ushers were usually ordained and often held posts in plurality with a small parish or curacy and boys were required to accompany the Master to Church on Sundays and Holy days.[82]

Public schools with their multiplicity of pupils were seen by many as fostering a morally corrupting atmosphere which, along with their use of the rod and championing of a classical education through rote learning, fell woefully short of both Lockean and Rousseauian ideals.[83] Certainly the frequently quoted statement of Samuel Johnson that 'My Master whipped me very well – without that I should have done nothing' suggests a somewhat violent approach to learning. That Johnson undoubtedly remembered Hunter, the Master to whom he referred, with fear contending: 'He was not severe Sir, a Master ought to be severe Sir, he was cruel', Smith points out that other pupils at school with Johnson spoke of Hunter as a learned man who was a lover of music.[84]

While a public school education may not have failed all, or even a majority of students, the anarchic and brutal nature of the great public schools of this period was widely acknowledged. Elliott-Binns described life there as 'a simple alternative of Classics and cuffs', its aim to produce the type of masculine role model portrayed in the classical literature that formed a large part of the curriculum.[85] Although Langford claims that life at the great public schools was considered a kind of primitive subculture, which nurtured immorality and indiscipline, Vicesimus Knox, argued that this was preferable to the domestic environment that endangered boys' manliness.[86] In Knox's view, a well-conducted school not only taught boys to be virtuous, but gave them an understanding of the world that taught them virtue in practice. When attending university, it was argued, a privately educated boy would be in much more danger of being infected with vices than if he had been inoculated against them while still at school.[87]

Eighteenth-century thinking considered the presence of women indispensable for shaping the gentleman; but, it also raised deep anxiety about effeminacy. Politeness, a complete system of manners and conduct based on the art of conversation, was at the heart of sociability and was central to the fashioning of a gentleman. Men were required to soften their manners and refine their conversation; something it was considered best achieved in conversation with, and in the company of women. At the same time, young men were required to exercise self-control and be constantly vigilant to the discipline of their body and tongue if they were not to run the risk of 'effeminacy', defined by eighteenth-century culture as a tendency to behave like women.[88] Perhaps wishing to distance pupils from the risk of effeminacy, the public school environment was considered by many as 'a godless world of cold, hunger, competition and endurance', a place where boys were neglected and allowed freedom outside academic hours and where fighting and violence between the boys were regarded as tolerated pastimes that fostered 'manliness'.[89]

Public schools, traditionally suited to providing a classical education for the sons of gentry who were destined for a life of honourable leisure or a career in one of the professions, were additionally criticised for failing to provide a 'modern' education. Non-conformist preacher and hymn writer Isaac Watts, in his *A Discourse on the Education of Children and Youth* published posthumously in 1754, stated: 'In our nation I confess it is a custom to educate the children of noblemen and the eldest sons of the gentry to no proper business or profession, but only to an acquaintance with some of the ornaments and accomplishments of life'.[90] The Classics were regarded by many parents, particularly among the 'middling sort', as of dubious value. There was an increasing expectation that children's education should include English and mathematics, together with lessons in history, geography and science, as well as instruction in what were regarded as 'socially valuable' attainments such as drawing, dancing and foreign languages.[91]

One of the places where this 'modern' education was available was in Dissenting schools and academies, which although small both in number and size, offered an education that was very different from most ordinary schools of the day.[92] Dissenting academies, founded by Independents, Presbyterians, Quakers and Baptists, had grown in stature throughout the early part of the eighteenth century to a point when they not only rivalled the grammar schools, but were regarded as institutions of university standing rivalling the great universities of the day.[93] Nevertheless, Rack argues that many were under-funded and understaffed, and claims about them should not be exaggerated.[94]

In the period between 1661 and 1729, learning at Dissenting academies followed no fixed pattern. Tutors, who had previously taught at Oxford or Cambridge, transferred much of the content and method of their university teaching to their private academies. The small scale of these academies made it difficult for all subjects to be taught with equal effectiveness and the different knowledge and skills of each tutor, Burden contends, explains why many students chose to attend more than one academy. There was considerable traffic between universities and private academies across the period 1660–1729 and neither side lay claim to being the chief engine of intellectual change.[95] There were no tests of religious doctrine exacted on students. Some entered Dissenting academies at fourteen to complete their formal education, while others pursued a more rigorous higher education lasting for up to five years.[96] The number of Dissenting academies was small, with only thirty four established in the period from 1691–1750. Despite this, their impact was significant since they provided an education not just for boys destined to become professional men, but for those seeking a good general education in preparation for a life in commerce. Although Classics remained important, lectures were generally in English rather than Latin, which was only spoken at certain times of the day.[97]

Discipline in the Dissenting academies was rigorous, not only in demanding strict attention to study, but, unlike the universities of the day, in ensuring the good conduct of students outside the academies. The writings of Locke were widely read, and tutors took time not simply to provide their students with facts, but to train them to think for themselves; and perhaps more importantly, to then allow students to express their thoughts. By offering a practical, modern education and at the same time adopting a high moral tone, the Dissenting academies, Parker argued, satisfied the needs of many families in a way that the universities were failing to do.[98]

It was not until 1779 that the Dissenting Schoolmasters' Relief Act finally legalised the activities of the Non-conformist teachers working in the Dissenting schools and academies.[99]

Pauper children – eighteenth-century philanthropy and education

Locke argued that if poor boys and girls were to develop their future potential, they needed to be taken away from the corrupting influence of their parents.

He regarded working schools as a way of breaking the cycle of dependency on parish relief by creating a new generation of rational, reliable workers.[100] In 1697 he wrote a memorandum on poor relief for the Board of Trade in which he proposed that working schools be set up in every parish to instruct pauper children in the skills required for the textile industry. This scheme was advocated by Locke not only as a way of securing their future path, but of ensuring their moral integrity.[101] Children above three and below fourteen years of age would be obliged to attend. Supplied with a 'plentiful amount of bread' instead of scanty rations from their parents, the report claimed that they would not only acquire the discipline of manual labour, but be instructed in Christian living through regular attendance at Church on Sundays.[102] Locke contended that by the age of fourteen children would have more than paid off the initial expenses of the scheme. Although schools of industry were set up during the eighteenth century, they never achieved the sort of results Locke anticipated.[103]

New concepts of childhood presented an image of children as deserving of sympathy and support, and whose poverty was not their own fault. Consequently, Cunningham describes as the 'greatest philanthropic passion of the day' the desire of eighteenth-century benefactors to ensure that children from poor families received an education.[104] By the end of the eighteenth century wealthy aristocratic women, along with those of lesser means, often took the lead in the founding of charity schools, and were prominent as managers, trustees and school teachers.[105] Although the efforts of Dissenters were largely concentrated on providing an education for the 'middling sort', Matthew Henry, minister of More Street Meeting House, Hackney, urged his fellow Non-conformists to follow the example of the Church and set up charity schools. His death in 1714 put an end to any organised effort and although Isaac Watts, Samuel Chandler and Philip Doddridge encouraged their establishment, the number of Dissenting charity schools set up throughout the eighteenth century was small.[106]

The charity school movement did not arise solely in response to new images of childhood. An earlier impetus had been the desire to ensure pauper children were instructed in Christian values. Drawing on the Mosaic assumption that some are destined to be 'hewers of wood and drawers of water',[107] charity schools had come into being largely as a way of fashioning children of the lower orders into good Christians and faithful servants. The guiding principle of the charity school movement was 'Train up a child in the way he should go and when he is old, he will not depart from it', a principle that suggested it was better to 'form' the child than 'reform' the man.[108] Although many bishops supported charitable and philanthropic projects, and annually delivered what Soloway describes as 'uninspiring' sermons on behalf of the charity schools, few of them regarded this as a move towards social improvement.[109]

The Church backed the establishment of charity schools through a co-ordinated and well publicised national campaign in collaboration with the Society for Promoting Christian Knowledge.[110] John Lewis's *Exposition of the Catechism* was written for the SPCK and alongside *The Christian Schoolmaster* outlined a four-year course of instruction.[111] The SPCK not only supplied charity schools with books, but developed an extremely ambitious programme which included the establishing of a corresponding society for disseminating ideas and materials for promoting more effective parochial ministry, donating Bibles to the poor and publishing and distributing religious tracts and pamphlets as a way of spreading religious education. The SPCK regularly distributed *The Whole Duty of Man*; although theologically complex, the expectation was that it would either be read by parents to their children, or children would read it themselves.[112] This was to be done on a regular basis, not only so that children might understand it, but use it as a guide to Christian living. The sale and widespread distribution of Bibles and other religious literature by the SPCK suggests the desire of many people to develop their religious understanding and devotional lives.[113]

One of the commonest means of fund-raising for charity schools was a collection taken after a sermon preached at an annual service before the mayor, corporation and leading citizens at which the children sang psalms and, in major churches, a setting of the canticles and an anthem. These were well-attended social occasions, when preachers reminded the better-off of their duty towards their less well-off neighbours; and reminded the poor that the Gospel gave them a proper expectation of generosity and fair dealing from the better-off.[114] The Bishop of Bristol, Joseph Butler, suggested in his annual sermon to charity schools in London in 1745, that the poor now felt a sense of stigma if they could not read and write, since 'the ordinary affairs of the world are now put in a way which requires that they should have some knowledge of letters'.[115]

Critics of the charity school movement raised concerns that children should not be educated beyond their needs or above their station.[116] Bishop Butler, while supporting the schools, stressed that they did not in any way 'remove poor children out of the rank in which they were born, but, keeping them in it, to give them the assistance which their circumstances plainly called for, by educating them in the principles of religion as well as civil life'.[117] Bernard Mandeville ignited fierce debate with his publication *The Fable of the Bees, or, Private Vices, Public Benefits*, which contained the 'Essay on Charity and Charity Schools' of 1723. He contended that:

> Every hour those poor people spend at their book is so much time lost to the society. Going to school, in comparison to working, is idleness, and the longer boys continue in this easy form of life, the more unfit they will be when grown up for down-right labour... A man who has had some education... will not make a good hireling, and serve a farmer for a pitiful reward.[118]

Mandeville saw the problem of education as primarily an issue of economics, and argued that far from beneficial, forced education was harmful to the public. He acknowledged the need for religious instruction if the poor were to lead a

Christian life, but contended that this could be achieved without having to teach poor children to read and write. Christian teaching, he argued, was to be provided not in school, but in Church; 'I would not have the meanest of a parish that is able to walk to it be absent on Sundays', he stated.[119] Despite his instance that the poor should attend their local Church, critics regarded Mandeville's publication as an attack on Christian values, and Andrew suggests that some of the greatest minds of the age wrote refutations of Mandeville's *Fable* in an attempt to restore the system of Christian morality that he appeared to have ridiculed.[120]

While Jones suggested that much of the strength of Mandeville's essay was due to his antagonism to the High Church party, there was enough agreement with his economics to keep public opinion running strongly in favour of his view.[121] Mindful of this, the charity schools sought to ensure that teachers concentrated on the most basic accomplishments, which were unlikely to provide a platform for potentially threatening learning, and which gave the pupils instruction in submission to political authority and social deference.[122]

The charity school movement expanded rapidly, to a point in 1729 when there were 1,419 schools with 22,303 pupils.[123] The minimal population growth in the 1730s and 1740s, combined with higher living standards and signs of a labour shortage, meant that the necessity to establish schools on anything like the scale they had been previously was diminished.[124] Marquardt also suggests that after 1730, as the interest of the SPCK turned more strongly to foreign missions, the quality of teachers and instruction in many of the established schools deteriorated.[125]

Towards the end of the eighteenth century, children were more readily defined by their association with the state of poverty than the state of childhood. Increasing urbanisation, combined with a population that doubled in the period from 1760 to 1830, saw the number of children and young people in Britain rise to an unprecedented level.[126] Not only was the scale of the poverty problem and its intensity increasing, but children themselves were becoming victims of social and economic changes.[127] As a result, the growing number of children who were receiving no education at all became a matter of increasing concern. With half the population under twenty years of age, and half of these children under ten, Hilton suggests, there were children everywhere, more visible and audible than they had ever been. What became a priority, as far as those in authority were concerned, was not only providing an education for the young, but maintaining social control.[128]

Educating children became a matter of public concern because, in shaping the individual, society could be shaped.[129] Since every child who died young or who followed his or her parents into dependency and poverty was a cumulative drain on society, the child's potential needed to be harnessed through instruction both in the ways of the Church and in a work ethic. Enlightenment and commercialism projected a concept of value on the bodies of children which was partly based on their future potential as productive and well-rounded adults.[130]

Although the Church had remained the oldest and largest sponsor of educational institutions, the charity schools were no longer large enough, or numerous enough, to educate the vast new numbers of poor children. Even among education reformers like Sarah Trimmer, it was not deemed appropriate to educate all poor children. Trimmer claimed that 'those who have the mental abilities to benefit from the education offered at charity schools should not be consigned to labour in the field', but that the 'dull and stupid should be, not put to school'. It seems she saw a clear demarcation between those among the poor children of a parish who have been 'born to good prospects' for whom it would be 'an act of particular kindness to place [them] in charity schools', and those who 'could not be admitted into charity schools on account of the expense of attending them'. 'It cannot be right', she argued 'to train them all in a way which will most probably raise their ideas above the very lowest occupations of life and disqualify them for those servile offices which must be filled by some of the members of the community'.[131]

Many families had little option but to send their children to work since the income they could bring in was essential to raise their household income above a level of bare subsistence. Pollock contends that the increasing social differentiation resulting from industrialisation ensured that many of the middling and upper ranks were wholly unfamiliar with the lives of the poor and were, she suggests, liable to misinterpret what they saw.[132] As the gulf between rich and poor became increasingly visible, it was blamed upon the failings of the poor themselves.[133] With the rise of manufacturing, and fundamental changes in technology combined with urbanisation, children were increasingly regarded as a natural component of the workforce. Trimmer claimed in 1787 that it was 'a disgrace to any parish, to see the children of the poor, who are old enough to do any kind of work, running about the streets ragged and dirty'.[134]

In the final decades of the eighteenth century, anxieties grew over problems arising from the expanding and unsustainable population. Fears about the moral state of the nation and the security and efficiency of the Church brought about a resurgence of evangelicalism from within the Church, as well as among Dissenters. Evangelicals, as they had done earlier in the century, campaigned for the suppression of immorality and vice, encouraged support for Sunday schools, and argued for reform of the Poor Law as well as reform of the Church.[135]

It was not just the observable unruly behaviour of poor children that made the governing classes anxious; as Shefrin points out, fears of civil unrest during the French Revolution, and following the Napoleonic Wars prompted attempts to exercise social control over the poor amid fears of political insurrection.[136] As the century drew to a close, the political establishment, fearful that the secular radicalism of the French Revolution might bring about a fundamental assault on Christian civilisation, closed ranks to contest Thomas Paine's ferocious attack on the British constitution in his *Rights of Man*, published in 1791.[137] Efforts by Evangelicals began to be viewed with suspicion; Mather suggests that 'the itinerant Evangelism which spread as a wave through the English villages in 1797–8', was increasingly seen as 'a circumstance which gives much ground for suspicion that sedition and atheism are the real objects of these institutions rather than religion'.[138]

Conclusion

The eighteenth century marked a period of considerable change in how children were raised and educated. While questions of gender, class and religious affiliation defined and contained educational practice, changing concepts of childhood influenced the way children were regarded, and impacted the level of parental choice and responsibility within these divisions. New concepts of childhood expounded by Locke, and later by Rousseau, brought about an acknowledgement of the individuality of the child. Yet, while Locke's writings suggested there need be little difference in the way elite parents educated their sons and daughters, it is clear that boys and girls were not considered educational equals.

The evidence suggests that the level of education for girls of the wealthy and 'middling sort' is easy to underestimate since girls' schools often fell between definitions of private and public education. Indeed, that Mary Astell's *A Serious Proposal* was widely read and discussed suggests that female education may not have been as superficial or as unavailable as some commentators have argued. Nevertheless, the prevailing sentiment of the period deemed that the education girls generally received was one that would foster their future role as wives and mothers.

Within the political, religious and ideological context of the eighteenth century, while the widening philosophical and educational debate presented many parents with a fresh approach, it also gave them an increased responsibility in their role of how their children were raised and educated. New arguments about the nature of childhood led many parents to take a more positive role in child-rearing. Private education, which gave parents the opportunity to raise, or have raised, their children in a family unit, remained popular throughout the century.[139]

The acquisition of a classical education not only divided society along social and religious lines, it also did so by gender. Although the anarchic and immoral nature of public schools and universities of the day was widely acknowledged, supporters of the public school regime argued that it taught manly ideals of endurance and self-reliance. The classical education offered at grammar schools was challenged by Dissenting academies, which provided an education not just for boys destined to become professional men, but for those seeking a good general education in preparation for a life in commerce.

New concepts of childhood brought about a sympathetic response to the plight of pauper children. The growing emphasis on the innocence of children increased the sentimental response to groups of the poor, notably through the charity school movement. Although clerics were important in setting the tone and practice of eighteenth-century charity, writers on economic policy and affairs were also significant. The commercial ideals of profit and loss, however, remained entrenched. Towards the end of the century, the onset of industrialisation, fears of civil unrest and the desire for moral reform, all had a significant influence on both the perception and the treatment of children. While childhood was on the one hand increasingly being regarded as a time of innocence, as the century progressed, attitudes to those in poverty were hardening.

It would seem that throughout the century, educational initiatives for the poor tended to be private, local and usually derived from the Church. Social pressures resulting from the rapid urban growth revealed the inadequacies of the provisions, with educational initiatives designed largely to regulate and reform the poor rather than ameliorate their condition. Indeed, the evidence in this chapter appears to support Roy Porter's claims that in the educational free market of the eighteenth century 'the instruction children got, determined by parental choice and pocket, tended to reinforce existing social, cultural, and gender distinctions, rather than break them down and make new ones'.[140]

Notes

1. Cunningham, Hugh (2005) *Children and Childhood in Western Society since 1500* London: Pearson Longman p. 121
2. Bygrave, Stephen (2009) *Uses of Education* Lewisburg: Bucknell University Press p. 98
3. Locke, John (1693) *Some Thoughts Concerning Education* London: A. & J. Churchill p. 194, A6
4. Ibid. p. 1–8, 16, 67
5. Fletcher (2008) *Growing up in England* p. 7
6. Rand (ed.) (1927) *The Correspondence of John Locke and Edward Clarke* p. 121
7. Ibid. p. 234–9, 103–4
8. Butler, Melissa A. (2007) 'Early Liberal Roots of Feminism' in Hirschmann, Nancy J. & McClure, Kirstie M. (eds.) *Feminist Interpretations of John Locke* Pennsylvania: The Pennsylvania State University Press p. 116
9. Locke (1693) *Some Thoughts Concerning Education* p. 33, 261
10. Bailey (2012) *Parenting in England c1760–1830* p. 72–3
11. Fletcher (2008) *Growing up in England* p. 6
12. Cunningham (2005) *Children and Childhood in Western Society since 1500* p. 61
13. Locke (1693) *Some Thoughts Concerning Education* p. 157–8
14. Ibid. p. 134, 261
15. Ezell, Margaret (1983) 'John Locke's Images of Childhood' in *Eighteenth-Century Studies 17* John Hopkins University Press p. 150–5
16. Paxman, David B. (2015) 'Imaging the Child' in *Journal for Eighteenth-Century Studies* 38.1 p. 135–51
17. Hilton (2007) *Women and the Shaping of the Nation's Young* p. 22
18. Bailey (2012) *Parenting in England c1760–1830* p. 184
19. Fletcher (2008) *Growing up in England* p. 7
20. Cunningham (2005) *Children and Childhood in Western Society since 1500* p. 65
21. Woodley, Sophia (2009) 'Oh Miserable and Most Ruinous Measure' in Hilton & Shefrin (eds.) *Educating the Child in Enlightenment Britain* p. 24
22. Rousseau (1762) *Emilius and Sophia* p. 9
23. Ibid. p. 107, 29
24. Ibid. p. 35, 100–16
25. Woodley (2009) 'Oh Miserable and Most Ruinous Measure' p. 25–35; Rousseau (1762) *Emilius and Sophia* p. 19

Child-rearing and education 31

26 Houswitschka, Christophe (2006) 'Locke's Education or Rousseau's Freedom' in Muller, Anja (ed.) *Fashioning Childhood in the Eighteenth Century* Aldershot: Ashgate Press p. 86
27 Fletcher (2008) *Growing up in England* p. 8; Muller, Anja (2009) *Framing Childhood in Eighteenth-Century Periodicals and Prints 1689–1789* Farnham: Ashgate Press p. 69
28 Levene (2012) *The Childhood of the Poor* p. 3–4
29 Hilton (2007) *Women and the Shaping of the Nation's Young* p. 26
30 Levene (2012) *The Childhood of the Poor* p. 4
31 Bygrave (2009) *Uses of Education* p. 34
32 Barker-Benfield, G. J. (1992) *The Culture of Sensibility* London: University of Chicago Press p. 102
33 Buchanan, James (1770) *Plan of an English Grammar School Education* London: E. & C. Dilly p. 33
34 More, Hannah (1799) *Strictures on the Modern System of Female Education* vol. 1 London: T. Cadell, Jun and W. Davies p. 64
35 Cunningham (2005) *Children and Childhood in Western Society since 1500* p. 59–67
36 While Rousseau implicitly argued against children being confined in institutions, Locke felt public schools valued classical knowledge above moral development, and argued that the company a child kept at school was a potential threat to virtue. Rousseau (1762) *Emilius and Sophia* p. 19; Locke (1693) *Some Thoughts Concerning Education* p. 111

   Porter suggests that Locke's loathing of his six years at Westminster School under 'the sadistic Dr Busby' was also influential in his favouring of personal tutors. Porter (2000) *Enlightenment* p. 347
37 Smith, Adam (1790) *The Theory of Moral Sentiments* London: A. Strahan; A. Cadell; W. Creech, and J. Bell & Co. p. 79
38 Woodley (2009) 'Oh Miserable and Most Ruinous Measure' p. 35–7
39 Bennett, John (1787) *Strictures on Female Education* London: T. Cadell; et al. p. 138
40 Gordon, Felicia (2005) '*Filles publiques* or Public Women' in Knot, Sarah & Taylor, Barbara (eds.) *Women, Gender and Enlightenment* Basingstoke: Palgrave Macmillan p. 611

   Rousseau viewed women's options as entirely limited to the roles of wife and mother. He insisted: 'A woman's education must be planned in relation to man'; 'She will always be in subjection to a man and she will never be free to set her own opinion above his'. Rousseau (1762) *Emilius and Sophia* p. 322–5
41 John Gregory defined religion as a peculiarly feminine province, arguing that it was 'rather a matter of sentiment than reasoning', and suggested that women were 'peculiarly susceptible to the feelings of devotion'. Gregory, John (1774) *A Father's Legacy to his Daughters* Edinburgh: W. Creech p. 10–13
42 More (1799) *Strictures on the Modern System of Female Education* p. 184–6
43 Hilton (2007) *Women and the Shaping of the Nation's Young* p. 139
44 Hirschmann, Nancy J. (2007) 'Intersectionality Before Intersectionality was Cool' in Hirschmann *Feminist Interpretations of John Locke* p. 174
45 Hilton (2007) *Women and the Shaping of the Nation's Young* p. 45
46 Astell, Mary (1697) *A Serious Proposal to the Ladies* London: Richard Wilkin p. 7–36
47 Goodman, Joyce (2010) 'Class and Religion' in Albisetti, James C. (ed.) et al. *Girls' Secondary Education in the Western World* New York: Palgrave Macmillan p. 165–7, 54–60
48 Gregory (1774) *A Father's Legacy to his Daughters* p. 31–2
49 Moran, Mary Catherine (2005) 'Between the Savage and the Civil' in Knott *Women, Gender and Enlightenment* p. 8
50 Knox, Vicesimus (1781) *Liberal Education* London: Charles Dilly p. 250
51 Although not from a rich family, Sarah Trimmer's father, artist Joshua Kirby, moved in distinguished circles. As a young child, Trimmer remembered visits to

Child-rearing and education

her house by Samuel Johnson, when theological and intellectual discussions would take place. Andrews, Robert M. (2015) 'Women of the Seventeenth- and Eighteenth-century High Church Tradition', in *Anglican and Episcopal History* p. 60–1
52 Cohen, Michelle (2009) 'Familiar Conversation' in Hilton *Educating the Child in Enlightenment Britain* p. 14
53 More (1799) *Strictures on the Modern System of Female Education* p. 176
54 Cohen (2009) 'Familiar Conversation' p. 99–105
55 Hilton (2009) *Educating the Child in Enlightenment Britain* p. 15
56 Hindmarsh (2005) *The Evangelical Conversion Narrative* p. 72–320
57 Ibid. p. 99–105
58 More (1799) *Strictures on the Modern System of Female Education* p. 184
59 Glaser, Brigitte (2006) 'Gendered Childhoods' in Muller *Fashioning Childhood in the Eighteenth Century* p. 191–2
60 Bygrave (2009) *Uses of Education* p. 83
61 Borsay, Peter (2006) 'Children, Adolescents and Fashionable Urban Society in Eighteenth-Century England' in Muller *Fashioning Childhood in the Eighteenth Century* p. 57
62 cited in Picard, Liza (2000) *Dr Johnson's London* London: Phoenix Press p. 176
63 Hilton (2007) *Women and the Shaping of the Nation's Young* p. 44; Hilton (2009) *Educating the Child in Enlightenment Britain* p. 13
64 Streiff, Patrick (2001) *Reluctant Saint?* Peterborough: Epworth Press p. 48
65 Mandeville (1723) 'An Essay on Charity and Charity Schools' p. 336
66 Streiff (2001) *Reluctant Saint?* p. 48
67 Brokesby, Francis (1701) *Of Education with Respect to Grammar Schools and the Universities* London: John Hartley p. A4–5
68 Jacob (2007) *The Clerical Profession in the Long Eighteenth Century* p. 10
 Although the smaller tutorial establishments for boys blurred the distinction between private and public education, the term 'public' education generally referred to attendance at one of the great public schools, or one of the numerous private schools which operated under a similar regime, rather than a private tutor. Woodley (2009) 'Oh Miserable and Most Ruinous Measure' p. 21
69 Percy, Carol (2009) 'Learning and Virtue' in Hilton *Educating the Child in Enlightenment Britain* p. 86
70 Langford (1989) *A Polite and Commercial People* p. 86
71 Brokesby (1701) *Of Education with Respect to Grammar Schools and the Universities* p. 44
72 Woodley (2009) 'Oh Miserable and Most Ruinous Measure' p. 35
73 Neuburg, Victor E. (1971) *Popular Education in Eighteenth Century England* London: The Woburn Press p. 18
74 Langford (1989) *A Polite and Commercial People* p. 86
75 Cunningham (2005) *Children and Childhood in Western Society Since 1500* p. 100
76 Shenstone, William (1742) *The School-mistress* London: R. Dodsley p. 4
77 Hilton (2007) *Women and the Shaping of the Nation's Young* p. 137
78 Percy (2009) 'Learning and Virtue' p. 83
79 Kennett, White (1706) *The Charity of Schools for Poor Children* Joseph Downing: London p. 24
80 Tompson, Richard S. (1971) *Classics or Charity?* Manchester: Manchester University Press p. 33
81 Muller (2009) *Framing Childhood in Eighteenth-century Periodicals and Prints 1689–1789* p. 70
82 Jacob (2007) *The Clerical Profession in the Long Eighteenth Century* p. 41–2
83 Woodley (2009) 'Oh Miserable and Most Ruinous Measure' p. 23
84 Smith, Timothy Wilson (2004) *Johnson* London: Hans Publishing p. 8
85 Elliott-Binns, Leonard E. (1953) *The Early Evangelicals* London: Lutterworth Press p. 67

86 Langford (1989) *A Polite and Commercial People* p. 88; Knox (1781) *Liberal Education* p. 30–42
87 Woodley (2009) 'Oh Miserable and Most Ruinous Measure' p. 29
88 Cohen, Michele (2000) *Masculinity* Marlborough: Adam Matthew Publications p. 4–5
89 Fletcher (2008) *Growing up in England* p. 196–8
90 cited in Bygrave (2009) *Uses of Education* p. 113
91 Langford (1989) *A Polite and Commercial People* p. 79–82
92 Parker, Irene (1914) *Dissenting Academies in England* Cambridge: Cambridge University Press p. 56
93 Marquardt, Manfred (1992) *John Wesley's Social Ethics* Nashville: Abingdon Press p. 50

Dissenters could not matriculate at Oxford or graduate at Cambridge without subscribing to the Thirty-Nine Articles of the Church of England.

94 Rack, Henry D. (2002) *Reasonable Enthusiast, Third Edition* London: Epworth Press p. 357
95 Burden, Mark (2013) *A Biographical Dictionary of Tutors at the Dissenters' Private Academies* Dr Williams's Centre for Dissenting Studies p. 29, 45
96 Deacon, Malcolm (1980) *Philip Doddridge of Northampton 1702–51* Northampton: Northamptonshire Libraries p. 24
97 Parker (1914) *Dissenting Academies in England* p. 76–134
98 Ibid. p. 76–134
99 Tranter, Donald (1996) 'John Wesley and the Education of Children' in Macquiban, Tim (ed.) *Issues in Education* Oxford: Applied Theology Press p. 18
100 Hirschman (2007) *Feminist Interpretations of John Locke* p. 165–72
101 Levene (2012) *The Childhood of the Poor* p. 3
102 Andrew (1989) *Philanthropy and Police* p. 31–2
103 Levene (2012) *The Childhood of the Poor* p. 7
104 Cunningham (2005) *Children and Childhood in Western Society Since 1500* p. 121
105 Gill, Sean (1994) *Women and the Church of England* London: SPCK p. 47

Charity schools were supervised by governors who were responsible to the subscribers and despite this system not being under the direct responsibility of parochial or ecclesiastical authorities, the parish clergy nearly always chaired trustees of charity schools. Jacob (2007) *The Clerical Profession in the Long Eighteenth Century* p. 10

106 Jones (1964) *The Charity School Movement* p. 131–4

In 1738 Philip Doddridge persuaded his congregation to support him in establishing a charity school in Northampton. Although the location of the school is unknown, the venture was successful from the beginning. Doddridge proposed having girls at the school, but there is no record of this being done. Twenty boys were put under the care of a pious, skilful master, John Browne, who taught them to read, write and learn their catechism. Deacon (1980) *Philip Doddridge of Northampton 1702–51* p. 103

107 Deuteronomy 29:11
108 Jones (1964) *The Charity School Movement* p. 4–22
109 Soloway (1969) *Prelates and People* p. 19
110 The SPCK had grown out of a meeting at Lincoln's Inn on 8 March 1699, when Thomas Bray and four lay Anglican friends had come together 'by due lawful methods to promote Christian knowledge'. Bray's primary enthusiasm was the teaching of the catechism to children. He was concerned with the poor, who he felt were too often neglected by the Church. The SPCK grew slowly and steadily into a numerous and influential body which operated outside the formal structure of the Church and in which the laity predominated.

Thompson, H. P. (1954) *Thomas Bray* London: SPCK p. 38–88

34 *Child-rearing and education*

111 Payne, Dianne (2006) 'London's Charity School Children' in *British Journal for Eighteenth-Century Studies 29* Wiley-Blackwell p. 389
112 *The Whole Duty of Man* stated: 'Catechizing is generally look'd on as a thing belonging only to the youth, and so indeed it ought, not because the oldest are not to learn, if they be ignorant, but because all children should be so instructed that it should be impossible for them to be ignorant when they come to years'. Anon (1704) *The Whole Duty of Man* London: W. Norton p. 55
113 Thomas Bray, in his *Essay towards Promoting all Necessary and Useful Knowledge* of 1697, outlined a programme for lending libraries in market towns in each rural deanery, with books to the value of thirty pounds, purchased by local subscription, for loan to clergy and the gentry. He also set up a committee, which functioned from 1705 until 1730, to raise funds and collect books for libraries to enable poorer clergy to continue their education. Jacob (2007) *The Clerical Profession in the Long Eighteenth Century* p. 62
114 Ibid. p. 244
    In 1706, White Kennett preached a sermon at a gathering of charity school children, in which he commended the school to its supporters by declaring 'some thousands of poor children, arm'd with their own innocence, adorn'd with your charity' had 'illustrated with the first rudiments of learning, virtue and religion'. Kennett (1706) *The Charity of Schools for Poor Children* p. 4
115 Butler, Joseph (1745) *A Sermon Preached in the Parish Church of Christ-Church London, on Thursday May 9th 1745* London: J. Oliver p. 14
116 *An Account of Charity Schools Lately Erected* suggested that children simply be taught to read, instructed in Christian religion and 'such other things as are suitable to their condition and capacity'. Anon (1706) *An Account of Charity-schools Lately Erected* London: Joseph Downing p. 22
117 cited in Briggs, Asa (1981) 'Innovation and Adaption' in Ferguson, John (ed.) *Christianity, Society and Education* London: SPCK p. 15–16
118 Mandeville (1723) 'An Essay on Charity and Charity Schools' p. 329–30
119 Ibid. p. 325, 352
120 Andrew (1989) *Philanthropy and Police* p. 32–5
121 Jones (1964) *The Charity School Movement* p. 86
122 *An Account of Charity-schools Lately Erected* of 1708 suggested that schoolmasters should be: 'A member of the Church of England… of sober life and conversation… a meek temper and humble behaviour… have a good genius for teaching… understand well the grounds and principles of the Christian religion… write in a good hand, and understand the grounds of arithmetic… [and] one who keeps good orders in his family'. Anon (1708) *An Account of Charity -schools Lately Erected* London: Joseph Downing p. 4
123 Cunningham (2005) *Children and Childhood in Western Society since 1500* p. 121
124 Langford (1989) *A Polite and Commercial People* p. 133
    There is evidence that the SPCK continued to support charity schools after this date; late in the 1730s the SPCK still included charity school activities in their annual report, and in 1744 noted 'two charity schools, newly erected, the one at Ely, the other at Orwell, Cambridgeshire'. Tye (2014) 'Religion, The SPCK and the Westminster Workhouses' p. 95–6
125 Marquardt (1992) *John Wesley's Social Ethics* p. 50
126 Ibid. p. 135
127 Pollock, Linda A. (1983) *Forgotten Children* Cambridge: Cambridge University Press p. 62
128 Hilton (2009) *Educating the Child in Enlightenment Britain* p. 11, 135
129 Samuel Parr, curate of Hatton, Warwickshire warned in *A Discourse on Education* 'Where education has been entirely neglected, or improperly managed, we see the worst persons ruling with uncontrolled and incessant sway… profane swearing,

lewd conversation, a contempt of order and decorum, a perverse and pertinacious resistance to authority, shameless debauchery and tumultuous riot swell the hateful catalogue... no reasoning, however just, no expostulation, however tender, can restore them to their natural vigour'. Parr, Samuel (1785) *A Discourse on Education and on the Plans Pursued in Charity-schools* London: T. Cadell and T. Evans p. 9

130 Laurence Braddon, solicitor to the wine excise board, calculated that: 'Every poor young child... as soon as born, and likely to live, upon a political account, may be valued at £15... when well bred up [these children] may be made the greatest wealth and strength of the nation'. cited in Andrew (1989) *Philanthropy and Police* p. 23–4

131 Trimmer, Sarah (1792) *Reflections upon the Education of Children in Charity Schools* London: Longman p. 7–9

132 Pollock (1983) *Forgotten Children* p. 61

133 King (2000) *Poverty and Welfare in England 1700–1850* p. 105

134 cited in Horn, Pamela (1994) *Children's Work and Welfare 1780–1890* Cambridge: Cambridge University Press p. 1

135 Jacob (2007) *The Clerical Profession in the Long Eighteenth Century* p. 19

136 Hilton (2007) *Women and the Shaping of the Nation's Young* p. 135; Shefrin (2009) 'Adapted for and Used in Infants' Schools' p. 166

137 Stott, Anne (2003) *Hannah More* Oxford: Oxford University Press p. 130–2

138 Mather (1992) *High Church Prophet* p. 282

139 Woodley (2009) 'Oh Miserable and Most Ruinous Measure' p. 35

140 Porter (1998) *England in the Eighteenth Century* p. 156–7

2 Influences that helped shape John Wesley's educational thinking

John Wesley left a considerable written record over his lifetime. His extensive catalogue of published literature, letters, *Journal* and sermons demonstrate his continuing interest in child-rearing and education. As chapter one has shown, the century in which he was writing was one of considerable social, religious and economic change. This chapter reassesses the influences that helped shape Wesley's thinking on how children were to be raised and educated. It demonstrates that his mother Susanna Wesley's educational thinking was more compassionate than some commentators have thitherto suggested, and argues that John Wesley's upbringing at Epworth had an impact on his views on female education.

Although Wesley's educational thinking crossed gender and class boundaries, his own attendance at public school and university gave him an education beyond that available to his sisters, and one denied to Dissenters, or children of the poor. Despite this, the chapter demonstrates that his time at Charterhouse and Oxford was influential in the development of Wesley's thinking on education, gender, class and piety. Although his thinking resonates with Puritan and Lockean influences, the chapter concludes by evaluating non-Anglican influences, particularly the significance of Wesley's encounter with the Moravian Church.

Wesley's thinking on child-rearing and education

Wesley's views on how children were to be raised and educated were complex and in some ways contradictory. He championed an early education of children within a family unit. Parents were expected to instruct their offspring in Christian values of virtue, morality and piety, alongside Puritan values of industriousness, sobriety, frugality and temperance. This inevitably led to a tension between the desire to educate children and the need to evangelise their parents. Indeed, the evidence suggests that, particularly towards the end of his life, Wesley's educational practice was more strongly Evangelical than intellectual, more pious than academic. He advocated the thinking of Locke and encouraged reading and learning. His Arminian doctrines of free will and universal salvation asserted that salvation lay not in the predestination of God, but in the individual's pursuit of a life of holiness. This inspired in his followers, particularly women and the poor, a desire to seek self-improvement and self-advancement. However, 'free will' without the constraints of reason, Wesley argued, manifested itself in the young as 'self-will', something to be conquered if children were to be governed by the reason and piety of their parents. His views on child-rearing, grounded in Puritan traditions of the seventeenth century, failed to acknowledge new concepts of the innocence of childhood which became increasingly influential during the eighteenth century.

The place of the family in instructing children was, for Wesley, paramount. He asked his listeners and readers to consider what the consequence would be if family religion was neglected, and suggested that if they did not take care of the rising generation, 'the present revival of religion would in a short time die away'. He warned parents that it was their responsibility to watch over their children with utmost care, 'that when you are called to give account of each to the Father of Spirits you may give your accounts with joy and not with grief'. He asserted that the wickedness of children was generally due to the fault or neglect of their parents; and that taking too soft and tender a line with their children would be like 'offering up their sons and their daughters unto the devil'.[1]

Perhaps unsurprisingly, some parents reacted to this by pointing out that Wesley had no children of his own.[2] Adam Clarke responded to such criticism by stressing the significant influence on Wesley of his mother Susanna:

> It has been wondered at that a man who had no children of his own could have known so well how they should be managed and educated; but that wonder will at once cease, when it is recollected by whom he was himself educated; and who was his instructress in all things, during his infancy and youth.[3]

Despite the importance he placed on family, Wesley's views on the parent/child relationship appear to be ambivalent. While the salvation of the child's soul depended on piety and virtue learned in relationship with, and by example of parents, this does not appear to have necessitated, in Wesley's view, the sort of deep emotional attachment brought about by parenthood. Wesley adopted the two daughters of his wife Mary Vazeille as step-daughters, and later delighted in seeing his step-grandchildren, about whom he showed concern and for whom he felt much love.[4] However, Wesley's love for children was always subordinate to his primary concern to save their souls.

Wesley's seemingly underdeveloped sense of the impact of parenthood was evident in his reaction to his sister Martha, whose children died of fever.[5] Though he expressed fondness for Martha, Wesley told her that the death of her children was 'a great instance of the goodness of God toward you'; he reasoned that she was always complaining about them, and would now have more time to devote to her own religious concerns.[6] Although Wesley's remarks appear to demonstrate a lack of feeling, they were spoken in affection; indeed Rack suggests that this sort of sentiment was commonplace at the time.[7] With child mortality high, avoiding excessive attachment to one's offspring may have served as an emotional defence mechanism.[8] Puritan religious conviction had led parents to regard children as having been temporarily entrusted to them by God, and Christian doctrine offered consolation on a child's death that he or she had moved to a better place.[9]

Perhaps for this reason, Wesley rarely discussed parental relationships in his writings, and when he referred to them regarding the death of a child, he focused on the triumph of faith rather than the emotion of bereavement.[10] A letter written by Charles Wesley to the Selina, Countess of Huntingdon after the death of his infant daughter on 28 July 1755 revealed that his brother's lack of emotional empathy had its consequences:

> He cannot feel my reasons for staying with my wife. I sent him word, as soon as she was delivered. He has never since taken the least notice of her, or her child. I did not particularly mention the child because I would not give him, or his wife, pain. I do not inform him of her death, because I would not give them pleasure.[11]

Indeed, Mack suggests that Charles Wesley's experience of bereavement gave him greater empathy and compassion than his brother, and enabled him to enter other people's suffering more than John. Writing to Mrs Jones on 13 January 1750, Charles stated: 'He that shall come will come, and wipe away all tears from your eyes. I bear your burthen till then, as your brother and companion in tribulation'.[12] John Wesley's emotional detachment appears not to have changed over his lifetime. In 1791 he wrote to Adam Clarke following the death of Clarke's eldest daughter, stating 'You startle me when you talk of grieving so much for the death of an infant… if you love them thus all your children will die'.[13]

What was important to Wesley was the way in which parents instructed their children. In *Lessons for Children*, published in 1746, he stated:

> I cannot but earnestly intreat [sic] you, to take good heed, how you teach these deep things of God. Beware of that common, but accursed way of making children parrots, instead of Christians. Labour that, as far as is possible, they may understand every single sentence which they read.[14]

Forty years later, addressing parents in his sermon *On Family Religion,* published in 1783, Wesley reiterated this by telling parents to instruct their children 'early, plainly, frequently and patiently'. He contended that children, even from an early age, must be able to read the Bible. Such knowledge, he argued, was necessary 'for forming, training and practising of children in such a course of life as the sublimest doctrines of Christianity require'.[15] He conceded that although there may be some use in teaching even very young children to say their prayers daily, it would be 'utterly impossible to teach any to practice prayer till they are awakened'.[16]

Wesley wrote in his *Journal* of July 1743 that 'the following days I had time to finish the *Instructions for Children*'.[17] The first edition was published in 1745;

and by 1755 Wesley had published a fourth edition. *Instructions for Children* concluded that children could, and should, be 'taught the knowledge of God, and the knowledge of letters at the same time'.[18] Intended for children of the poor, it advised them: 'You ought to be content, tho' you should have little or nothing in the World. And you ought not to desire anything more than you have, for you have now more than you deserve'. Parents were to ensure that their children lived simply, did not eat between meals or desire abundance in anything. Children were expected to pray for a 'humble, submissive, simple and obedient heart'; they were to pray for their parents, and for their 'superiors'; to 'obey without murmuring'; and to 'think everyone better' than themselves. They were to avoid idleness, take responsibility for their actions and, when they were wilfully wrong, expect to be punished.[19] Wesley followed *Instructions for Children* by publishing, between 1746 and 1756, a four volume *Lessons for Children*.[20] Written to encourage young readers, the opening remarks in volume I advised parents and schoolmasters that the *Lessons* were 'the plainest and the most useful portions of scripture, such as children may the most easily understand, and such as it most concerns them to know'.[21]

Despite the somewhat autocratic tone of Wesley's *Instructions*, his writings resonate with Lockean influences.[22] This is perhaps not surprising since his mother Susanna had commended 'the wise Mr Locke' to her son, and frequently referred to him in her *Journals*.[23] Wesley's reaction to Rousseau was rather less favourable. In his *Journal* of February 1770 Wesley concluded: 'I read with much expectation a celebrated book, Rousseau *On Education*. But how was I disappointed! Surely a more consummate coxcomb never saw the sun! Many of his oracles are palpably false'. He suggested that Rousseau's view was 'whimsical to the last degree, grounded neither upon reason, or experience'.[24]

Despite his admiration of Locke, Wesley contended that 'a wise parent should begin to break their child's will the first moment it appears'. To do this, he suggested, needed firmness and resolution, adding 'my own mother had ten children each of whom had spirit enough'.[25] Evidence from Wesley's writings suggests that his child-rearing methods were not based solely on punishment. Writing that 'the duty of educating children requires first encouragement, second correction' he added:

> Endeavour to make children in love with duty by offering them rewards and invitations, and whenever they do well, encouraging them to go on… the second means is correction… when all fair means prevail not, then there is a necessity of using sharper, and let that be first tried in words, I mean not by railing and foul language, but in sober, yet sharp reproof, but if that fail too, then proceed to blows, 'He that spareth his rod hateth his son'.[26]

Indeed, Wesley's remarks appear to be less severe than those of Quaker George Fox who, despite acceptance of the principle of non-violence, claimed: 'Withhold not correction from thy child, for if thou beatest him with the rod he shall not die'.[27] Nevertheless, Wesley's tone contrasts with that of Dissenting educator, preacher and hymn writer Philip Doddridge who cautioned: 'take heed, that your corrections be not too frequent, or too severe, and that they be not given in an unbecoming manner'.[28]

Telling parents that they needed to equip their children for 'the world to come', Wesley advised them to send their sons to a private school, kept by a pious man, who would instruct a small number of children in religion and learning. Sending them to large public schools, he contended, would be little better than sending them to the devil, since they were 'nurseries of all manner of wickedness'. Daughters, Wesley stated, were not to be sent to large boarding schools which taught 'pride, vanity and affectation, intrigue, artifice and in short, everything which a Christian woman ought not to learn', adding that he did not know of a pious, sensible woman who had been educated at a large boarding school.[29]

That is not to suggest that Wesley was opposed to young women acquiring an education. His attitude to the education of girls was undoubtedly influenced by his experiences at Epworth. Indeed Bowden suggests that Susanna Wesley's attitude to her daughters' education may have influenced John Wesley's decision to appoint a number of women preachers.[30] Baker contended that Wesley's lifelong dedication to female education was sparked by the discovery of Mary Astell's *A Serious Proposal to Ladies*, published in 1697. Correspondence between Wesley, Ann Granville and Nancy Griffiths in June 1731 noted 'surely her plan of female life must have pleased all the thinking part of her sex'.[31] However, it was not until 1780 that Wesley published in *The Arminian Magazine*, 'A Female Course of Study', and even then, his thoughts were addressed only to those elite young ladies who 'had a good understanding and much leisure'.[32]

Indeed, Wesley's course of study would only be possible in better-off households where daughters had access to the sort of reading material he recommended, or were able to purchase the books he advocated. Assuring them that the Bible contained all the knowledge they needed, Wesley reminded young ladies that 'all you learn is to be referred to this, as either directly, or remotely conducive to it'. Wesley advised young women that, if their constitutions could bear it, they should study for five or six hours a day. They were to begin and end with divinity. He told them that whenever they began to tire with books that required a strong and deep attention, they could relax their minds by interposing history or poetry, 'or something of a lighter nature'. Wesley set out an extensive list of subjects that they might follow over the three to five years it would take them to complete their studies, depending on their 'health and application'. Beginning with grammar and arithmetic, they were advised to move on to logic, ethics, natural philosophy, chronology, ancient history and metaphysics; Wesley concluded 'you will then have knowledge enough for any reasonable Christian'.[33]

Where it was not possible for parents to educate their daughters at home, Wesley suggested that girls might instead be sent to a 'mistress who truly fears God, one whose life is a pattern to her scholars, and who has only so many that she can watch over each as one that must give account to God'.[34] Discussed in more detail in chapter three, Wesley frequently corresponded with Mistresses who ran small boarding schools for daughters from Methodist homes, and the reading list he supplied for Mary Bishop, who sought his advice on how to extend her library for twelve to twenty year old girls, suggests his desire to advance their learning. He recommended the *Concise History of England*; the *Concise History of the Church*; Rollin's *Ancient History*, Hooke's *Roman History*; and 'for the elder and more sensible children' Malebranchi's *Search after Truth* and Locke's *Essay on the Human Understanding...* et al. However, to Bishop's request that she 'mix instruction with delight' at her 'good school of orderly affectionate children', Wesley warned: 'I would recommend very few novels for fear they would be desirous of more'.[35]

Wesley's Anglican upbringing at Epworth

Susanna Wesley spent twenty years educating her children at home. Clarke noted in his *Memoirs of the Wesley Family* that as 'their circumstances were narrow and confined, the education of their progeny fell particularly upon themselves, and especially Mrs Wesley, who seems to have possessed every qualification requisite for either a public or private teacher'.[36] There is little doubt that John Wesley's thinking on how children should be raised and educated was profoundly influenced by his mother.[37] All the Wesley children, both sons and daughters, were instructed in a strong and rational foundation of religious education. 'There is nothing I now desire to live for', Susanna Wesley stated in a letter to her son Samuel on 11 October 1709, 'but to do some small service to my children; that as I have brought them into the world, I may, if it please God, be an instrument of doing good to their souls'.[38]

John Wesley's early childhood was spent predominantly in a feminine atmosphere where his sisters were both lively and literate. The relationship between John and his sisters was affectionate and mutually supportive.[39] Susanna Wesley's attitude towards her daughters' education was, Bowden suggests, striking for the time since she placed great significance on the education of girls. Susanna Wesley believed that:

> No girl be taught to work till she can read very well, and then that she be kept to her work with the same application, and for the same time, that she was held to in reading. This rule also is much to be observed; for the putting children to learn sewing before they can read perfectly is the very reason why so few women can read fit to be heard, and never to be well understood.[40]

Nevertheless, the male and female children in the Wesley household were not educational equals. While the expectation was that the boys would go on to receive a public school education designed to prepare them for university, for the Wesley girls, their mother's tuition was the only schooling they received.

Although she believed that it was important for her daughters to be heard and understood, and she gave them an education equal to their brothers at home, during the eighteenth century the opportunity of a university education was available to males only. Nevertheless, it was John Wesley's 'sonship' to Susanna, Brantley argues, that set the pattern for his lifetime of intellectual relationships with women.[41]

Both Samuel and Susanna Wesley had been brought up in Dissenting families, their fathers having been among over two thousand clergy expelled from their livings under the Act of Uniformity in 1662. Susanna had been instructed by her father Samuel Annesley to a level far beyond that which was customary for her time and sex.[42] Despite this, she wrote a report regarding her decision to conform to the Church of England when she was just twelve years old.[43] Gregory argues that this independence in religious matters was a precursor to John Wesley's religious position.[44] Samuel Wesley received a Dissenting education at Veal's Academy in Stepney and Morton's Academy at Newington Green. Both Edward Veal and Charles Morton were men of considerable scholarship and were held in high regard by him. Morton was one of the most important Dissenting educators of the late seventeenth century, and his academy was the most considerable among the Dissenters in England, having annexed 'a fine garden, bowling green, fish-pond, and within a laboratory' in which were 'air pumps, thermometers, and all sorts of mathematical instruments'.[45]

Samuel Wesley entered Exeter College, Oxford as a servitor in August 1683.[46] While there, he was persuaded to write an account of his experiences at the Dissenting academies. Perhaps in an opinion coloured by his own political sensitivities, after meeting some students, Wesley reported that he had taken offence not only at their vulgarity, but at their republicanism.[47] Although Burden argues that few of the early Dissenting academies earned a reputation for political radicalism, and many of their students later took up posts within the Church, Samuel Wesley was later to claim that the Dissenting academies made accessible 'Republican books to confirm and encourage' these tendencies.[48] He also claimed that although he had 'kept no such lewd company' during his time at Morton's or Veal's Academies, he owed it 'one of the happiest providences' of his life that he had a 'narrow escape from debauchery and ruin'.[49]

A pious man of principle, Samuel Wesley was a diligent pastor, and from 1699 an enthusiastic correspondent for the SPCK.[50] He was actively involved in their work in establishing charity schools for the poor,[51] and expressed concerns, which his son John would later echo, that the procurement of 'men of known and approved piety' to teach at these schools was not easily achievable.[52] Samuel Wesley instructed his sons in Latin, Greek and classical literature, laying the foundation for their future learning at Westminster, Charterhouse and Oxford.[53] He was also happy for his daughters to use his extensive library.[54] Through his father, John Wesley was not only exposed to a store of classical knowledge, but a broad religious and political heritage which focused on loyalty, monarchism and passive obedience, factors which would inform his future life.[55] The exposure his sisters had to their father's library may also have influenced John Wesley's thinking towards female education.

John Wesley's growing interest in education prompted him to write to his mother for an account of her Epworth system. Her reply, dated 24 July 1732, has come to be regarded as one of her most important pieces of writing. The precise text of this 'Education Letter' is uncertain since the original letter has been lost, and Lynch claims that there is no convincing evidence that any Wesley family biographer beyond Adam Clarke had access to it.[56] The methods Susanna Wesley outlined to her son have been criticised by scholars as puritanical and austere. Bowen in *Wrestling Jacob*, published in 1937, claimed that Susanna Wesley's ideas of education 'were welded in the hands of her son into an evil thing that did unrecorded harm to thousands of children'.[57] Plumb contended that 'love was alien to her heart'.[58] The evidence suggests to the contrary, indicating instead that her practices were in fact governed by affection and respect for her children.[59]

The 'Education Letter' was reproduced by John Wesley in two published forms, the earliest and longer version in the 1749 instalment of his *Journal*, and the second, published thirty five years later, in *The Arminian Magazine* in 1784.[60] A problem arises on comparing the two versions, when Lynch suggests there is difficulty discerning 'where the mother's voice ends and the son's begins'.[61] The most striking difference is an additional paragraph that appears in the later version, but which is neither in the earlier version, nor in Clarke's *Memoirs of the Wesley Family*.[62] Lynch contends that the paragraph was added by John Wesley to reinforce his message on parental authority given in his sermon *On Obedience to Parents*, and published in *The Arminian Magazine* in September and October 1784. By removing from Susanna Wesley's authorship the paragraph exhorting: 'if you whip him ten times running to effect it let none persuade you it is cruelty to do this…', her practices appear more compassionate than commentators have hitherto suggested. Certainly the Puritan emphasis on conquering the child's will remains, but, Lynch argues, rather than turning first and frequently to the rod, Susanna's methods were directed towards minimising the need for punishment.[63] Susanna wrote that although 'the education of so many children must create abundance of trouble'; it was 'no small honour… to be entrusted with the care of so many souls'.[64] John Wesley was to record in 1766:

> I remember to have heard my father asking my mother 'How could you have the patience to tell that blockhead the same thing twenty times over?' She answered 'Why, if I had told him but nineteen times, I should have lost all my labour'. What patience indeed, what love, what knowledge is requisite for this![65]

In stating that children: 'should be always commended and frequently rewarded' for obedience, Susanna Wesley's practices appear to show affection and respect for their efforts.[66] Samuel Wesley, writing to his eldest son Samuel, stated 'You know what you owe to one of the best mothers... [I have] often reflected on the tender and peculiar love which your mother has always expressed towards you... the particular care she took of your education'.[67] Rather than austere and puritanical, Wallace argues that Susanna Wesley drew on some of the latest theories of education of her time, and that she was an early reader of Locke's *Some Thoughts Concerning Education* of 1693.[68] She treated her children as individuals; writing to her husband in February 1712, she stated 'I take such a proportion of time as I can best spare every night to discourse with each child by itself on something that relates to its principal concerns'. The time the children spent individually with her was not, Potter argues, intended for teaching or instruction, but advice, and listening to the issues that were of concern to each of them.[69] She did not seek to shut down their minds in order to claim their souls; 'breaking the will' did not mean extinguishing the child's personality.[70]

Susanna Wesley insisted on 'a regular method of living'.[71] While Bowden comments that with nine children in her care at Epworth, the alternative to a regulated life would have been 'complete chaos', she adds that the sense of order in the schoolroom at Epworth is nevertheless striking.[72] Potter suggests that this methodical and structured approach to learning owed much to the influence of the Danish missionaries, whose work in India had been outlined in a letter that Emiliá Wesley found in her father's study in 1712. Although Susanna Wesley's education method had begun in earnest after the Epworth fire in 1709, and she did not read the letter until later, Potter argues 'the missionaries work relating to the education of children did not so much change Susanna's own methods, as confirm them and inspire her to develop them further'.[73]

An important part of upbringing for the Wesley children was to learn self-discipline and self-control. Regulation in eating and sleeping was a feature of the Epworth household and Susanna stated that her children 'might have nothing they cry'd for'. Drinking or eating between meals was forbidden and the children, from the age of one, were taught 'to fear the rod, and cry softly'.[74] She did not supply toys for her family, but they did play cards, and a dancing master came to Epworth.[75] Despite this, John Wesley grew up in an environment where the children were deliberately deprived of contact with other boys and girls of their own age who might encourage frivolity in them.[76]

Susanna Wesley taught her children to read at the age of five, and expected them to learn prayers, catechism and portions of scripture 'as their memories could bear'.[77] Classes were conducted six days a week, from nine to twelve and from two until five.[78] Pairs of older and younger siblings read one another a chapter of each testament and the 'Psalms for the day' as appointed in the Book of Common Prayer.[79] Writing to John in a letter dated 21 February 1731/2, Susanna declared 'There are few, if any, that would entirely devote above twenty years of the prime of life in hopes to save the souls of their children... for that was my principle intention, however unskilfully or unsuccessfully managed'.[80]

While Dallimore suggests that John Wesley's upbringing at Epworth was not as idyllic as some have previously suggested, Susanna Wesley's vigour of mind and talent for discipline, combined with Samuel Wesley's intensity of purpose and aptitude for learning, were to prove important qualities inherited by their son.[81] Wesley believed that the family was the seat of virtue and piety.[82] His mother's example had shown the young Wesley that the interaction of a parent with a child in the domestic setting could be transformed into an effective educational vehicle.[83]

Wesley at Charterhouse and Oxford

Educated at Charterhouse School from the age of ten, Wesley was described by Thompson as 'unusually well behaved, obedient and of excellent manners'. Between sixty and seventy boys attended the school in Wesley's day. The staff consisted of the schoolmaster, Dr Thomas Walker, and the Usher, Andrew Tooke. Although Walker, 'a most exact scholar in Greek, Latin and Hebrew', may have laid the foundation of Wesley's classical learning, Thompson suggested that it was Tooke, not only a classical scholar but a mathematician and scientist, who gave him a width and variety of intellectual interests unusual in his age.[84] Unfortunately, despite having been a constant correspondent, no letters from Wesley's time at Charterhouse have survived.[85]

Wesley claimed to have been happy at Charterhouse.[86] He was, however, to confess in his *Journal* on 28 June 1770 that 'From ten to thirteen or fourteen, I had little but bread to eat, and not great plenty of that'. Despite the fact that Wesley appears to have been a victim of the bullying that was experienced by the younger boys, who were deprived of their meat by the older boys, he was subsequently to regard this experience in rather a different light, writing in July 1770 'far from hurting me… [it] laid the foundation of lasting health'.[87] Indeed, this enforced deprivation came to be regarded by Wesley as an important act of self-denial, which thereafter was not only adopted by him voluntarily, but which, for the members of the Holy Club, became a way of seeking holiness.[88]

In later life, Wesley was often to return to Charterhouse, which he referred to as 'that great school wherein I had been educated'; and made a practice of walking through the school every year.[89] He nevertheless described many of the public schools of his day as places where children not only learned to read and write, but learned 'all kind of vice so that it had been better for them to have been without their knowledge than to have bought it at so dear a price'.[90] On leaving Charterhouse and prior to going up to Oxford, Wesley spent time with his elder brother Samuel.[91] He was thereafter an undergraduate at Christ Church from 1720, and a Fellow at Lincoln College, Oxford University from 17 March 1726. Professors and Fellows at Oxford were mostly clergy, and all undergraduates were educated in the Classics and received a basic grounding in theology.[92] Wesley was ordained at Oxford in 1728, and carried out his duties as a tutor and as a lecturer in Classics, logic and divinity conscientiously.[93]

Throughout the eighteenth century Oxford University functioned largely hierarchically, with privileges, freedoms and disciplines conferred according to social rank. While *The Gentleman's Magazine* of 1798 declared that 'Nothing [is] so beneficial in a wise state as properly keeping up the distinction of different ranks in society', such distinctions, Midgley suggests, 'spawned a sub-culture of flatterers seeking to climb the social ladder; and of privileged louts secure in their idleness and dissipation'. Young noblemen often led lives of excess; and gentlemen commoners were notorious for misbehaviour and wildness, leading *The Gentleman's Magazine* to suggest, 'They are perfectly their own masters, and take the lead in every disgraceful frolic of juvenile debauchery'.[94]

Such behaviour was by no means universal; the large body of commoners, though in no way innocent of frolic and juvenile high spirits, were undoubtedly under discipline and tutorial supervision. Each had his assigned tutor, and was required to attend lectures, to write impositions and to attend Chapel regularly.[95] Undergraduates, bachelors and fellows were required to daily attend Morning Prayer in the College chapel, usually at 6am in spring and summer, and 7am in autumn and winter, and Evening Prayer at 5 or 5.30pm, and were fined for non-attendance; they were also expected to attend university sermons.[96] There was an expectation that Oxford University would pass on received wisdom and maintain the established order in Church and State.[97] Above all, Oxford was the trustee of orthodoxy in the Church; it trained the clergy and defended the Church intellectually against subversive religious and political opinions.[98]

Preachers were regarded as role models for young clergy and, when invited to speak, were expected to deliver sermons at the University that followed orthodox thinking and to avoid any extremes of opinion.[99] Nevertheless, when university officials invited Wesley to preach in Oxford on 25 July 1741, he had initially intended to deliver a long-considered diatribe against the University entitled 'How is the faithful city become an harlot', outlining what he considered were its manifold lapses in doctrine.[100] In the event, he was dissuaded from doing so by Lady Huntingdon.[101] Instead he delivered the sermon *The Almost Christian,* in which he made no reference to the University but declared that a 'pattern of holy living' might bring about the 'almost Christian'; but only through the love and grace of God might someone become the 'altogether Christian'.[102]

When he returned to St Mary's for the last time in 1744, having by then been away from Oxford for nine years, Wesley was to couch his denunciation of the University not in terms of its doctrine, but its conduct and lack of piety.[103] In his sermon *Scriptural Christianity* delivered to the University on 24 August 1744, Wesley declared to the assembled students and staff that 'iniquity had overspread [them] like a flood'. He questioned the attitude of the students who, he contended, rather than being 'humble, teachable, and advisable', were 'stubborn, self-willed, heady and high-minded'. He reprimanded the masters for their lack of Christian love, asserting that 'without love, all learning is but splendid ignorance'.[104] Wesley's condemnation was not of the University itself, but of those who failed to conduct themselves in accordance with its Statutes. While some university officials may have sympathised with some of his views, even Samuel Johnson, who Turberville suggests respected Wesley personally, felt that in the University of Oxford such a display of pietism and enthusiasm was out of place, and therefore totally unacceptable to the authorities.[105]

John Wesley was not alone in his determination to uphold the University Statutes. His brother Charles noted in a letter dated 5 May 1729 that 'Diligence led me into serious thinking… and to observe the method of study prescribed by the Statutes of the University. This gained me the harmless nickname of Methodist'.[106] Both Charles and John Wesley had, by the 1730s, committed themselves to a pattern of 'holy living'. This quest for holiness, purity of intention and Christian perfection followed the guidance of William Law's *Serious Call to a Devout and Holy Life,* which was published in 1729.[107] Law's work evoked the classic High Church message that life was to be taken seriously, filled with good works, with no room for pleasure or relaxation, and with regular self-examination and resolutions to do better.[108] Law contended that Christianity was not a school for the teaching of moral virtues, the polishing of manners or forming a life of decency and gentility, it was the training for a life of holiness which demanded nothing less than a change of heart and mind.[109]

While much has been written concerning the society which became known as the Holy Club, the image of a single group of people meeting in John Wesley's room at Lincoln College is, Heitzenrater contends, 'incomplete and even misleading'.[110] The complex development of the Holy Club took place over the period from summer 1729 to autumn 1730.[111] Originally intended as a fellowship for the study of the New Testament and classical literature, the interests of the group shifted towards the cultivation of piety.[112] John Wesley, who returned to Oxford in November 1729, having taken a leave of absence from his fellowship to assist his father at Epworth, assumed leadership and the group grew into what Rack refers to as a 'shifting network' of small societies.[113] These societies were comprised of between three and six people, whose purpose, frequency and pattern of meeting varied, but whose aim was the pursuit of a pattern of holy living through the practice of meditation, self-examination and prayer.[114] This kind of religious society was by no means unique,[115] but generally comprised of groups of young men since it was not thought proper for women to form any sort of religious associations of their own.[116]

Regarding scholarship as a Christian virtue, John Wesley conducted small gatherings in his rooms at Lincoln College in an atmosphere of intellectual learning.[117] He argued that by developing better habits of eating, exercise, sleeping, reading and thinking, Holy Club members could master negative feelings like anger or envy, while nurturing positive feelings of compassion or tenderness.[118] He encouraged them into practices that included regular fasting, early rising and meticulous diary keeping.[119] These practices were coupled with a desire to enact a practical expression of Christian faith through charitable activities.[120] Those involved spent a good deal of their time, money and energy in a ministry of mercy among the Oxford poor.[121] Although both in spirit and aim the Holy Club was akin to the Religious Societies of England and the *Collegia Pietatis* of Germany,[122] what drew attention, derision and even hostility to the Holy Club was the intensity and persistence with which their 'methods' permeated the lives of those involved.[123]

Despite the fact that Wesley was inclined to impose parts of his private disciplines upon his students, Green suggests that the impact of the Holy Club should not be exaggerated. Although many young undergraduates and graduates were interested in their activities, the majority of the senior members of the University had hardly heard of the Holy Club.[124]

Non-Anglican influences on Wesley's educational principles

Although Wesley took an interest in Roman Catholic Port Royal Schools, established in France between 1646 and 1660, he was particularly keen to discover more about the educational work of the German Pietists.[125] He learned German in order to converse with them.[126] As chapter five demonstrates, there were marked similarities between the work of the Port Royal Schools and that of the Pietists in rules Wesley later instigated at his boarding school in Kingswood. The Salzburgers followed the teachings of August Hermann Francke who founded a community which Campbell describes as 'a kind of pietistic empire' in Halle.[127] Francke established several institutions, including two schools for commoners, publishing houses and an orphanage.[128] Educators respected the schools as the most progressive educational institutions in Germany and Francke's work exercised a remarkable influence upon the charity school movement in England.[129] Wesley visited Halle in August 1738; he knew something of the work being done since the Holy Club had made much of the *Pietas Hallensis*, Professor Francke's account of the Orphan House, there.[130]

In rules laid down by Francke in his *Short and Simple Instructions*, published in 1707, the first essential was to place in the hands of a child the means by which he could prepare his soul for salvation. Franke met with the orphans every evening and examined their consciences.[131] The intention was that children of the poor 'who lived their lives like cattle without any knowledge of God and spiritual things' were provided with 'food for the soul as well as the body'. Children were trained in discipline and industry. In a school day of seven hours, more than half was devoted to the religious discipline of the Bible. The hours of the day were marked off with precision and only necessary activities were permitted. At first the only other subjects taught were reading, writing and simple arithmetic, but when Wesley visited Halle in 1738, Latin, Greek, Hebrew, French, English, history and geography had been added. All subjects were graded for the many classes with the intention of leading each child at his own level.[132]

The Moravians traditionally placed a strong emphasis on education, and Count Nikolaus Ludwig von Zinzendorf laid the foundation for a rapid expansion of Moravian schools in Europe and North America in the eighteenth and nineteenth centuries.[133] His theology was not a religion of the head, but of the heart. Faith was shaped by inner experience, intuition and feeling; and emphasised introspection and feeling over dogma or ritual.[134] Wesley first encountered the Moravians on his way to Georgia in 1735 when the boat in which he was sailing was hit by a fierce storm. Struck by their calm faith, the Moravian notion of an 'inward' religion was to have a significant effect on him.[135] In 1738 Wesley visited the Moravian schools at both Herrnhut and Jena to see at first hand their educational systems in operation. On his return to England Wesley wrote to the Moravian brethren expressing approval of their 'method of instructing children', and the 'great care of the souls committed to your charge'.[136]

For Zinzendorf, education was a much larger enterprise than training intellectual or practical skills, and he was increasingly sceptical of the benefits of scholarly pursuits. He criticised the discipline that had characterised his own education at Halle since he did not believe that breaking a child's will was the correct way to educate; what he required was 'the conquest of the heart'.[137] Zinzendorf believed that children should be allowed to develop in an atmosphere of freedom and love, unconfined by social background, class differences or geographical origin.[138] The children lived, and were educated, communally with all activities, prayer, singing, sleeping, eating and work conducted in groups.[139] They were bound by rules which stipulated early rising and daily walking.[140] They were not 'converted' but were kept in 'innocence' since the Moravians maintained that salvation arose not through works or piety, but solely by awaiting God's grace.[141] Wesley came to regard the Moravian settlement at Herrnhut, near Dresden as a truly Christian community.[142]

Although Wesley admired much about the Moravian system, his thinking did not entirely accord with that of Zinzendorf. Wesley maintained that children should be 'taught the knowledge of God and the knowledge of letters at the same time'.[143] For Zinzendorf, faith and reason were diametrically opposed. He considered reason to be a 'science of the head' and argued that the reality of God lay outside the sphere of human understanding. He claimed that the experience of a 'personal connection' with Christ superseded all efforts of studious scholarship, and declared that 'the personal connection with the Saviour... should not entail any bookishness or coerced learning... we have let go of the study of books and we have ceased to defend the truth with rational arguments'.[144]

The Moravian Church was at the heart of the English spiritual revival of the 1730s.[145] On 1 May 1738 Wesley, along with several members of the Holy Club, joined the Moravians in London where they had established the Fetter Lane Society. The Society was Moravian in foundation and character, although initially largely Anglican in membership. The Society's services were attended by several well-to-do families, who, under an arrangement with the Archbishop of Canterbury, were able to retain their status as members of the Church of England, yet avail themselves of the warmth of the Moravians.[146]

Although Wesley's admiration of the Moravians continued, he separated from the Fetter Lane Society in 1740 when the Moravian August Gottlieb Spangenberg introduced the doctrine of 'stillness'. Spangenberg's radical interpretation was built on a belief that those who had not yet found faith should 'be still', that is, abstain from communion, Bible reading and attendance at

Church and await God's grace.[147] Wesley rejected this radical quietism, believing the ordinances to be both means of grace and commands of God.[148] He concluded that prayer, communion and attendance at sermons were actually efficacious in bringing people to contrition and faith, and that passivity led to despair or to a spirituality that was virtually inert.[149] The Moravians, on the other hand, Hindmarsh argues, regarded the move to stillness as a reaction against what they saw as the problem of English 'enthusiasm', which Philip Molther described as involving the 'convulsions, cryings out, and groaning' happening at the Fetter Lane meetings.[150]

While the Fetter Lane Society had professed to be in union with the Church of England, and members had received communion at St Paul's Cathedral, they now began to assume the character of a distinct community.[151] Possibly in anticipation of the split with the Fetter Lane Society, Wesley bought in 1740 the 'vast, uncouth heap of ruins' known as the Foundery, a former factory for making cannons, having preached there in November 1739.[152] The first phase of work on the redundant building, to prepare a large preaching place able to accommodate one thousand five hundred people, was completed in February 1740.[153] Its location in Moorfields was strategic since it was close enough to the Fetter Lane Society that the people from there could also attend the Foundery if they wished.[154] It was at the Foundery that Wesley established his own 'United Society', and where he opened a day school for local children.[155]

Conclusion

As a prodigious author, John Wesley left an extensive catalogue of literature from which it is evident that he maintained an interest in how children were to be raised and educated through his life. Wesley's Anglican upbringing at Epworth undoubtedly informed his belief in the importance of the family in instructing children in piety and learning. Raised in a predominantly female household, Wesley was exposed not only to his mother's educational influence, but to female siblings who were able and intelligent. The gender constraints of the eighteenth century meant that while the male members of the Wesley household were destined for public school and university, this option was not available to their sisters.

John Wesley's thinking on the education of girls was far from straightforward. Although he encouraged young women to improve themselves through learning, his insistence that they always 'begin and end' with divinity suggests that his primary concern was with their piety rather than their intellect. Although his course of study for young ladies was, for its day, comprehensive, and he encouraged Mistresses in small boarding schools to develop girl's intellect, gender constraints meant that this did not include subjects like Latin, Greek and Hebrew which were taught to boys in grammar schools, and at Wesley's boarding school in Kingswood.

Although raised in a Puritan environment, Susanna Wesley's educational method resonates with Lockean influences. The Puritan virtues of industry, sobriety, frugality and temperance were combined with a recognition of the individuality of the child; and as the work of Elizabeth Lynch and others demonstrates, an affection and respect for her children. At Charterhouse and Oxford, Wesley was exposed to an education bound by specific social and gender parameters. His subsequent condemnation of both public schools and universities arose from a belief that they were failing to educate pupils for 'the world to come', something he, and his brother Charles, tried to address through their efforts with the Holy Club.

In not wishing to compromise his strongly held Christian principles, and favouring the thinking of Locke, Wesley's educational writings shared similar origins to those of his own upbringing and education. Nevertheless, Wesley was undoubtedly influenced by the work of the German Pietists. Although he distanced himself from the Moravians in the 1740s, Wesley's encounter with their education system at Herrnhut and Jena laid the foundations for much of the subsequent practical application of his educational thinking. As a consequence, William Warburton, Bishop of Gloucester, stated of Methodism: 'William Law was its father and Count Zinzendorf rocked the cradle'.[156]

Notes

1 Baker (1984) *BCE* vol. 3 p. 335–7
   Wesley was not alone in this view; Bernard Mandeville claimed that 'No pity does more mischief in the world, than is excited by the tenderness of parents, and hinders them from managing their children'. Mandeville (1723) 'An Essay on Charity and Charity Schools' p. 294
2 Baker (1984) *BCE* vol. 22 p. 63
3 Clarke, Adam (1832) *Memoirs of the Wesley Family* New York: J. Collord p. 174
4 Lenton, John (2009) *John Wesley's Preachers* Milton Keynes: Paternoster p. 111
5 The correspondence between members of the Wesley family, Potter suggests, gives the impression of very close knit relationships, with each taking a keen interest in the lives and thoughts of the others. Potter, Claire (2013) 'The Influence of Danish Missionaries to India', Unpublished paper given at the Oxford Institute of Methodist Theological Studies, August 2013 p. 2
6 Baker (1984) *BCE* vol. 26 p. 90–1
7 Rack (2002) *Reasonable Enthusiast* p. 354
8 Porter (1998) *England in the Eighteenth Century* p. 30
9 Bailey (2012) *Parenting in England c1760–1830* p. 40
10 Mack, Phyllis (2008) *Heart Religion in the British Enlightenment* Cambridge: Cambridge University Press p. 91
11 cited in Lloyd, Gareth (2007) *Charles Wesley and the Struggle for Methodist Identity* Oxford: Oxford University Press p. 138
12 cited in Mack (2008) *Heart Religion in the British Enlightenment* p. 210
13 John Wesley letter to Adam Clarke dated 3 Jan. 1791 in Telford, John (ed.) (1931) *The Letters of the Rev. John Wesley* London: The Epworth Press p. 253
14 Wesley, John (1746) *Lessons for Children* Bristol: Felix Farley p. 2
15 Baker (1984) *BCE* vol. 3 p. 340, 349
16 Telford (1931) *The Letters of the Rev. John Wesley* vol. 6 p. 39
   Wesley included in *The Arminian Magazine 1782* p. 78 'A Short Account of a Child' dated 28 June 1746, which suggested that the three-year-old son of Mrs Nowers was independently prayerful.

17 Baker (1984) *BCE* vol. 19 p. 328
    This was not an original document, having been taken largely from a French text by Abbe Fleury and M. Poiret. Burton, Vicki Tolar (2008) *Spiritual Literacy in John Wesley's Methodism* Waco: Baylor University Press p. 255
18 Addressed 'To all Parents and Schoolmasters', *Instructions for Children* began with 'Lessons I and II of God', a brief nine-point catechism for children to memorize; then set out in Lessons III to XII simple questions and answer sections on 'the Creation and Fall of Man', 'The Redemption of Man', 'the Means of Grace', 'Of Hell' and 'Of Heaven'. This was followed by short lessons on theological concepts; with the final lessons on the Ten Commandments, all written in a simple language that children could understand. Wesley (1755) *Instructions for Children, Fourth Edition* p. iii, 6–32
19 Ibid. p. 14–38
20 Wesley (1746) *Lessons for Children*; Wesley, John (1747) *Lessons for Children, Part II* Bristol: Felix Farley; Wesley, John (1748) *Lessons for Children, Part III* Bristol: Felix Farley; Wesley, John (1754a) *Lessons for Children, Part IV* London: Henry Cock
21 Wesley (1746) *Lessons for Children* p. 2
22 Wesley printed parts of Locke's 'On the Understanding' in *The Arminian Magazine 1783* p. 30, p. 86… and *The Arminian Magazine 1784* p. 32, p. 91… et al.
23 Susanna Wesley's letter to John of 14 Feb. 1734 in Wallace, Charles (ed.) (1997) *Susanna Wesley* New York: Oxford University Press p. 368
24 Baker (1984) *BCE* vol. 22 p. 214–5
    Wesley was not alone in his criticism; Sarah Trimmer referred to *Emile* as 'a conspiracy against Christianity and all social order'. cited in Woodley (2009) 'Oh Miserable and Most Ruinous Measure' p. 35
25 Baker (1984) *BCE* vol. 3 p. 348
26 Wesley, John (1749a) *A Christian Library* vol. 21 Bristol: Felix Farley p. 156
27 G. Fox and E. Hookes (1670) *A Primer and Catechisme for Children* p. 91 cited in Stewart, W. A. Campbell (1953) *Quakers and Education* London: The Epworth Press p. 58
28 cited in Dallimore, Arnold (1980) *George Whitefield* vol. 1 Edinburgh: The Banner of Truth Trust p. 108
29 Baker (1984) *BCE* vol. 3 p. 341–3
30 Bowden, Martha F. (2002) 'Susanna Wesley's Educational Method' in *Journal of the Canadian Church Historical Society* 44.1, Toronto: Canadian Church Historical Society p. 61
31 Baker (1984) *BCE* vol. 25 p. 285–9
32 Wesley, John (1780) 'A Female Course of Study' in *The Arminian Magazine 1780* London: J. Paramore p. 602
33 Ibid. p. 602–4
    The list of subjects, although comprehensive for female education of the day, did not include Classics taught to boys of a similar class in grammar schools or at home, and to boys in Wesley's boarding school at Kingswood.
34 Baker (1984) *BCE* vol. 3 p. 341–3
35 Wesley, John (1792) 'Letter from Mary Bishop to John Wesley dated 18 Aug 1784' in *The Arminian Magazine* p. 51–2
36 Clarke (1832) *Memoirs of the Wesley Family* p. 256
37 Potter (2013) 'The Influence of Danish Missionaries to India' p. 2
38 Clarke (1832) *Memoirs of the Wesley Family* p. 281
39 Ibid. p. 302–47
    Adam Clarke referred to John Wesley's sisters as Emilia (Emily), Mary, Anne, Susanna (Sukey), Mehetabel (Hetty, and sometimes Kitty), Martha (Patty, or Pat) and Kezzia (Kezze, or Kez in family papers). Clarke (1832) *Memoirs of the Wesley Family* p. 466–540

40 Wallace (1997) *Susanna Wesley* p. 373
41 Brantley, Richard E. (1984) *Locke, Wesley, and the Method of English Romanticism* Gainesville: University of Florida p. 16
42 Samuel Annesley was an important figure among Puritan Dissenters. Having been among the two thousand ministers driven out of their livings for refusing to conform under the Act of Uniformity of 1662, he leased a meeting house in London and built up a flourishing congregation. As a result, Dallimore states, 'the forces of Non-conformity looked upon him as their most prominent figure'. Dallimore, Arnold A. (1992) *Susanna* Darlington: Evangelical Press p. 89
43 Susanna Wesley wrote: 'Because I had been educated among the Dissenters… I had drawn up an account of the whole transaction, under which I included the main of the controversy between them and the Established Church, as far as it had come to my knowledge'. Although the account was destroyed in the Epworth rectory fire of 1709, it appears in Kirk, John (1868) *The Mother of the Wesleys* Jarrold p. 5. cited in Dallimore (1992) *Susanna* p. 16
44 Gregory (2005) 'In the Church I will Live and Die' p. 159
45 Burden contends that Charles Morton contributed to a growing sense that English was a suitable language for higher education, and remained abreast of many developments in natural philosophy, including experimental science and pneumatology. Burden (2013) *A Biographical Dictionary of Tutors at the Dissenters' Private Academies* p. 381–4, 505–6
46 Social distinctions were very strong and there was a wide gap between servitors and other undergraduates for whom they performed menial duties. This was voiced by Samuel Johnson: 'The difference, sir, between us Servitors and gentlemen Commoners is this, that we are men of wit and no fortune, and they are men of fortune and not wit'. cited in Elliott-Binns (1953) *The Early Evangelicals* p. 65
47 Gibson, William (2009) 'Samuel Wesley's Conformity Reconsidered' in *Methodist History* Madison: The General Commission on Archives p. 69–82
    Adam Clarke suggested that although Samuel Wesley stated that he witnessed lewdness and profanity, and villainous principles and practices in his encounter with the 'calves-head club', the proceedings were 'not fairly chargeable upon the Dissenters'. Clarke concluded that 'Mr S. Wesley in his controversial writings often overstepped the bounds of Christian moderation'. Clarke (1832) *Memoirs of the Wesley Family* p. 64–5
48 Burden (2013) *A Biographical Dictionary of Tutors at the Dissenters' Private Academies* p. 12
49 Wesley, Samuel (1707) *Reply to Mr Palmer's Vindication of the Learning* London: Robert Clavel p. 26, 154
50 Rack (2002) *Reasonable Enthusiast* p. 46, 52
51 Hempton, David (2003) 'John Wesley and the Rise of Methodism' in Gregory, Jeremy (ed.) *John Wesley: Tercentenary Essays* Manchester: The John Rylands University Library p. 57
    Samuel Wesley wrote to his Bishop in 1700 stating that the creation of a school for the poor at Epworth would be 'a mighty advantage, for the people are so extream [sic] ignorant that not one in twenty can say the Lord's Prayer right, not one in thirty the Beliefs'. cited in Gill (1994) *Women and the Church of England* p. 53
52 Wesley, Samuel 'An Account of the Religious Society begun in Epworth in the Isle of Axholm, Lincolnshire, Feb 1, 1701–2', sent by him to the SPCK. cited in Jones (1964) *The Charity School Movement* p. 100
53 Dallimore (1992) *Susanna* p. 89
54 Best, Gary Martin (2012) *Seven Sisters* Weston-Super-Mare: Woodspring Resource Centre p. 2
55 Gibson (2009) 'Samuel Wesley's Conformity Reconsidered' p. 68
56 Lynch (2003) 'John Wesley's Editorial Hand' p. 176, 196

57 cited in Wearmouth, Robert F. (1945) *Methodism and the Common People of the Eighteenth Century* London: The Epworth Press p. 207
58 Plumb (1950) *England in the Eighteenth Century* p. 91
59 Lynch (2003) 'John Wesley's Editorial Hand' p. 176
60 Susanna's letter is in John Wesley's *Journal*: Baker (1984) *BCE* vol. 19 p. 286–8; The letter forms part of John Wesley's 'Sermon on Colos iii 20 – Children, Obey your Parents in all things': *The Arminian Magazine 1784* p. 457–64
61 Lynch (2003) 'John Wesley's Editorial Hand' p. 196–7
62 Clarke (1832) *Memoirs of the Wesley Family* p. 261–7
63 Lynch (2003) 'John Wesley's Editorial Hand' p. 197–206
64 Wallace (1997) *Susanna Wesley* p. 210
65 Rack, Henry D. (ed.) (2011) *Bi-centennial Edition: The Works of John Wesley* vol. 10 Nashville: Abingdon Press p. 341
66 Lynch (2003) 'John Wesley's Editorial Hand' p. 206
67 cited in Dallimore (1992) *Susanna* p. 95
68 Wallace (1997) *Susanna Wesley* p. 368
69 Potter (2013) 'The Influence of Danish Missionaries to India' p. 3–4
  When the Epworth fire split the household to different locations, Susanna wrote to her daughter Sukey stating 'Since our misfortunes have separated us from each other, and we can no longer enjoy the opportunities we once had of conversing together, I can no other way discharge the duty of a parent, or comply with my inclination of doing you all the good I can, but by writing. You know very well how I love you'. Clarke (1832) *Memoirs of the Wesley Family* p. 283
70 Bowden (2002) 'Susanna Wesley's Educational Method' p. 60–2
71 'As she was a woman that lived by rule, she methodized and arranged everything so exactly, that to each operation she had a time; and time sufficient to transact all the business of the family'. Clarke (1832) *Memoirs of the Wesley Family* p. 174
72 Bowden (2002) 'Susanna Wesley's Educational Method' p. 51
73 Potter (2013) 'The Influence of Danish Missionaries to India' p. 3–15
74 Baker (1984) *BCE* vol. 19 p. 286
75 Dallimore (1992) *Susanna* p. 65
  Wesley was subsequently to reflect that the use of a dancing master might teach his preachers courtesy and grace of movement. Snowden, Rita F. (1963) *Such a Woman* London: Epworth Press p. 22
76 Lloyd (2007) *Charles Wesley and the Struggle for Methodist Identity* p. 8
77 Baker (1984) *BCE* vol. 19 p. 288
78 Dallimore (1992) *Susanna* p. 57
79 Wallace, Charles (2007) 'Charles Wesley and Susanna' in Newport, Kenneth G. C. (ed.) & Campbell, Ted A. (ed.), *Charles Wesley: Life, Literature & Legacy* Peterborough: Epworth Press p. 73
80 Wallace (1997) *Susanna Wesley* p. 150
81 Dallimore (1980) *George Whitefield* vol. 2. p. 10, 22
82 Baker (1984) *BCE* vol. 3 p. 335–7
83 Cohen (2009) 'Familiar Conversation' p. 113
84 Dr Thomas Walker was sixty-seven years old when Wesley entered Charterhouse, and the quote 'a most exact scholar in Greek, Latin and Hebrew' was inscribed on his tomb; Andrew Tooke was Professor of Geometry at Gresham College and a Fellow of the Royal Society. Thompson, Edgar W. (1938) *Wesley at Charterhouse* London: Epworth Press p. 5–8
85 Green, Vivian Hubert Howard (1961) *The Young Mr Wesley* London: Edward Arnold p. 55
86 Thompson (1938) *Wesley at Charterhouse* p. 11

87 Baker (1984) *BCE* vol. 22 p. 237
88 Podmore, Colin (1998) *The Moravian Church in England 1728–1760* Oxford: Clarendon Press p. 40
89 Wesley, John (1781) 'A Plain Account of Kingswood School near Bristol' in *The Arminian Magazine* p. 382; Bett, Henry (1911) 'John Wesley and Charterhouse School' article in *Methodist Recorder* 7 December 1911: London
90 Baker (1984) *BCE* vol. 9 p. 278
91 Thompson (1938) *Wesley at Charterhouse* p. 5
92 Oxford colleges were small; Jacob notes that in 1745/6 Christ Church matriculated 25 undergraduates. Jacob (2007) *The Clerical Profession in the Long Eighteenth Century* p. 2–47
93 Green (1961) *The Young Mr Wesley* p. 100
Little is known of Wesley's undergraduate experience, other than that he was on friendly terms with his tutors George Wigan and Henry Sherman, and his academic reading extended beyond formal tutorial needs in pursuit of personal interest. Rack (2002) *Reasonable Enthusiast* p. 69–77
94 Midgley, Graham (1996) *University Life in Eighteenth-Century Oxford* New Haven: Yale University Press p. 1–15
95 Ibid. p. 3
96 Jacob (2007) *The Clerical Profession in the Long Eighteenth Century* p. 48
97 Most clergy were educated at grammar schools, which were Anglican institutions that provided access to the universities. The universities had responsibility for training Church of England clergy, and Oxford made a considerable contribution to Anglican thought and the defence of Christian religion during the eighteenth century. Ibid. p. 42–7
98 Rack (2002) *Reasonable Enthusiast* p. 62
99 Green (1961) *The Young Mr Wesley* p. 29
100 Turnbull, Richard (2012) *Reviving the Heart* Oxford: Lion Hudson p. 109
101 Wesley visited Lady Huntingdon on nine occasions between 15 April and 4 August 1741. She urged him to abandon his sermon on Isaiah 1:21, and to adopt one based on Acts 26:28 'Almost thou persuadest me to be a Christian'. Rogal, Samuel J. (1994) 'Ladies Huntingdon, Glenorchy, and Maxwell: Militant Methodist Women' in *Methodist History* 32:2 p. 127
102 Baker (1984) *BCE* vol. 1 p. 131
103 Ibid. vol. 4 p. 392
104 Ibid. vol. 1 p. 176–9
105 Turberville, Arthur Stanley (ed.) (1952) *Johnson's England* vol. 2 Oxford: Clarendon Press p. 239; Green (1961) *The Young Mr Wesley* p. 29
106 Baker, Frank (1948) *Charles Wesley As Revealed by His Letters* The Wesley Historical Society Lectures No.14 London: The Epworth Press p. 14
107 Elliott-Binns argued that Law exercised a deeper and more persistent influence on religion than any writer of the century, and although Wesley visited him in Putney, he was later to turn against Law's work, writing a condemnation in his *Journal* of 27 July 1749 of his tract *The Spirit of Prayer* published that year. Elliott-Binns (1953) *The Early Evangelicals* p. 121
108 Harding, Alan (2007) *Selina, Countess of Huntingdon* Peterborough: Epworth p. 14
109 Brown-Lawson, Albert (1994) *John Wesley and the Anglican Evangelicals of the Eighteenth Century* Bishop Auckland: The Pentland Press p. 142
110 Heitzenrater, Richard P. (ed.) (1985) *Diary of an Oxford Methodist* Durham: Duke University Press p. 7–12
111 Baker (1948) *Charles Wesley As Revealed by His Letters* p. 14
112 Campbell, Ted A. (1991) *John Wesley and Christian Antiquity* Nashville: Kingswood Books p. 27
113 Rack (2002) *Reasonable Enthusiast* p. 87

Wesley's *Arminian Magazine, 1787* suggested that 'In the year 1729, four young students in Oxford agreed to spend their evenings together. They were all zealous members of the Church of England, and had no peculiar opinions, but were distinguished only by their constant attendance on the Church and sacrament. In 1735, they were increased to fifteen. Wesley, John (1787c) 'Thoughts on Methodism' in *The Arminian Magazine* p. 100–1

114 Heitzenrater (1985) *Diary of an Oxford Methodist* p. 11–23

115 Men in these societies committed themselves to meet regularly, attend daily prayers in Church, receive communion and support acts of charity, often charity schools. From the late 1730s there is little evidence for the continuation of these societies, except in parishes of clergy influenced by the Evangelical movement. Jacob (2007) *The Clerical Profession in the Long Eighteenth Century* p. 222–4

116 Samuel Wesley stipulated that women should not attend the meetings at Epworth because of the risk of scandal, and should instead content themselves with receiving instruction at home. Gill (1994) *Women and the Church of England* p. 60

117 Dallimore (1980) *George Whitefield* vol. 1 p. 69–70

118 Mack (2008) *Heart Religion in the British Enlightenment* p. 15

119 Heitzenrater (1985) *Diary of an Oxford Methodist* p. 11–23

120 Wesley prepared for the library at his school in Kingswood *The Manners of the Antient [sic] Christians* in which he wrote 'What time they could spare… they employ'd in works of charity, in visiting the sick or afflicted, and assisting whoever stood in need of their assistance. So that the life of a Christian was a continued course of prayer, reading and labour, succeeding each other, as little as possible interrupted by the necessities of life'. Wesley (1749c) *The Manners of the Antient Christians* p. 13

121 Heitzenrater, Richard P. (1995) *Wesley and the People called Methodists* Nashville: Abingdon Press p. 125

In 1736 George Whitefield took charge of the two small charity schools in Oxford maintained by early Methodists. He was frequently called upon to preach charity school sermons since he had the power to 'loosen the purse-strings of his hearers'. Jones (1964) *The Charity School Movement* p. 136–7

122 *Collegia Pietatis* meaning 'gatherings for piety'

123 Heitzenrater (1985) *Diary of an Oxford Methodist* p. 12, 26

124 Green (1961) *The Young Mr Wesley* p. 141

125 Regulations at Port Royal schools stipulated that the moral and spiritual capacity of each child should be carefully monitored by masters, and that a close watch be kept on children at all times; requirements that Wesley later implemented in his Kingswood boarding school. Aries, Philippe (1996) *Centuries of Childhood* London: Pimlico p. 119

126 Heitzenrater (1995) *Wesley and the People called Methodists* p. 68

127 cited in Turnbull (2012) *Reviving the Heart* p. 171

128 Lempa, Heikki (2010) 'Moravian Education in an Eighteenth-Century Context' in Lempa, Heikki & Peucker, Paul (eds.) *Self, Community, World* Cranbury: Associated University Presses p. 273

129 Jones (1964) *The Charity School Movement* p. 136

130 Franke, August (1705) *Pietas Hallensis* Charles Wesley noted in his Journal on 7 November 1737 'I read over *Pietas Hallensis* and desired our orphan-house might be begun in the power of faith'. Kimbrough, ST Jnr. & Newport, Kennett, G. C. (2008) *The Manuscript Journal of the Reverend Charles Wesley M.A.* vol. 1 Nashville: Abingdon Press p. 93

131 Naglee, David Ingersoll (1987) *From Font to Faith* New York: Peter Lang p. 175

132 Jones (1964) *The Charity School Movement* p. 37

133 Vogt, Peter (2010) 'Headless and Un-Erudite' in Lempa *Self, Community, World* p. 118

134 Hindmarsh (2005) *The Evangelical Conversion Narrative* p. 73
135 Mack (2008) *Heart Religion in the British Enlightenment* p. 36
136 John Wesley letter to the Moravians 27–8 Sept 1738 in Baker (1984) *BCE* vol. 25 p. 566
137 Lempa (2010) 'Moravian Education in an Eighteenth-Century Context' in Lempa *Self, Community, World* p. 282
138 Schunka, Alexander (2010) 'A Missing Link' in Lempa *Self, Community, World* p. 67
139 Schmid, Pia (2010) 'Moravian Memoirs as a Source for the History of Education' in Lempa *Self, Community, World* p. 177
140 Burton (2008) *Spiritual Literacy in John Wesley's Methodism* p. 87
141 Podmore (1998) *The Moravian Church in England 1728–1760* p. 142
142 Ives (1970) *Kingswood School in Wesley's Day and Since* p. 236
143 Wesley (1755) *Instructions for Children* p. iii
144 cited in Vogt (2010) 'Headless and Un-Erudite' p. 107–114
   Zinzendorf's views, Vogt argues, should not be considered representative of Moravian pedagogical traditions as a whole. After his death, the Moravian Church experienced a surprising surge in scientific studies, especially in botany and the earth sciences. Ibid. p. 118
145 Yonan, Jonathan (2010) 'Evangelicalism and Enlightenment' in Lempa *Self, Community, World* p. 128
146 Podmore (1998) *The Moravian Church in England 1728–1760* p. 30–51
147 Ibid. p. 57–75
148 Kimbrough (2008) *The Manuscript Journal of the Reverend Charles Wesley* p. 248
149 Mack (2008) *Heart Religion in the British Enlightenment* p. 37
150 Hindmarsh (2005) *The Evangelical Conversion Narrative* p. 163
151 Jackson, Thomas (1862) *Memoirs of the Rev. Charles Wesley* London: Wesleyan Conference Office p. 100
   Charles Wesley contended 'they trample upon the ordinances, and despise the commands of Christ'; adding 'I see no middle point wherein we can meet'. Kimbrough (2008) *The Manuscript Journal of the Reverend Charles Wesley* p. 248
152 Heitzenrater (1995) *Wesley and the People called Methodists* p. 34
153 Best, Gary Martin (2006) *Charles Wesley* Peterborough: Epworth p. 129
154 Dallimore (1980) *George Whitefield* vol. 2 p. 29
155 Gentry (2007) *Bold as a Lion* p. 31
156 cited in Elliott-Binns (1953) *The Early Evangelicals* p. 121

3 The implementation of John Wesley's thinking on education

Earlier scholars have tended to focus on specific aspects of John Wesley's educational practice, particularly the schools he established at Kingswood, near Bristol, primarily because of the emphasis Wesley himself placed on them. Although the colliers' school, established in 1739, and the boarding school established seven years later, may be regarded as 'models' of Wesley's educational practice for the offspring of the poor and wealthier families respectively, they do not provide the full picture. Indeed, as chapter four demonstrates, Wesley's work with children of the poor extended far beyond the confines of the colliers' school. The boarding school at Kingswood, discussed in chapter five, was predominantly for boy boarders, and its significance has too often overshadowed Methodist boarding schools for girls, which have frequently been overlooked by scholars.

Rather than focusing on one particular aspect of his work, this chapter demonstrates that Wesley's educational practice was governed by key themes. It argues that, although he was not opposed to female education, Wesley's primary concern was to instil attitudes of piety and virtue, along with such knowledge as was necessary to secure salvation, rather than develop intellect.[1] Tension in his thinking between piety and academic learning led Wesley to consistently employing Masters for their piety rather than their pedagogical credentials. Although he recognised Oxford as a seat of academic learning and defender of Anglican thought, the expulsion of six students from St Edmund Hall not only compelled Wesley to extend his educational programme at Kingswood, but highlighted the growing divisions in the Methodist movement between Arminians and Calvinists.

The chapter demonstrates that Wesley not only regarded education as a training for a life of holiness, but considered it a pathway to the kind of conversion he himself had experienced. He placed emphasis on ascetic self-denial, introspection and emotion as features of religious and educational development, but overlooked their effects on the minds of adolescent boys. Wesley's thinking on what constituted suitable reading material was complex and, as a consequence, he wrote and published huge quantities of material which undoubtedly enhanced the religious and academic knowledge of his readers. Nevertheless, this chapter argues that the tension in Wesley's thinking between piety and learning meant that his educational practice was frequently more strongly Evangelical than intellectual, more pious than academic.

Education of girls and young women

John Wesley believed that the education of both boys and girls should 'fit them for the enjoyment of God in eternity'.[2] He wrote in 1776: 'I lament over every pious young woman who is not as active as possible, seeing every one shall receive his [sic] own reward according to his own labour'.[3] Although Wesley encouraged female education, the primary purpose of instruction was to ensure girls were pious and virtuous. On a visit to Dublin in April 1785, he noted with joy the conversion of a number of girls who were 'as serious and staid in their whole behaviour as if they were thirty or forty years old'.[4] The most suitable place where a daughter's piety and virtue could be nurtured and protected was in the family home. Girls, Wesley contended, should be instructed at home 'as my mother did, who bred up seven daughters to years of maturity'.[5] Even though girls were frequently educated at home, their education was seldom as rigorous as Susanna Wesley's for her daughters. Wesley seems to have overlooked the fact that Susanna herself stated that 'there's few (if any) that would entirely devote above twenty years of the prime of life in hope to save the souls of their children'.[6]

Clarke suggested in his *Memoirs of the Wesley Family*, that both Samuel and Susanna Wesley intended their daughters to become governesses. He described Emilia as having a 'strong sense, much wit, prodigious memory and a talent for poetry', adding that she was a 'classical scholar who wrote in a beautiful hand'. Kezzia was described by Clarke as 'capable of high cultivation', but 'prevented from improving her mind' by ill health throughout her life; and Martha as 'distinguished for deep thoughtfulness'. A particular accolade was pronounced by Clarke on Hetty:

> The pains taken with her education were crowned with success, for at the early age of eight years she had made such proficiency in the learned languages that she could read the Greek text. She has naturally a fine poetic genius, which, though common to the whole family, shone forth in her with peculiar splendour and was heightened by her knowledge of the fine models of antiquity.[7]

The adult lives of the Wesley girls were far from happy. Although it would be unfair to single blame, Best concludes that their education eventually proved a curse rather than a blessing because most of the men with whom they came into contact with were intellectually far inferior to them.[8] Indeed, Clarke recorded of Hetty 'She appears to have had many suitors, but they were generally of the airy and thoughtless class, and ill-suited to make her either happy or useful in a matrimonial life'.

Both Emilia and Kezzia became teachers for limited periods at boarding schools in Lincoln, although in neither case does it appear to have been a happy or rewarding experience. Clarke recorded that Emilia, 'though she had the whole care of the school, was not well used and was worse paid'. Kezzia, writing to John Wesley on 3 July 1731, stated: 'I am entirely of your opinion, that the pursuit of knowledge and virtue will most improve the mind: but how to pursue these is the question. Cut off indeed I am from all means which most men, and many women, have of acquiring them'. She described, having 'a thirst for knowledge', but complained of struggling 'against many disadvantages, among which comparative poverty and bad health were none of the least'.[9]

Charles Wesley, undoubtedly influenced by the level of education his sisters received at Epworth, ensured that his daughter Sally had an education beyond that expected of most girls, including a strong grasp of Latin.[10] In a letter to his eighteen-year-old daughter in 1777, Charles reminded Sally:

> I think you may avail yourself of my small knowledge of books and poetry. I am not yet too old to assist you a little in your reading, and perhaps improve your taste in versifying… Witness your brothers; who I do not love a jot better than you. O be you as ready to show me your verses, as they their music.[11]

When John Wesley opened his boarding school at Kingswood in 1746, his intention was that it would accept only boys.[12] Perhaps under pressure from his friends for places for their daughters as well as their sons, a small number of girl boarders were accepted.[13] They were accommodated during the night in the eight school rooms in Kingswood House, which was used during the day by the colliers' children.[14] Wesley drew up rules for the school specifically for girls.[15] Unlike those for the boys, these rules were never published. Graham contends that there were a number of substantial and important differences between the rules for girls and boys.[16] Wesley intended his boarding school for the offspring of his more affluent followers and, in keeping with eighteenth-century thinking and expectations on female education, the restricted curriculum for daughters of the middling and wealthier sort meant that they were instructed by a Mistress only in 'such things as are needful for them' i.e. 'reading, writing, English grammar, arithmetic, sewing and needlework'.[17]

Despite the fact that a small number of girls were admitted to Kingswood boarding school in the early years, and women were among the staff, the demand for places appears to have been limited and short-lived. The register of names, in itself not complete, only included boys enrolled at the school, although it is known that Samuel Lloyd sent his niece Molly to Kingswood for a short time.[18] Wesley's friend and fellow Evangelical, William Grimshaw not only sent his son John, but his thirteen year old daughter Jane. Sadly, Grimshaw, who was by then twice widowed, was to face further tragedy when Jane became ill and died at the school in January 1750.[19]

It would seem that Molly Lloyd's experience at Kingswood was far from satisfactory. In a letter to Samuel Lloyd of 3 July 1751, Wesley referred to news he had received from another parent which alleged that 'the boys and girls committed wickedness together, and destroyed one another, both body and soul'.[20] Dismissing such accusations as 'senseless tales' Wesley advised Lloyd, who had by then withdrawn Molly from the school, that his niece 'might board for twelve pounds a year at Mrs Robertson's, a serious and prudent woman, and for forty shillings a year more may be by day at one of the best schools in Bristol'. 'Senseless tales' or not, the Kingswood roll had by then reduced to just two Masters and eleven boys, and there are no further references to girls being educated at the school.[21]

There was an increased prevalence of small girls' boarding schools in the mid-eighteenth century. By 1759 an anonymous writer in the *Annual Register* noted that:

> Every village in the neighbourhood... has one or two little boarding schools... the expense is small and hither the blacksmith, the alehouse-keeper, the shoemaker, etc., sends his daughter, who, from the moment she enters these walls becomes a 'young lady'.[22]

Although he advised parents against sending their daughters to large boarding schools that taught 'pride, vanity and affectation',[23] Wesley supported several smaller boarding establishments run by governesses. He declared of Mary Bosanquet's school in 1765 'I rode to Leytonstone and found one truly Christian family... what that at Kingswood should be, and would be if it had such governors'.[24] He wrote in 1782 that he had 'spent an agreeable hour at the boarding school in Sheriffhales', adding that 'the Misses Yeomans are well qualified in their office', and 'several of the children are under strong drawings'.[25] Mrs Edwards, who Wesley described as 'a person of no extraordinary natural abilities' taught 'near a hundred children' in her school in Lambeth, keeping them 'in as good, if not better, order than most school mistresses in the kingdom'.[26]

The school run by Mrs Owen and her daughters in Publow, Somerset, six miles south of Kingswood, was described by Wesley as 'perhaps the best boarding school for girls in Great Britain'.[27] He commended Frances Owen for limiting her boarders to twenty so that she could look after them properly.[28] Nevertheless, in a letter dated 6 September 1772, published in *The Arminian Magazine for 1785*, Owen suggested that, as several of the children's parents were not spiritual and were consequently 'pleased with trifles', they had begun to teach the children 'to make artificial flowers, network, and little pieces of embroidery'.[29] Unhappy with the inclusion of such 'worldly' accomplishments, Wesley's early support for the school appears to have declined, since he suggested that the school had lost its 'original simplicity'.[30]

Wesley frequently corresponded with Mary Bishop; and a letter from her dated 4 March 1777 appeared in *The Arminian Magazine for 1788*. Bishop confirmed that she was able to keep 'all eye and all ear' on her charges and save them from the 'contagion of bad example'. But, again it seems, parents were applying pressure in order to influence what was being taught in the school.

Bishop told Wesley that parents were expecting her, against her better judgement, to teach young children to repeat the catechism and creeds. 'Is it not useless, if not absurd', she contended, 'to teach children of six or seven years old, the answers to the question on the sacrament of the Lord's Supper?'.[31] Wesley agreed, advised her not to go against her own judgement, but instead to use his short catechism prefixed to the *Instructions for Children*.[32]

In a further letter to Bishop dated 21 May 1781, Wesley referred to Mrs Molly Maddern who taught a few children at Kingswood.[33] 'To make the children Christians was her first care', he contended, 'afterwards, they were taught what women need to learn'. But Wesley again lamented the expectations of parents. 'Good breeding I love', he stated, 'but how difficult it is to keep quite clear of affectation'. Referring her to girls taught by Miss Bosanquet, who he described as very genteel, but with a manner which 'belonged to another world', Wesley advised Bishop: 'Let it be said of the young women you educate: Grace was in all her steps, heaven in her eye; In all her gestures sanctity and love'.[34]

Wesley condemned as unwise and unkind those parents who desired to make their daughters 'finer than themselves'. Threatening to 'make their ears tingle', he warned Bishop on 17 July 1781 not to be influenced by the 'fashions of the world', but to set an example herself, and thereby train her pupils by 'all mildness and firmness' to a Christian life of primitive simplicity.[35] He argued that the sole end of life, and consequently of education, was to prepare for eternity: 'for this and no other purpose is our life either given or continued', he stated.[36] In a further letter to Wesley, Bishop once again complained about parents who were threatening to remove their daughters because they were not being instructed in dancing.[37] Wesley responded 'If dancing be not evil in itself, it leads young women to numberless evils... you have chosen the more excellent way'.[38]

Tension between academic learning and piety

One of the most striking themes which ran through Wesley's educational thinking and practice was a tension between academic learning and piety. This is perhaps nowhere more apparent than in his thinking concerning those charged with educating children. Wesley contended that scholarship was a Christian virtue. He argued that children could, and should, be 'taught the knowledge of God, and the knowledge of letters at the same time'.[39] On the other hand, in the *Minutes* of the Methodist Conference in Leeds on 12 August 1766, he advised his preachers:

> Gaining knowledge is a good thing: but saving souls is a better. By this very thing you will gain the most excellent knowledge of God and eternity... If you can do but one, either follow your studies, or instruct the ignorant, let your studies alone. I would throw by all the libraries in the world, rather than be guilty of the perdition of one soul.[40]

This apparent tension between a desire to safeguard the moral and spiritual wellbeing of children in his care, while at the same time providing academic learning, resulted in Wesley consistently elevating piety over pedagogical qualification when employing Masters and Mistresses, whether at his boarding school, or his day schools for poorer children. 'A diligent master', he told Lady Darcy Maxwell in Feb 1770, 'may manage 20 or perhaps 30 children'.[41] Wesley appears to have seen no distinction between a pious Master and one who could both manage and instruct children. This even applied to the Master in charge of Wesley's boarding school; he declared in 1783: 'The Head Master should have nothing to do with temporal things'.[42] When schoolmaster Thomas Welch offered himself for a vacancy at Kingswood in 1783, he was advised by Wesley: 'Do not come for money. Do not come at all, unless purely to raise a Christian school'.[43] Wesley was not alone in believing that teachers were responsible not only for the academic nurture, but the spiritual development of their pupils; White Kennett suggested early in the eighteenth century that the 'Christian Scholar' should 'look upon thy teachers as thy second parents'.[44] Wesley went further, contending that those charged with educating children should imitate their 'guardian angels'.[45]

The procurement of 'men of known and approved piety' was not easy to achieve. The status of the teaching profession was comparatively low, particularly where instruction of poorer children was concerned. In many charity schools facilities were meagre, and teachers were expected to deal with all levels of age, ability and attainment together.[46] Teaching posts were not well paid, and James Barclay, rector of Dalkeith Grammar School, in his *Treatise on Education* of 1743 remarked that 'if anything can excuse negligence in masters, it is the reward given for their labour'.[47] Oliver Goldsmith observed in *Critical Review* of 10 November 1759:

> Any man unfit for any of the professions, he finds his last resource in setting up a school... of all the professions in Society I do not know a more useful or more honourable one than a schoolmaster: at the same time I do not see any more generally despised... or so ill rewarded.[48]

As a consequence of his difficulties in securing Masters of whom he approved, Wesley was to write of his boarding school at Kingswood on 8 September 1781, 'What trouble has it cost me for above these thirty years! I can plan, but who will execute?'.[49] It seems there was a point in 1787 when the lack of a suitable Master for Kingswood School brought Wesley to despair. In a letter to Thomas McGeary dated 15 February 1787 he wrote:

> It is a wonderful strange thing, that in all the kingdoms we cannot find such a schoolmaster as we want!... I shall be weary and say to let it go as it will: I will trouble myself about it no more... the labour of near forty years is lost! But I trust, that will not be the case yet.[50]

This apparent lack of competent Masters and Mistresses not only thwarted Wesley; it similarly handicapped other education endeavours throughout the eighteenth century.[51]

It was not just in charity schools, or small boarding schools, that tension between piety and academic learning were evident. Oxford University was a seat of academic learning; it was also responsible for training Anglican clergy. As discussed in chapter two, Wesley condemned both Masters and students for their lack of piety.[52] His condemnation was not of the University itself, but of those who failed to conduct themselves according to its Statutes. He claimed in his *Plain Account of Kingswood School* published in 1781:

> I love the very sight of Oxford; I love the manner of life; I love and esteem many of its institutions... I had so strong a prejudice in favour of our own Universities, that of Oxford in particular, that I could hardly think of any one's finishing his education without spending some years there... but my prejudice in its favour is considerably abated: I do not admire it as I once did.[53]

The reasons behind Wesley's change of heart are far from straightforward. Wesley argued that he thought it 'highly expedient for every youth to begin and finish his education at the same place'. Despite this, in its first twenty years, Kingswood School did not offer an education beyond that available at grammar schools; Wesley's intention being that students might go up to Oxford to complete their studies. Indeed, his 'academical course', designed to offer boys an alternative to university education, was not instigated at Kingwood until, in Wesley's words, he was 'constrained to make a virtue of necessity'.[54] This 'necessity' arose not only out of a growing tension between piety and learning at Oxford, but a deepening tension between Calvinists and Arminians which came to a head following the expulsion of six students from St Edmund Hall, Oxford in 1768.

Oxford University was expected to maintain the established order in the Church and State and train clergy to defend the Church intellectually against subversive religious and political opinions.[55] Having already attacked the university authorities in his pamphlet *Pietas Oxoniensis*, published in 1768, prominent Calvinist Tory MP Sir Richard Hill claimed in *Goliath Slain* that between 1765 and 1768 St Edmund Hall 'lay under the odium of there being too much religion there'.[56] While the Principal, Dr George Dixon, was sympathetic towards the new Methodist movement, but not connected with it, the Vice-Principal John Higson was not. When Lady Huntingdon proposed a student for admission, Higson decided to take action.[57]

Described by Ollard as a man of strong prejudices, Higson was responsible for most of the tuition and discipline of the Hall. He claimed that some students had 'rudely and violently disputed their tutor's opinions in his lectures upon the Articles of the Church of England' and confronted the young men with various allegations.[58] Charges were laid against the seven students who, on

29 February 1768, were variously charged with being 'destitute of such knowledge in the learned languages as is necessary for performing the usual exercises of the Hall and of the University'; being of 'humble birth'; and of 'behaving indecently' by either neglecting to attend lectures or misbehaving when at them.[59] The crux of the matter was the charge of being Methodists and, therefore, by implication, potential enemies to the doctrine and discipline of the Church of England. The accused men were, for the most part, Calvinists. There was some suggestion that the poorer students had been sponsored by Lady Huntingdon, something she denied. They were, significantly as far as Wesley's subsequent reaction to these claims was concerned, supporters of his, by then, great rival George Whitefield.[60]

The charges against one of the students, Benjamin Blatch, were abandoned since he chose to leave the University, but the other six were cited to appear before the Vice-Chancellor and his assessors on 11 March 1768.[61] At the Court of Enquiry the students were found guilty and expelled from Oxford. Although primarily expelled for their 'irregular' preaching and teaching, the additional charge of illiteracy was proved in only two cases and the charge of humble birth in three.[62] The events caused considerable public interest and pamphlets were published for and against the University's actions. The *London Chronicle* printed warnings to undergraduates:

> So drink, ye jovial souls, and swear,
> And all shall then go well;
> But oh! Take heed of Hymns and Prayer
> These cry aloud – E-X-P-E-L.[63]

Public opinion was by no means sympathetic to these young men, whose humble birth and education seem in part to have prejudiced their case. Social status, defined by such considerations as family (by birth or marriage), property or profession, played a significant role in eighteenth-century society.[64] Judgements were made not on their character, but on their suitability for Oxford. Dr Johnson concluded: 'I believe they might be good beings, but they were not fit to be in the University of Oxford. A cow is a very good animal in the field, but we turn her out of a garden'.[65] Whitefield's reaction to the expulsion, addressed to the Vice-Chancellor, was:

> It is to be hoped that as some have been expelled for extempore praying, we shall hear of some few others of a contrary stamp, being expelled for extempore swearing, which by all impartial judges must undoubtedly be acknowledged to be the greater crime of the two.[66]

Despite Whitefield's reaction, and possibly because of it, Wesley offered neither support to the Calvinists, or criticism of the University. He appears to have been pleased with the line taken by the University, viewing the expulsions as a decision centred on whether the Thirty Nine Articles of the Church of

England taught predestination.[67] It seems that this assumption was far from accurate. Although as early as 1711 Richard Roots had declared that 'the crumbling walls of Oxford Calvinism had fallen', an edition of Edward Welchman's commentary on the Thirty Nine Articles published in 1793 conceded, as regards article 17 on predestination, that 'the grace of election is asserted in it'.[68]

Although the emergence of Calvinistic Methodism had led, from the 1750s onwards, to an increasingly strident Oxford Arminianism, Wesley soon found the University closing its doors to Arminian Methodists. Little more than a year after the expulsions, a pupil from Kingswood, Stephen Seager, was due to matriculate. Perhaps looking for support from within Oxford, Wesley stated in a letter to Joseph Benson 'Those hot-heads at Oxford will constrain me to beat them. But first let Dr Dixon speak'.[69] In an undated letter, Benson wrote to Dixon at St Edmund Hall, inviting him to make known his views on the 'late affair at Oxford'. He suggested that Dixon and Wesley might agree on a concerted course of action, or at the very least that Dixon might consult with Wesley before publishing his opinions.[70]

A week later, Benson wrote to Wesley with details of Dixon's reply, which read:

> It was an unprecedented and irregular step by the Vice-Chancellor to bring the affair before the convocation… Are these not sufficient grounds for the Principal of St Edmund Hall to apply to the Court of King's Bench for a redress of grievances in this case by moving for a mandamus in order to compel the Vice-Chancellor to matriculate the said Stephen Seager.

Despite this, Wesley appears not to have acted on Dixon's suggestion to appeal the case. A note on the reverse of the letter, not in Benson's hand, but attributed to Wesley stated 'Too technical to use them'.[71] Instead, Wesley declared that he knew not 'by what rule of prudence… law or equity' the refusal to admit Seager was based, and claimed that 'neither I, nor any of my friends must expect either favour or justice' at Oxford.[72]

Wesley's hand had been forced, and he instigated the academical course at Kingswood, outlining his rules for it in his *Short Account of the School in Kingswood, near Bristol* of 1768. Whatever his aspirations, however, there were too few staff to provide adequate teaching and the twenty four-hour supervision that Wesley demanded.[73] The difficulties were compounded by the arrival at Kingswood, in increasing numbers, of the sons of Wesley's preachers; the consequences of which will be discussed further in chapter six. As far as Seager was concerned, although his name appears in the register of Kingswood in 1768–1769, and an old account book dated 1764–1770 lists an entry for him – 'January 1770: ¼ of year board £5', there are no further details of his progress.[74]

Despite Wesley's claim that his academical course would advance students 'more in three years than the generality of students at Oxford or Cambridge do in seven', there were too few students enrolled to draw any firm conclusions.[75] Oxford University, on the other hand, saw an increase in students from an annual average of one hundred and eighty two matriculations between 1750 and 1759, to two hundred and forty five between 1790 and 1799.[76]

Ascetic self-denial

During the eighteenth century, physical self-denial was a practice widely valued as morally beneficial. Frugality, temperance and sobriety were not only indicators of piety, but were forms of self-discipline which enhanced the ability to 'feel'. Physical restraint allowed emotions to flourish whereas overloading the body with food produced numbness. Parents were warned not to over-indulge their offspring, for it rendered their bodies diseased and ineffectual. The advice for genteel parents was to lead simpler, less luxurious lives and bring up their children in a like manner.[77] Rejection of excessive food consumption was considered to be evidence of the distance between civilised society and a former state of boorish gluttony born of want.[78]

William Law, in his *Serious Call to a Devout and Holy Life,* stated that Christianity called all men to a state of self-denial; and Wesley declared in his sermon *The Duty and Advantage of Early Rising* of 1783 that 'Self-denial of all kinds is the very life and soul of piety'.[79] He regarded early rising as an act of self-denial, arguing that to take more sleep than was necessary was contrary to piety, 'prepared the soul for every other kind of intemperance' and 'occasioned universal softness and faintness of spirit'. It would be no sacrifice, Wesley argued, 'to rise to prayer at such a time as the drudging part of the world are content to rise to their labour'.[80]

Masters as well as pupils at Wesley's day schools at the Foundery and the Orphan House, and the boarding school in Kingswood, were expected to rise before 5am. Early rising, Wesley suggested 'by constant observation and by long experience, to be admirable use, either for preserving a good, or improving a bad constitution'.[81] In a letter to Samuel Furley, dated 30 March 1754, Wesley advised the twenty two year old:

> I suppose you to rise not later than five, to allow an hour in the morning and another in the evening for Private Exercises. An hour before dinner and one in the afternoon (suppose from four to five) for walking and to go to bed between nine and ten.[82]

Susanna Wesley regarded fasting as a means of 'purifying the mind of sin… subjecting appetite to the superior power of the mind… and a penance for former excess'.[83] Perhaps with this in mind, John Wesley often confessed in his diary to 'over-eating' during his time with the Holy Club in Oxford. Consequently he argued:

> If there are two dishes set before you, by the rule of self-denial you ought to eat of that which you like the least. And this rule I desire to observe myself: always choose what is least pleasing and cheapest… self-indulgence (not in food only) is practised by too many.[84]

The physician George Cheyne, in his popular work *Essay on Health and Long Life* published 1724, argued that a plain diet, refined to its essentials of milk, vegetables and seeds, could 'return the corrupt body to Adamic purity'.[85] A 'plain and simple' diet was stipulated for the boys at Kingswood School, where Wesley was determined to protect his pupils from what he regarded as the sins and dangers of over-indulgence.[86]

In his sermon *On Visiting the Sick*, Wesley asserted that without industry men were 'neither fit for this world or the world to come'.[87] In order to safeguard their moral and spiritual wellbeing, children, Wesley argued, were to be kept at the 'utmost distance from idleness'. Pupils at Kingswood were expected to be industrious, and their day was structured to ensure they would have no opportunity to be idle. Wesley contended that 'he that plays when he is a child, will play when he is a man'. He did, however recognise the need, if not for play, for some form of physical exercise. Periods away from lessons were designated as times when pupils at the school might walk around the grounds, or work in the garden.[88]

The impact of Wesley's regime of self-denial at Kingswood School was described by one of its pupils. Thomas Maurice, in his poem *The Schoolboy* published in 1775, wrote of his time there as being:

> ...a life exposed,
> To all the woes of hunger, toil, distress.
> Cut off from every source of bliss,
> From every bland amusement want to soothe
> The youthful breast.[89]

In a statement perhaps typical of the nineteenth century reaction to Wesley's regime at Kingswood, Hastling contended that it was their meagre diet, lack of physical exercise and boyish recreation, and enforced prayer and meditation both morning and evening, which brought about the unusually morbid and sensitive nature of the boys which manifested itself in the emotional outbursts of the 'religious revivals' of the 1760s–1770s.[90] While Maurice's sentiments provide an informed personal testament, investigation into the circumstances surrounding the 'religious revivals' throws further light on Hastling's claim.

Religious revivals

While those charged with educating children were to be men of piety, Wesley was nevertheless to contend 'We have the clearest proof, when we have to do with children, that the help which is done upon earth God doeth it Himself. All our wisdom will not even make them understand, much less feel the things of God'. Although Wesley insisted that his *Instructions for Children* contained 'the best matter that we can possibly teach them', he contended that 'nothing less than the finger of God can write it on their hearts'.[91]

Wesley's association with the 'heart religion' of the Moravians convinced him of the importance of introspection, feeling and emotion in religious development. Unlike Zinzendorf, who considered emotion and reason as opposing forces, Wesley regarded them as complementary, declaring "Tis plain God begins his work at the heart, then the inspiration of the Highest giveth understanding'.[92] He believed that even a young child could 'feel the things of God' through a profound religious experience. Indeed, Wesley regarded an emotional response arising from a religious experience as an indicator that a child had been 'moved'; and he searched diligently for edifying accounts of such religious experiences. He also encouraged the Masters at Kingswood to supply him with accounts of revivals among the children there, which he subsequently published in *The Arminian Magazine*.[93]

One such incident, recorded in *The Arminian Magazine*, occurred in August 1748 when 'some of the boys were pricked to the heart and cried out – what shall we do to be saved'. Jacky Williams was said to have asked his fellow pupils: 'If the Lord should require your soul of you this night, what would become of you?'. Jackey Standworth was said to have 'likewise received a fresh sense of pardon'.[94] Suspecting that the sort of manifestations of religious experiences that his brother was so eager to find were of human rather than divine origin, Charles Wesley appears to have been more sceptical. Writing in his Journal on 5 August 1740, he stated: 'I talked sharply to Jenny Deschamps, a girl of twelve years old, who confessed that her fits and cryings out (above thirty of them) were all feigned, that Mr Wesley might take notice of her'.[95]

Charles Wesley's scepticism seems to have been justified. Little more than a year after the Jacky Williams incident, he wrote to Mary Jones, whose son was under threat of expulsion and had been given 'one week to display a change in attitude', suggesting that he had been 'seduced by that wicked boy Williams'.[96] Charles's concerns were not limited to shows of emotion in children. At Methodist revival meetings, while John was sympathetic to extreme displays of emotion, his brother suggested following preachers with buckets of water in order to subdue the most unruly of them.[97]

The death from smallpox of a Kingswood pupil on in September 1763 was said by John Wesley to have caused God to 'touch many of their hearts in a manner they never knew before'.[98] Nevertheless, when Joseph Benson arrived at the school in 1766, he stated that although 'some of them do desire to fear God, I hope to see it more so… O when shall we see a lasting change'.[99] Between April 1768 to September 1773 four 'religious revivals' were recorded at Kingswood, when pupils were said to have 'experienced' God in their lives. Although Tranter points to a link between Wesley's autumn visits to Kingswood and three of the recorded 'revivals', they also coincided with James Hindmarsh's time at the school.[100] Hindmarsh joined Kingswood in 1765 as writing master, and his wife was appointed housekeeper.[101] On 27 April 1768 Hindmarsh, by then chief English and mathematics master, wrote to Wesley advising that:

> On Wednesday 20th God broke in upon our boys in a surprising manner. The power of God came upon them like a mighty, rushing wind, which made them cry aloud for mercy... about twenty were in the utmost distress... we have no need to exhort them to pray, for the spirit runs through the whole school... the cries of the boys are sounding in my ears.[102]

There followed shortly afterwards a letter to Wesley from another Master, who stated: 'I have had frequent opportunities of conversing alone with the boys and find the work has taken deep root in many hearts... The whole behaviour of the children strongly speaks of God...'.[103] Hindmarsh, described by Hastling as the 'chief agent in stirring up tremendous excitement', wrote again to Wesley, specifically identifying two boys as having apparently been spoken to by God; John Glascott and Thomas Maurice 'rejoice with joy unspeakable', he claimed.[104]

While this experience may have had a lasting effect on John Glascott, who was subsequently to become a Wesleyan minister, the 'joy unspeakable' was certainly not Maurice's interpretation of his time at Kingswood.[105] Maurice, a pupil at Kingswood from 1767–1769, wrote of his feelings, not of joy, but of misery while there. He found no fault with the running of the school, stating that 'the presiding classical master [Joseph Benson] was by no means deficient in learning, in talents and in zeal to promote the improvement of the pupils'. In an age when sympathy and feelings were at the heart of sensibility, Maurice criticised 'those unfeeling friends who permitted me to be sent to such a barbarous place for mental improvement'. The habit of early rising and the strict discipline were, he suggested, good and salutary, but he criticised 'the long prayers, the occasional fastings, and restraint from the usual sports of school boys'. Of the isolated location of the school, he wrote:

> Bleak and terrific was the prospect of the barren desert that surrounded us; and the only human beings we beheld, or could converse with, without the walls of this holy Bastille, were the sooty delvers of the coalpits that extended for miles on every side of it. Two miserable years were passed in the bosom of this howling wilderness, the solitude of which was alleviated only by occasional visits to Bristol.[106]

The most dramatic revival at Kingswood occurred following an incident on 18 September 1770. On that day, most of the school were taken in solemn procession to view the body of a near neighbour who had died some four or five days before. The children, who ranged in age from eight to fourteen, were, unsurprisingly, greatly affected by what they witnessed. On their return to Kingswood, the boys were said to be on their knees, praying and crying out in the company of three maids sent to restrain them.[107] This religious hysteria continued for some days and Hindmarsh writing on 28 September, reported that 'ten of the children quickly gathered roundabout me earnestly asking what they must do to be saved. All this time we observed, the children who were most affected learned faster and better than the rest'. This tension was maintained at the school until, some thirteen days after the incident began, physical exhaustion finally moderated it. Indeed Southey comments: 'It is a wonder that the boys were not driven mad by the conduct of their instructors. These insane persons urged them never to rest till they had obtained a clear sense of the pardoning love of God…'.[108]

Within a year of this incident, on 6 September 1771, Wesley was asking himself the same question that seems to have followed every revival 'What is become of the wonderful work which God wrought in them last September? It is gone! It is lost! It is vanished away!'.[109] One final incident was recorded two years later. On 10 September 1773, the year that James Hindmarsh left Kingswood, Wesley claimed to have seen several boys who had 'the clear light of God's countenance' on them.[110] Wesley made few visits to the school between 1773 and 1780, a period when no further religious revivals were reported. This coincided with a time when Wesley had decided to disavow excessive behaviour, and it no longer characterised the emotional landscape among Methodists.[111]

Adherence to both Methodism and the cult of sensibility had been demonstrated by the capacity to feel, and to signify feeling by tears, groans, sighs and trembling.[112] Despite being gratified by such displays of emotional religious fervour among newly converted followers, Wesley had become aware of the effect such demonstrativeness had on the reputations of his movement's male leaders, who were often criticised as unmanly. Influenced perhaps by the Moravian belief that women had privileged access to emotions at the core of spirituality, Wesley continued to encourage women to cultivate 'sensibility'.[113] Increasingly recognising that this could be deemed a 'weakness' in men, Wesley now expected them to maintain a balance between emotional expression and 'hysteria', which was considered a feminine 'malady'.[114]

While the reasons behind the periods of religious hysteria may be complex, that Wesley searched for edifying accounts of religious experiences and celebrated their occurrence might suggest that Masters, keen to please him, would encourage rather than moderate any such religious fervour in the boys. That the revivals appear to have intensified during Hindmarsh's time at the school may be significant; on the other hand it might also suggest that Wesley's expectation that Masters could 'move' pupils to experience such religious excitement had intensified during this period. Wesley, despite the many opportunities he had of observing the behaviour of children, appears to have been unaware that in an introverted and pressurised atmosphere such at that at Kingswood, they might aim to please adults by imitating their words and behaviour, and was often taken aback by the decline that followed a Kingswood revival.[115]

This sort of adolescent religious 'awakening' was by no means confined to Kingswood, or to Methodism. There is evidence that small religious societies were formed by pupils in the Dissenting academies for boys run by John Ryland senior, and girls by Martha Smith, in Northampton where Ryland served as a Baptist minister from 1759 to 1786. These societies were a way for pupils to test spiritual gifts, and to narrate spiritual experience. 'Awakened' by the lectures of John Ryland senior, the pupils gathered in small groups to pray. Growing up as they did amid the piety and theology of their elders, they sought to reproduce this in their private introspective narratives. John Ryland junior kept a confessional diary from 1766 to 1768, in which he recounted in detail the fluctuating state of his soul. He described three episodes of strong convictions in the autumn of 1766; he also described more than a dozen occurrences of doubt prior to his baptism in September 1767 at the age of fourteen.[116] As with the displays of religious fervour at Kingswood, it is impossible to speculate on the authenticity of these emotions, set as they are against a backdrop of the lives of adolescent school children aiming to please adults by imitating their words and behaviour.

While Wesley included the names of pupils involved in religious revivals at Kingswood and elsewhere in his *Journal* and published accounts of these incidents in *The Arminian Magazine*, he did not acknowledge the academic distinction of any of his pupils. His emphasis on the spiritual effects of education rather than its academic value was highlighted in the case of John Henderson. Henderson, a pupil at Kingswood circa 1764, was at the age of eight teaching Latin to his Kingswood peers.[117] Four years later he was appointed to the Countess of Huntingdon's College at Trevecka to teach Classics, before going to Pembroke College, Oxford.[118] Despite this, he was never commended for this academic achievement by Wesley.[119] This could in part be as a consequence of the situation at the time, discussed more fully in chapter six, when his move from Kingswood to Trevecka may have been seen by Wesley as a betrayal.[120]

Wesley as author, editor and distributor of books

Wesley's chief literary monument was his *Journal*, published in twenty one instalments, or 'extracts', between 1740 and 1791, and running to over a million printed words.[121] During his time with the Moravians, Wesley had witnessed their practice of censoring books, and perhaps taking a lead from them; from 1739 he became an author, editor and distributor of books on a significant scale.[122] Although Wesley's procedures for choosing and distributing books, and the books he chose to edit and publish, differed in many respects from those of the SPCK, Rivers contends that there is no doubt that he learned from their practice of publishing and distributing religious tracts and pamphlets as a way of spreading religious education.[123]

Rivers argues that Wesley was the editor, author or publisher of more works than any other single figure in eighteenth-century Britain.[124] He recorded in his *Arminian Magazine* in 1781: 'Two and forty years ago, having a desire to furnish poor people with cheaper, shorter, and plainer books I wrote many small tracts, generally a penny a piece; and afterwards several larger... by this means I unawares became rich. But I never desired or endeavoured after it'.[125] The great majority of Wesley's publications were prepared for members of Methodist Societies and itinerant preachers, and their distribution became an important feature of his meeting houses. The Book Room at the Foundery, established in 1741, had by 1753 increased its activities to such an extent that Wesley appointed two book stewards, Thomas Butts and William Briggs, to run it.[126] Despite this, at the Methodist Conference in 1765, when asked: 'Do not they in general talk too much, and read too little?' Wesley responded: 'They do. Let them retrench but half the time they spend in talking, and they will have time enough to read'.[127]

Wesley argued that 'reading' Christians would be 'knowing' Christians, and contended that 'people who talk much will know little'.[128] Not only were people to be supplied with books to assist in their religious development, but the order in which books were read was to receive careful consideration. Writing to Ann Granville on 14 August 1731, Wesley told her that 'the shortest way to knowledge' was to:

> Consider what knowledge you desire to attain to… read no book which does not some way tend to the attainment of that knowledge unless it be the best in its kind… finish one before you begin another and read them all in such an order that every subsequent book may illustrate and confirm the preceding.[129]

In a letter to twenty two year old Samuel Furley on 30 March 1754, Wesley advised:

> With regard to your studies, I know no better method than to take the printed rules of Kingswood School, and to read all the authors therein mentioned in the same order as they occur there. The authors set down for those in the school you would probably read over (with application) in about a twelve month. And those afterwards named in a year or two more. And it will not be lost labour.[130]

Charles Wesley took a similarly systematic approach when advising his daughter Sally in her reading, although his letter to her suggests his disappointment in her application: 'you have a thirst after knowledge and a capacity for it', he wrote, but 'your want of resolution to rise, and to study regularly has discouraged me'. Perhaps in an attempt to remedy this, he suggested:

> The evenings I have set aside for reading with you… we should begin with history. A plan or order of study is absolutely necessary. Without that, the more you read the more you are confused, and never rise [above] a smattering in learning.[131]

Such a course of study was not always easy. Writing to John on 3 July 1731, his sister Kezzia Wesley responded to the letter in which he had sent her a suggested reading list by complaining:

> I could read all the books you mention, if it were in my power to buy them: but as it is not at present, nor have any of my acquaintance I can borrow them of, I must make easy without them if I can; but I had rather you had not told me of them, because it always occasions me some uneasiness that I have not books and opportunity to improve my mind.[132]

Schools often had libraries presented to them by a benefactor; but Wesley contended that the content of these books required careful consideration.[133] Having attended Westminster School, John Wesley's elder brother Samuel went on to become headmaster of Blundell's School in Tiverton, where he taught from 1732 until his death in 1739. Clarke noted that Samuel's 'diligence and able method of teaching was so evident and successful… that children were sent from all quarters to be placed under his tuition'.[134] Nevertheless, John Wesley advised Samuel that as 'most of the classics usually read in great schools… influence the lusts of the flesh…', he should 'banish all such books from your school'.[135] Wesley was determined to ensure that such classics as were used at his boarding school in Kingswood were scrupulously edited.[136]

Dissenter Philip Doddridge, on the other hand, argued that all knowledge was interrelated, and worked hard to build up his Northampton Academy library.[137] The payment of a guinea to the library when students entered the second year of their course gave them access to numerous books.[138] A designated student monitor was responsible 'every Saturday at 3 in the afternoon to call over the catalogue of books wanting'.[139] Although Wesley's father Samuel had claimed of his early education in a Dissenting academy that he had had, and transcribed, 'very lewd books', John Wesley recognised the excellence of Dissenting academies and in 1745 visited his friend Doddridge.[140] Doddridge, who described Wesley as 'not only a man of sterling piety, but of considerable genius'; told him: 'in order to defend the truth, it is very proper that a young minister should know the chief strength of error'.[141]

Following this visit, Doddridge provided Wesley with an extensive booklist, which he subsequently used as the basis for his *Christian Library*, the largest of his publications. The fifty volumes were issued at intervals from 1749–1755.[142] Wesley subsequently printed Doddridge's letter of 18 June 1746 in *The Arminian Magazine 1778*, at a time when he was keen to encourage his preachers to further their knowledge by constant study. The booklist, which Doddridge described as 'a collection of books chiefly relating to practical divinity' was, perhaps for this reason, given the title 'A scheme of study for a clergyman'.[143]

Wesley's close scrutiny of books often took place as he travelled the country and rather than transcribing passages, he marked with his pen what was to be printed, as well as altering or adding a few words here and there.[144] He ensured by such heavy editing that although works of Calvinist authors were included, all references to Calvinism were omitted.[145] He was to complain that, once printed, *A Christian Library* had a hundred passages left in that he had in fact scribbled out. *A Christian Library* was not only used at Kingswood. Wesley stated 'I desire assistants to take care that all the large Societies provide *A Christian Library* for the use of preachers... [and] for those that fear God'.[146]

In March 1766 Joseph Benson took over the teaching of Classics at Kingswood. Evidence in a letter from the school, written later that year by Benson to an unnamed correspondent, suggests that he was rather disappointed with what he found there. He claimed it had 'not yet answered his expectations'; adding 'with regard to learning, I believe in general they do profit and... I expect they will now make more proficiency than ever'.[147] By 1768 the twenty year old Benson had become headmaster and corresponded regularly with Wesley. A frequently quoted sentence from a letter Wesley wrote to Benson on 7 November 1768 stated: 'beware you be not swallowed up in books: an ounce of love is worth a pound of knowledge'.[148] In a letter to Benson the following month, Wesley advised him that he need 'not ramble, however learned the persons may be that advise you to do so. This does indulge curiosity, but does not minister to real improvement, as a stricter method would do'.[149] Taken in isolation, these statements appear to suggest that Wesley was intransigent towards Benson's proposal to expand the Kingswood library. Evidence from the school archive suggests otherwise. Wesley had in fact written in an earlier letter dated 7 November 1768, 'It would not be amiss if I had a catalogue of the books at Kingswood then I should know better what to buy. As fast as I can meet them at sales I shall procure what are yet wanting'.[150]

Tranter argues that the books available at Kingswood School demonstrated that Wesley believed no one should pursue any intellectual or aesthetic interest which might question, or fail to reinforce, his own theological understanding.[151] Despite this, Wesley appears to have recognised the importance of keeping abreast of contemporary scientific thinking. Not only did he have his own electrical therapy clinics in London, but he acquired *the Proceedings of the Royal Society* for the school and purchased titles including Benjamin Franklin's *New Experiments and Observations on Electricity 1754–1761*.[152] Indeed, Joseph Benson's *Memoirs* note on 25 July 1769, that 'Mr Benson wrote out a list of classic works, and of many of the most approved books that have appeared in the English language on a great variety of subjects, on which he was in the habit of making observations as he perused them'.[153]

Wesley began publication of his *Arminian Magazine* in 1778. This provocatively named publication was, Hindmarsh contends, a conscious effort on behalf of Wesley to challenge the periodicals of the Evangelical Calvinists, *The Gospel Magazine*, begun in 1766 and the *Spiritual Magazine* begun in 1761.[154] *Gemeinnachrichten*, the monthly Moravian journal, had a world-wide circulation and printed personal accounts, recorded in a 'memoir' to be shared with others, of experiences of spiritual awakening.[155] Although *The Arminian Magazine* was set in an adversarial context in which questions about conversion and spiritual experience were highly contested, the publishing of periodicals was an effective method of promoting the conversion narrative. It also made public the experience of conversion, an identifying trait of the Evangelical movement.

Conclusion

The key themes discussed in this chapter demonstrate the tension in Wesley's thinking between a desire to educate for 'the world to come', while ensuring learning in the 'here and now'. Wesley encouraged female education; but while this might appear progressive, it is clear that his thinking was far from straightforward. He advocated home education, but was not averse to girls going to school, albeit under the care and supervision of suitable Mistresses. He advised girls that all the knowledge they needed could be found in the Bible, yet he encouraged wider reading, albeit from a prescriptive reading list. His thinking on female education was rooted in a restrictive religious perspective, but this nevertheless gave girls an opportunity to expand their intellect. Although he admitted a small number of girls into his boarding school at Kingswood, supported several small girls' boarding schools run by Methodist ladies and agreed that daughters of his itinerant preachers receive money towards their education, it is clear that Wesley did not consider boys and girls educational equals.

The tension in Wesley's thinking between piety and academic learning was perhaps no more clearly demonstrated than in his insistence on employing Masters for their piety rather than their pedagogical credentials. While not unique to Wesley, this decision was not without its difficulties; there were few Masters who could match his expectations on piety and at the same time have the skills to deliver the level of academic learning he demanded. The circumstances surrounding the expulsion for six students from St Edmund Hall highlighted further the complexity of Wesley's thinking. Although he recognised Oxford as a seat of academic learning and defender of Anglican thought, Methodists were regarded by some as potential enemies to the doctrine and discipline of the Church. Further tension between Calvinists and Arminians compelled Wesley to extend his educational programme at Kingswood to provide an academical course to rival Oxford. There may be many reasons why few students were enrolled at the school, but the evidence suggests that in Oxford at this time, the University intake was thriving.

While religious instruction was paramount, Wesley regarded emotion as a significant feature of religiosity. Introspection, feeling and emotion coupled with qualities of seriousness, self-denial and industriousness were all aspects he believed necessary in the development of a pious child. It appears that Wesley not only regarded education as a training for a life of holiness, but considered it a pathway to the kind of conversion he himself had experienced. In expecting the children in his schools to be as he himself had been, Wesley was frequently dismayed when this proved not to be the case, and appears to have overlooked the effects of his regime on the minds of adolescent boys, aiming to please adults with their behaviour.

Despite his belief that the Bible contained all the knowledge needed, Wesley insisted that his preachers, followers and pupils read a plentiful supply of books. Nevertheless, he stressed that the content of each book needed careful consideration, as did the order in which they were read. As a result of his close scrutiny of texts, Wesley wrote and published huge quantities of material which, although heavily edited to his own way of thinking, undoubtedly enhanced the religious and academic knowledge of his readers.

Notes

1. In January 1771, Wesley advised Philothea Briggs, the teenage daughter of his book steward at the Foundery, that 'all the knowledge you want is comprised in one book – the Bible. When you understand this, you will know enough'. Telford (1931) *The Letters of the Rev. John Wesley* vol. 5 p. 221
2. Baker (1984) *BCE* vol. 3 p. 335–7
3. Telford (1931) *The Letters of the Rev. John Wesley* vol. 6 p. 245
4. Baker (1984) *BCE* vol. 23 p. 349
5. Ibid. vol. 3 p. 343
6. Wallace (1997) *Susanna Wesley* p. 150
7. Clarke (1832) *Memoirs of the Wesley Family* p. 466, 539, 511, 487
8. Best (2012) *Seven Sisters* p. 2
9. Clarke (1832) *Memoirs of the Wesley Family* p. 487, 466, 540–1
10. Best (2006) *Charles Wesley* p. 314–20
11. Baker (1948) *Charles Wesley As Revealed by His Letters* p. 115
12. John Wesley letter to Mary Jones dated 12 Feb. 1748 in Baker (1984) *BCE* vol. 26 p. 279
13. John Wesley's letter to Samuel Lloyd of 3 Jul. 1751 referred to 'boys and girls' at the school at this time. Baker (1984) *BCE* vol. 26 p. 468
14. Bishop, Michael (1977) 'A Detective Story' *The Kingswood School Magazine* Bath: Kingswood School (unpaginated)
15. Benson, Joseph (1766) Letter from Kingswood School to unnamed correspondent, dated 22 Dec. 1766, John Rylands Library 'Joseph Benson Papers' ref. GB 133PLP 7/6/1
16. Graham, William T. (1990) *Wesley's Early Experiments in Education* Ilkeston: Moorley's Publishing p. 11–12
17. 'Needlework' normally referred only to ornamental sewing for middling and upper classes, while 'sewing' on its own normally referred to 'work' with the needle by the poor in charity schools.
18. Hastling, Arthur Henry Lee (1898) *The History of Kingswood School* London: Charles H. Kelly p. 1–127
19. Ives (1970) *Kingswood School in Wesley's Day and Since* p. 39
20. John Wesley letter to Samuel Lloyd 3 Jul. 1751. The news had come from Mary Jones, who also claimed her son Bobby had been 'ruined by going to Kingswood'. Baker (1984) *BCE* vol. 26 p. 468
21. John Wesley letter dated 8 Jul 1751. Mrs Robertson is described by Baker as 'a devout Kingswood Methodist'. Baker (1984) *BCE* vol. 26 p. 470

    Although Ives suggests the 'best school in Bristol' is a reference to Kingswood, the preceding correspondence makes this unlikely; Wesley may have been referring to Mrs Owen's school in Publow. Ives (1970) *Kingswood School in Wesley's Day and Since* p. 40–1
22. cited in Hilton (2007) *Women and the Shaping of the Nation's Young* p. 45
23. Baker (1984) *BCE* vol. 3 p. 341–3
24. Ibid. vol. 22 p. 17
25. Curnock, Nehemiah (1909–1916) *The Journal of the Rev. John Wesley* vol. 6 London: Charles H. Kelly p. 345

26 Baker (1984) *BCE* vol. 24 p. 66
27 Rack (2011) *BCE* vol. 10 p. 432
28 Curnock (1909–1916) *The Journal of the Rev. John Wesley* vol. 6 p. 221
29 Wesley, John (1785)*The Arminian Magazine for the Year 1785, Consisting Chiefly of Extracts and Original Treatises on Universal Redemption* vol. 6, London: J. Paramore p. 551–2
30 Wesley, John (1827) *The Works of the Rev. John Wesley* vol. 10 New York: J. & J. Harper p. 36
31 Wesley, John (1788d) 'Letter from Mary Bishop to John Wesley dated 4 March 1777' in *The Arminian Magazine* p. 103
32 Curnock (1909–16) *The Journal of the Rev. John Wesley* vol. 6 p. 135
33 John Maddern was English master at *Kingswood School in 1760*. Ives (1970) *Kingswood School in Wesley's Day and Since* p. 40
34 Wesley (1827) *Works* vol. 10 p. 367
35 Telford (1931) *The Letters of the Rev. John Wesley* vol. 7 p. 74
36 Baker (1984) *BCE* vol. 3 p. 25
37 Wesley (1792) *The Arminian Magazine* p. 51
38 Telford (1931) *The Letters of the Rev. John Wesley* vol. 7 p. 228
39 Wesley (1755) *Instructions for Children, Fourth Edition* p. iii
40 Rack (2011) *BCE* vol. 10 p. 335
41 Telford (1931) *The Letters of the Rev. John Wesley* vol. 5 p. 182
42 Rack (2011) *BCE* vol. 10 p. 540
43 Hastling (1898) *The History of Kingswood School* p. 50
44 Kennett (1746) *The Christian Scholar* p. 30
45 Baker (1984) *BCE* vol. 3 p. 349
46 Payne (2006) 'London's Charity School Children' p. 391
47 Barclay, James (1743) *Treatise on Education* Edinburgh: James Cochran and Company p. 41
48 cited in Picard (2000) *Dr Johnson's London* p. 204
49 Baker (1984) *BCE* vol. 23 p. 222
50 Wesley, John (1787a) Letter to Thomas McGeary dated 15 Feb. 1787
51 Sarah Trimmer stated that 'All possible care is taken by the trustees of charity schools in the choice of teachers; the majority of them are incapable of giving verbal instructions on religious subjects'. Trimmer (1792) *Reflections upon the Education of Children in Charity Schools* p. 47
52 Baker (1984) *BCE* vol. 1 p. 176
   It would seem that little changed over the subsequent thirty years. Adam Smith contended in *The Wealth of Nations* that 'The discipline of colleges and universities is in general contrived, not for the benefit of students, but for the interest, or more properly speaking, for the ease of the masters'. Smith, Adam (1776) *An Inquiry into the Nature and Causes of the Wealth of Nations, Vol. I* Dublin: Messrs. Whitestone, Chamberlaine, et al. p. 347
53 Wesley (1781) 'A Plain Account of Kingswood School near Bristol' p. 487–8
54 Ibid. p. 487–8
55 Rack (2002) *Reasonable Enthusiast* p. 62
56 Ollard, Sidney Leslie (1911) *The Six Students of St Edmund Hall expelled from the University of Oxford in 1768* Oxford: A. R. Mowbray & Co. p. 4
57 Welch, Edwin (1995) *Spiritual Pilgrim* Cardiff: University of Wales p. 111
58 Ollard (1911) *The Six Students of St Edmund Hall* p. 6
   The students were John Matthews, Thomas Jones, Joseph Shipman, Erasmus Middleton, Benjamin Blatch, Benjamin Kay and Thomas Grove. Welch (1995) *Spiritual Pilgrim* p. 111–12
59 Ollard (1911) *The Six Students of St Edmund Hall* p. 7–8

Erasmus Middleton was also accused of breaking the 'Stamford Oath' by having taught at Kingswood, although his name does not appear on the register of masters at the school. Hastling (1898) *The History of Kingswood School* p. 1–127

60 Ollard (1911) *The Six Students of St Edmund Hall* p. 4–33
61 Welch (1995) *Spiritual Pilgrim* p. 112
62 Ollard (1911) *The Six Students of St Edmund Hall* p. 42
63 cited in Elliott-Binns (1953) *The Early Evangelicals* p. 355
64 Langford (1989) *A Polite and Commercial People* p. 62
65 cited in Ollard (1911) *The Six Students of St Edmund Hall* p. 48
66 cited in Ives (1970) *Kingswood School in Wesley's Day and Since* p. 72
67 Schlenther, Boyd Stanley (1997) *Queen of the Methodists* Durham: Durham Academic Press p. 76
68 Richard Roots (1711) 'St Paul's Epistle to the Romans Vindicated from Absolute or Unconditional Predestination', cited in Tyacke, Nicolas (2001) *Aspects of English Protestantism c1530–1700* Manchester: Manchester University Press p. 23
69 Wesley, John (1768?) Letter to Joseph Benson (undated) but attributed 1769 [author's note: the evidence suggests this letter was actually written in 1768]
70 Benson, Joseph (c1768a) Letter to Dr Dixon, undated, John Rylands Library 'Joseph Benson Papers' ref. GB 133PLP 7/6/2
71 Benson, Joseph (c1768b) Letter to John Wesley (attributed), undated, John Rylands Library 'Joseph Benson Papers' ref. GB 133PLP 7/12/28
72 Wesley (1781) 'A Plain Account of Kingswood School near Bristol' p. 488
73 Tranter (1996) 'John Wesley and the Education of Children' p. 21
74 Kingswood School archive: Account book dated 1764–1770
75 Wesley (1781) 'A Plain Account of Kingswood School near Bristol' p. 487–8

John Floyd (1769), John Undrell (1770) and Adam Clarke (1782) were enrolled on the academical course. Hastling (1898) *The History of Kingswood School* p. 1–127

Although all three went on to become Wesleyan Ministers, Clarke's short time at Kingswood was described by him as lasting 'only one month and two days; thirty-one days too much'. Clarke, Adam (1833) *An Account of the Infancy, Religious and Literary Life of Adam Clarke* London: T. S. Clarke p. 169

There are also traces in old account books of other students paying twenty pounds a year and being dignified by the title 'Mr', which Hastling suggested distinguishes them as academical students. Hastling (1898) *The History of Kingswood School* p. 66

Bishop claims a further six students were enrolled on the Academical course: Erasmus Middleton, Joseph Pilmoor, Mr Carrick, Boston King, Thomas Watson and James Alexander, but concludes 'few young men availed themselves of what was on offer'. Bishop, Michael (1996) 'Wesley's Four Schools at Kingswood' in Macquiban, Tim (ed.) *Issues in Education* Oxford: Applied Theology Press p. 58–9

76 Jacob (2007) *The Clerical Profession in the Long Eighteenth Century* p. 46
77 Bailey (2012) *Parenting in England c1760–1830* p. 106–7
78 Carter, Philip (2001) *Men and the Emergence of Polite Society* Harlow: Longman p. 65
79 Brown-Lawson (1994) *John Wesley and the Anglican Evangelicals of the Eighteenth Century* p. 142
80 Wesley, John (1783b) *The Duty and Advantage of Early Rising* J. Paramore: London p. 2–9

Writing in his diary in February 1745, Wesley claimed to have 'sunk into a gulf of sloth, which got the dominion over me in such a manner that I… was content frequently to lie in bed till eight…'. Baker (1984) *BCE* vol. 20 p. 52

81 Wesley (1781) 'A Plain Account of Kingswood School near Bristol' p. 434
82 Baker (1984) *BCE* vol. 26 p. 536
83 Wallace (1997) *Susanna Wesley* p. 210
84 Baker (1984) *BCE* vol. 20 p. 52

85 Guerrini, Anita (1999) 'A diet for a Sensitive Soul' in *Eighteenth-Century Life* vol. 23, The John Hopkins University Press p. 38
86 Hastling (1898) *The History of Kingswood School* p. 28
87 Baker (1984) *BCE* vol. 3 p. 392
88 Wesley (1749b) *A Short Account of the School in Kingswood, Near Bristol* p. 5
89 cited in Tranter (1996) 'John Wesley and the Education of Children' p. 22
90 Hastling (1898) *The History of Kingswood School* p. 58–9
91 Telford (1931) *The Letters of the Rev. John Wesley* vol. 6 p. 39
92 Baker (1984) *BCE* vol. 20 p. 274: quoting Job 32:8
93 Wesley published accounts of boys and girls, for example: *The Arminian Magazine* included 'A Short Account of Miss Sarah Butler', who was born in 1769, and at the age of eight was said to be 'very earnest with God'. Wesley (1787b) *The Arminian Magazine* p. 246

It also included 'An Account of the Work of God begun among the Children at Whittlebury' about the lives of several teenage boys in 1774. Wesley (1788b) *The Arminian Magazine* p. 491–4
94 Wesley, John (1788e) 'Letter to John Wesley from William Spencer dated 9 August 1748' in *The Arminian Magazine* p. 533–4
95 Kimbrough (2008) *The Manuscript Journal of the Reverend Charles Wesley* p. 276
96 Wesley, Charles (1749b) Letter to Mrs Mary Jones dated 7 Nov. 1749, John Rylands Library 'Charles Wesley Papers' [copy] reference GB133 DDCW/1/27
97 Mack (2008) *Heart Religion in the British Enlightenment* p. 57
98 Baker (1984) *BCE* vol. 21 p. 429
99 Benson (1766) Letter from Kingswood School to unnamed correspondent, dated 22 Dec 1766, John Rylands Library 'Joseph Benson Papers' ref. GB 133PLP 7/6/1
100 Tranter (1996) 'John Wesley and the Education of Children' p. 21
101 Rack (2011) *BCE* vol. 10 p. 319
102 Baker (1984) *BCE* vol. 22 p. 129

One of the pupils involved was Robert Hindmarsh, the Master's son. Rack (2002) *Reasonable Enthusiast* p. 359
103 Baker (1984) *BCE* vol. 22 p. 131
104 Hastling (1898) *The History of Kingswood School* p. 57; Baker (1984) *BCE* vol. 22 p. 129
105 Hastling (1898) *The History of Kingswood School* p. 46
106 cited in Ives (1970) *Kingswood School in Wesley's Day and Since* p. 84–5
107 Tranter (1996) 'John Wesley and the Education of Children' p. 22
108 cited in Hastling (1898) *The History of Kingswood School* p. 59–63
109 Baker (1984) *BCE* vol. 22 p. 254
110 Ibid. vol. 22 p. 388–9
111 Mack (2008) *Heart Religion in the British Enlightenment* p. 41
112 Barker-Benfield (1992) *The Culture of Sensibility* p. 268
113 Mettele, Gisela (2010) 'Erudition vs. Experience' in Lempa *Self, Community, World* p. 190–2
114 Mack (2008) *Heart Religion in the British Enlightenment* p. 90
115 Tranter (1996) 'John Wesley and the Education of Children' p. 31
116 Hindmarsh (2005) *The Evangelical Conversion Narrative* p. 301–18
117 Hastling (1898) *The History of Kingswood School* p. 54
118 Ives (1970) *Kingswood School in Wesley's Day and Since* p. 86
119 Tranter (1996) 'John Wesley and the Education of Children' p. 30
120 While John Henderson appears in secondary literature as a tutor at Trevecka, at the time an infant prodigy only twelve years old, his name does not appear on John Fletcher's report to Lady Huntingdon of April 1769. Streiff (2001) *Reluctant Saint?* p. 143
121 Hindmarsh (2005) *The Evangelical Conversion Narrative* p. 111

122 Norris comments that Wesley's 1740 booklist recorded only ten publications; a 1760 list covered 158; and by 1780 a published catalogue listed 264. By 1790 Wesley's Book Room had probably issued over 150,000 individual works, and it is estimated that over his lifetime Wesley dispersed over 20 million volumes and tracts. Norris, Clive Murray (2015) 'Prophets and Profits: The Financing of Wesleyan Methodism c1740–1800', PhD, Oxford Brookes University p. 196
123 Rivers (2010) 'John Wesley as Editor and Publisher' p. 148–53
124 Ibid. p. 145
125 Wesley (1781) 'A Plain Account of Kingswood School near Bristol' p. 75
126 Neuburg (1971) *Popular Education in 18th Century England* p. 133
127 Rack (2011) *BCE* vol. 10 p. 314
128 Letter to George Holder dated 8 Nov. 1790 in Telford (1931) *The Letters of the Rev. John Wesley* vol. 8 p. 247
129 John Wesley letter to Ann Granville 14 Aug. 1731 in Baker (1984) *BCE* vol. 25 p. 306
130 Wesley, John (1754b) Letter to Samuel Furley dated 30 March 1754
131 Baker (1948) *Charles Wesley As Revealed by His Letters* p. 115
132 Clarke (1832) *Memoirs of the Wesley Family* p. 540
133 Tompson (1971) *Classics or Charity?* p. 30
   Wesley may have been prompted by William Law who, in *A Serious Call to a Devout and Holy Life*, advised against the danger of reading 'vain, impertinent books'. Brown-Lawson (1994) *John Wesley and the Anglican Evangelicals of the Eighteenth Century* p. 143
134 Clarke (1832) *Memoirs of the Wesley Family* p. 394
135 Graham (1990) *Wesley's Early Experiments in Education* p. 1
136 Wesley (1781) 'A Plain Account of Kingswood School near Bristol' p. 435
   Edited versions, as well as books written specially by him were printed at Felix Farley press in Bristol. Ives (1970) *Kingswood School in Wesley's Day and Since* p. 28
137 Deacon (1980) *Philip Doddridge of Northampton 1702–51* p. 98
138 Doddridge had a notebook, originally owed by his tutor John Jennings (1687/8–1723), in which he had written a list of 162 books donated to the Northampton Academy library, together with the names of their donors. The booklist was written in Latin, and the notebook was subsequently passed to Thomas Belsham (1750–1829), tutor at Daventry Academy and New College, Hackney. Whitehouse, Tessa (2011) 'Introduction to John Jenning's Academy Timetable and Reading Lists' in Whitehouse, Tessa (ed.) *Dissenting Education and the Legacy of John Jennings, c.1720–c.1729, Second Edition* revised 2011, Dr Williams' Centre for Dissenting Studies p. 1
139 Parker (1914) *Dissenting Academies in England* p. 152
140 Wesley, Samuel (1707) *Reply to Mr Palmer's Vindication of the Learning* p. 151–2
141 Humphreys, John Doddridge (1830) *The Correspondence and Diary of Philip Doddridge* vol. 4 London: Henry Colburn and Richard Bentley p. 491–3
142 Wesley (1749a) *A Christian Library*
143 Wesley (1778) *The Arminian Magazine* p. 419–25
144 This editing could be extensive. John Foxe's *Acts and Monuments*, first published in England in 1563 to extol the heroic faith of two hundred and eighty two people burned at the stake, designed as a polemic for English Protestantism against Papist tyranny and described by Green as a 'huge work of three great folios', was reduced under Wesley's editorial penmanship to 'four duodecimos'. Hindmarsh (2005) *The Evangelical Conversion Narrative* p. 30
145 Tranter (1996) 'John Wesley and the Education of Children' p. 29
146 Green, Richard (1896) *The Works of John & Charles Wesley* London: C. H. Kelly p. 62
147 Benson, Joseph (1766) Letter from Kingswood School to unnamed correspondent, dated 22 Dec. 1766, John Rylands Library 'Joseph Benson Papers' ref. GB 133PLP 7/6/1

148 Wesley, John (1768b) Letter from John Wesley to Joseph Benson dated 7 Nov. 1768
149 Letter from John Wesley to Joseph Benson dated 22 Dec. 1768. Telford (1931) *The Letters of the Rev. John Wesley* vol. 5 p. 119
150 Wesley (1768b) Letter from John Wesley to Joseph Benson dated 7 Nov. 1768
151 Tranter (1996) 'John Wesley and the Education of Children' p. 28
152 Maddox, Randy L. (2002) 'Kingswood School Library Holdings (ca 1775)' in *Methodist History 41.1, October 2002* The General Commission on Archives and History: Wesley Studies Resource Centre, Duke University divinity.duke.edu, p. 343
153 MacDonald, James (1822) *Memoirs of the Rev. Joseph Benson* London: T. Cordeux p. 15
154 Hindmarsh (2005) *The Evangelical Conversion Narrative* p. 229
155 Mettele (2010) 'Erudition vs. Experience' in Lempa *Self, Community, World* p. 190–2

4 Educating pauper children: 1723–1780

Covering a period from his days at Oxford as a tutor, to a time which saw the emergence of the Sunday school movement, this chapter demonstrates that John Wesley's educational thinking and practice for pauper children was far from straightforward. His Arminian theology argued that salvation and grace were available to all. He expressed concern for the plight of the poor, and opened day schools that their offspring might receive religious instruction. Nevertheless, Wesley continued to champion family religion, and argued that it was the responsibility of parents to instruct their children in the family home.

Much of Wesley's thinking concerning education of children of the poor was in line with sentiments of the day. He understood the power of reading, writing and speaking in the formation of faith, but believed that the poor should be industrious and should show due deference to their social superiors. His aim in educating children of the poor was that they would be protected against the dangerous influences of a non-Christian way of life, rather than as a means by which they might improve their lot on earth. This chapter demonstrates that the education for children of the poor was frequently marked by tension between piety and a degree of learning that might elevate pauper children 'above their station'. It argues that Wesley's educational programme among the poor tended to reinforce social and gender boundaries, rather than breaking them down.

Children of the poor 'deserving' of an education

Samuel Johnson wrote that 'A decent provision for the poor is the true test of civilization – Gentlemen of education are pretty much the same in all countries; the condition of the lower orders, the poor especially, is the true mark of national discrimination'.[1] The eighteenth century was marked by a sense of responsibility to help those children whose physical and spiritual interests had previously been neglected. Despite this, opinions about the level of instruction to be given, and to whom, remained deeply divided. Mandeville suggested that 'to make the society happy, and people easy under the meanest circumstances, it is requisite that great numbers of them should be ignorant, as well as poor'.[2] On the other hand, economist Adam Smith contended that 'an instructed and intelligent people [besides] are always more decent and orderly than an ignorant and stupid one... they are less apt to be misled into any wanton or unnecessary opposition to the measures of government'.[3]

Over the course of the eighteenth century, the group that would have fallen under the category of 'poor' included more than half of the population of England.[4] John Locke, in his *Essay on the Poor Law* of 1699, blamed poverty on the moral corruption of the poor. He argued that their poverty was evidence of a failure to develop and use their God-given rationality. The development of full reason, he asserted, required a wide range of scholarship such as philosophy, theology, Latin and particularly mathematics, all of which required time that the labouring classes did not have. As children of the poor would not receive the kind of education that would produce full-blown reason, Locke argued, the important lesson they needed to learn was how to work, and how to value work.[5]

John Wesley wrote to Dorothy Furly on 25 September 1757, stating 'I love the poor, in many of them I find pure, genuine grace, unmixed with paint, folly and affection'.[6] Wearmouth argued that 'the Methodism of John Wesley proved itself to be the most powerful and active understanding friend the working masses had during the whole of the eighteenth century'.[7] Heitzenrater claims that Wesley did not have to search out the poor; 'they sat in front of him on the benches of his preaching houses'.[8] He was a frequent visitor to the poor, and recognised that poverty affected not only the 'idle' poor, but those who 'after a hard day's labour, come back to a poor, cold, dirty, uncomfortable lodging, and to find there not even the food which is needful to repair [his] wasted strength'.[9] Methodists were encouraged to share with Wesley in schemes of welfare among the poor, even though many were poor themselves.[10] He urged his followers to spend time with the poor in an effort to understanding their plight, writing in his *Journal* of 24 November 1760 that such an encounter 'Is far more apt to soften our heart, and to make us naturally care for each other'.[11] Samuel Johnson attributed the Methodists' success to 'their expressing themselves in a plain and familiar manner which is the only way to do good to the common people'.[12] That Wesley had an immense sympathy for the poor is not denied; but Heitzenrater contends, to say he had a 'preferential option for the poor' is simply to say that he did not categorise more than half of the population as 'outsiders' as some of his wealthy friends did.[13]

Even among education reformers, some children were considered more 'deserving' of an education than others. Children attending charity schools came, for the most part, from families of the 'deserving poor'. The majority did not come from workhouses, nor were they from destitute families.[14] Sarah Trimmer argued:

> It would be thought very cruel to send the child, or orphan, of a pious clergyman, or a respectable but reduced tradesman to be brought up among the offspring of thieves and vagabonds in schools so happily and judiciously founded for those most wretched of all poor children... Yet

nothing is more common than to mix poor children together in Charity Schools.[15]

Children of the 'undeserving poor' were to be educated only so far as to make them 'useful'. At the Foundling Hospital, for example, the governors proposed teaching their children to read, but not to write, arguing that they 'should not be educated in such a manner as may put them upon a level with the children of parents who have the humanity and virtue to preserve them, and the industry to support them'.[16]

Further distinctions were drawn by Isaac Watts, who declared that 'The poor who are bred in towns and cities should enjoy some small advantages in their education, beyond those who are born in far distant fields and villages'. He added:

> I will by no means contend for writing as a matter or equal necessity or advantage with that of reading... and there may also be some of the poor who dwell in very obscure villages, and are confined to rural labours, and others in towns or cities, and especially girls, whose business is most within doors at home, who may have but very little occasion, and as little inclination to use a pen. I would not therefore by any means have it made a necessary part of a charity-school that the children should be taught to write.[17]

It would seem that the provision of an education among the poor tended to reinforce existing social and gender boundaries rather than to break them down. Even where education was offered, there was general agreement that children should not be instructed in a manner that might give them aspirations 'above their station'. These sentiments were articulated by Thomas Hayter, Bishop of Norwich, when he stated:

> These poor children are born to be daily labourers, for the most part to earn their bread by the sweat of their brows. It is evident then, that if such children are, by charity, brought up in a manner that is only proper to qualify them for a rank, to which they ought not to aspire... such a charity would be, in reality, injurious to the children and to the community.[18]

Charity schools were intended to rescue poor children from idleness and vagrancy, to ensure they were washed, tidied and instructed in their duties through the Church catechism.[19] They varied considerably in size, from around twenty pupils, to as many as one hundred but, Kamm suggests, thirty was about the average.[20] Some of the charity schools took boarders, but the majority were day schools. It was usual for these schools to admit boys and girls between the ages of eight and twelve. Although some children had basic literacy on admission, children were taken with no particular regard to their capacity for learning.[21] The knowledge and practice of religion formed the foundation of instruction offered.[22]

The Bible, Book of Common Prayer and Anglican catechism were vital for religious instruction. *The Whole Duty of Man* was considered an important work for ensuring piety and maintaining social order among the poor.[23] It was intended 'to be a short and plain direction to the meanest readers, to behave themselves so in this world that they may be happy for ever in the next'.[24]

Prospective parents were expected to appear clean, co-operative and respectful. Even if they did not attend Church regularly, they were expected to give an impression of at least tacit religious observance. Children were taught to sing psalms and hymns emphasising meekness and obedience, chastity, patience and industry. On Sundays and holy days they attended Church where special pews were provided for them.[25] The usefulness of these schools in promoting religion and virtue was, Edmund Gibson, Bishop of London, stated in 1724 'so manifest that it must be the wish of all serious and good men to see them flourish and increase'.[26]

Idleness was generally considered 'the most odious and contemptible' of all vices and was to be nipped in the bud by severe punishments. Hand in hand with industriousness went submission to authority.[27] In delivering his charity school's sermon in 1755, Thomas Hayter, Bishop of Norwich, claimed that schools employed the gospels to render poor children 'sober, peaceful and industrious in their respective callings'. Addressing an audience already supportive of the work of charity schools, he claimed 'these schools… are of service to the public, in a civil view; because they are so eminently serviceable to the children, in a religious one'.[28]

The difference in rank between charity school children and children of tradesmen was stressed by the uniform they were obliged to wear. Dissenter Isaac Watts countered the claim that, by instructing charity school children in reading, writing and arithmetic, thereby rendering them qualified for clerkship or book-keeping, they might 'become competitors for such places with others of equal talents who have yet far better pretension to them' by stating:

> There are none of those poor who are, or ought to be, bred up to such an accomplished skill in writing and accompts [sic] as to be qualified for any of these posts, except here and there a single lad whose bright genius, and whole constant application and industry have outrun all his fellows.[29]

Despite its basic format, instruction was nevertheless divided along gender lines; boys were taught separately from girls, often in different schools. Boys, as soon as they could read competently, learned to write in 'a fair legible hand', and were taught 'the grounds of arithmetic to fit them for services or apprentices'. Girls were taught to read and although 'several learned to write', generally they were instructed in how to 'knit their stockings and gloves, to mark, sew, make and mend their clothes, and some to spin their clothes'.[30] Thomas Coram, who in 1741 opened the Foundling Hospital in London, wrote in March 1737:

> It is an evil amongst us here in England to think girls having learning given them is not so material as for boys to have it. I think and say it is more material, for girls when they come to be mothers will have the forming of their children's lives and if mothers be good or bad the children generally take after them, so giving girls a virtuous education is a vast advantage to their posterity as well as to the public.[31]

As a result of prevailing sentiments, and despite the desire in a growing economy for a better educated workforce, teachers in charity schools concentrated on the most basic accomplishments which were unlikely to provide a platform for potentially threatening learning.[32] This view was not only held by the Anglican establishment; Isaac Watts concluded:

> The masters and mistresses of these schools among us teach the children of the poor which are under their care to know what their station in life is, how mean their circumstances are, how necessary 'tis for them to be diligent, laborious, honest and faithful, humble and submissive, what duties they owe the rest of mankind and particularly their superiors.[33]

Joseph Priestley similarly argued 'those who have the poorest prospects in life can be taught contentment in their station, and a firm belief in the wisdom and goodness of Providence that has so disposed of them'.[34]

Despite his undoubted sympathy for the poor, there is much in Wesley's writing that suggests his attitude accorded with conventional thinking. Alongside religious instruction, teaching in Methodist schools was gender defined, with boys 'instructed in reading, writing and arithmetic', while girls were 'taught reading, writing and needlework'.[35] The provision of an education was not intended to give children aspirations above their station; nor did literacy, and even higher-order skills such as casting accounts, change traditional social hierarchies. In his *Instructions for Children*, Wesley stated that children of the poor were to remain submissive and obedient. He advised them to be content, even though they had 'little or nothing in the world', for they had 'more than they deserve'. Children, he stated, should pray for a 'humble, submissive, simple and obedient heart'. They were to 'obey without murmuring' and to 'think everyone better than themselves'.[36]

Evangelising the colliers at Kingswood

As a result of their frequent involvement in riotous protests during the 1740s and 1750s the Kingswood colliers had earned something of a reputation.[37] George Heath noted in 1794 that:

> The colliers of the forest were 40 or 50 years ago, so barbarous and savage, that they were a terror to the City of Bristol, which they several times

invaded; it was dangerous to go among them, and their dialect was the roughest and rudest in the Nation.

Heath went on to state that by 1794:

> By the labours of Messrs. Whitefield and Wesley, by the erection of a parish Church and some meeting-houses, and the establishment of several Sunday and daily schools, they are much civilized and improved in principles, morals and pronunciation.[38]

This view of 'barbarous and savage' colliers 'civilized' by Whitefield and Wesley through preaching and education is somewhat simplistic, and fails to tell the whole story. Disturbances in Bristol during the 1740s, and 1750s arose primarily when the Kingswood colliers were faced with severe hardship and even starvation.[39] Wesley undoubtedly felt some sympathy for their situation. In 1773 his *Thoughts on the Present Scarcity of Provisions* asked: 'Why are thousands of people starving, perishing for want, in every part of the nation?'. The causes, he claimed, were 'distilling', 'taxes' and 'luxury'; the remedy, a reduction in the price of basic provisions, and the prohibition of distilling.[40] In common with other Evangelicals, Wesley's primary concern was with reforming the individual; but while piety might 'civilise' the poor, it would not ameliorate their condition. Although economic reform via political action seams implicit in his words, Wesley did not regard himself as a political reformer.[41] Indeed, he argued that piety demanded a position of passive obedience and submission to authority; the poor were told to await the time when 'God must arise and maintain his own cause'.[42] That social order was restored at Kingswood, may have been as a result of a more pious and educated populace, but, Malcolmson argues, it could equally have been because commodities became more plentiful, and prices remained fairly stable.[43]

It is to George Whitefield that the credit of proposing a school for colliers' children at Kingswood should be given, although Wesley was later to claim the school as his own.[44] Whitefield used his preaching skills as an effective way of raising money for charity schools, and while in Savannah had witnessed the work of the Saltzburgers in training children in discipline and industry. He wrote: 'I am setting little schools in and about Savannah, that the rising generation may be bred upon the nurture and admonition of the Lord'. Having raised large sums of money in America without difficulties, Whitefield believed an appeal for orphaned children in England would bring a still greater response.[45] He knew something of the work being done in Halle and on returning to England in 1737, had in mind a project to build an Orphan House along similar lines at Kingswood.[46]

On broaching the idea to the colliers Whitefield received considerable support, which included money towards its cost, and the promise of labour and materials. A piece of ground was donated, and on 2 April 1739 Whitefield prayed over a dedicatory stone erected on the spot. The following day, he wrote to John Wesley, stating 'I suppose you have heard of my proceedings in Kingswood. Be pleased to go thither and forward the good work as much as possible'. On 23 April 1739 Wesley travelled to Bristol to take over the school project that Whitefield had begun. Despite this, by June 1739, he had instead begun building a preaching house for the two Methodist Societies in Bristol.[47]

The New Room, as the preaching house in Bristol became known, operated as a multi-function facility for the poor. The pattern of Wesley's preaching house, which he would follow elsewhere, had important implications for education. Wesley believed that the sole end of life, and consequently of education, was to prepare for eternity. His preaching house school rooms were places where children were to be 'trained and practiced in such a course of life as the sublimest doctrines of Christianity require'.[48] Above all, Wesley believed that salvation and grace were available to all, and rejected the Calvinist doctrine that salvation was predestined only though God's election. By incorporating school rooms within preaching houses, not only was Wesley able to ensure that it was his fellow Arminians who preached to Methodist Societies, but he had control of what was taught in the school.[49] As discussed in chapter three, Wesley's demands over the piety of Masters and Mistresses, and tight control of publications used, could all be managed by him within the confines of his preaching houses.

Instead of the 'little schools' that Whitefield had envisaged for Kingswood, as he had done in the New Room, Wesley incorporated school rooms into a preaching house for the Kingswood colliers. The eventual site for the building was 'in the middle of the wood, between the London and Bath roads, not far from that called Two-Mile-Hill, about three measured miles from Bristol'.[50] Kingswood House, as the building became known, is described by Bishop as a 'handsome, free-standing, commodious affair' and comprised a roomy preaching-hall for the local society with four small rooms at either end.[51] Wesley's actions were strongly resented by Whitefield's supporters in Bristol.[52] Although Whitefield preached 'within the roofless shell' of the construction in July 1739, once Wesley had laid claim to Kingswood House, Whitefield was no longer permitted to preach his Calvinist doctrine there.[53]

Wesley's determination that teaching at Kingswood would reflect his Arminian doctrine was brought into question when Whitefield selected John Cennick, a young man of twenty, to serve as its first Master. On arrival in Kingswood on 11 June 1739 Cennick discovered that, in the absence of both Wesley and Whitefield, there was no one to preach to the colliers and their children. Attracted to Cennick's youthful preaching the colliers flocked in large numbers to his services. Wesley, who had by then returned to Bristol, noted in his *Journal*: 'My congregation was gone to hear Mr Cennick so that except for a few from Bristol I had not above two or three men and as many women'. The situation was exacerbated when, on 17 January 1741, Cennick wrote to Whitefield complaining of Wesley's Arminian doctrines, and urged him to return from America. Wesley got hold of the letter before it was sent, and in a provocative gesture, on 22 February 1741, read it aloud at a meeting of the

Kingswood Society. Wesley charged Cennick and his supporters with 'scoffing at the Word and ministers of God' and announced: 'I, John Wesley, by the consent and approbation of the band-society in Kingswood, do declare the persons above-mentioned, to be no longer members thereof'.[54]

Determined that Kingswood children would not come under the influence of a Master who might question his Arminian thinking, Wesley also refused to allow Cennick to teach at the school. He wrote to Whitefield on 27 April 1741 stating: 'you sent down Brother Cennick to be schoolmaster, whom I have turned out – what, from being schoolmaster? You know he never was so at all'.[55] Cennick, with backing from Whitefield, chose a site half a mile from Kingswood where land was purchased from a local collier, and on 6 March 1741 the first Calvinistic Methodist Society was established.[56] The Tabernacle, opened in 1742, incorporated a school for the colliers' children to rival that of Wesley's Kingswood.[57]

Other than two early references to the colliers and their children at Kingswood, Charles Wesley made scant reference to Kingswood School in his *Journal*.[58] He did, however, refer to the rift between Wesley's Arminians and Whitefield's Calvinists in April 1741, and the intensity of his feelings is clear:

> News was brought to me that the predestinarians had a design to get Kingswood School into their hands, and had made sure of the mistress, Hannah Barrow, a bold confident Pharisee, a liar, backbiter, swearer, drunkard, and if she is not a whore, it is because others have more grace than herself.

The following day, Charles Wesley rode to Kingswood, 'paid her above her wages and quickly dismissed her'. Later that year, he recorded in his Journal 'Met with Kingswood bands and rejoiced on their steadfastness, none having turned either to the right-hand or the left, either to still-ness or predestination'.[59]

The theological schism between Wesley and Whitefield was never resolved, and John Cennick's work continued to distress Wesley, who wrote in October 1760:

> I visited the classes at Kingswood. Here there is no increase. And yet where was there such a prospect till that weak man John Cennick confounded the poor people with strange ideas! O what mischief may be done by one that means well!.[60]

Wesley's preaching house schools

Wesley declared that his Kingswood colliers' day school would 'teach chiefly the poorer children to read, write and cast accounts, but more especially (by God's assistance) to know God, and Jesus Christ, whom he hath sent'.[61] Girls as well as boys were instructed, and although they were taught separately, they were housed in the same building.[62] Under the tutelage of Sarah Dimmock and James Harding respectively, Wesley recorded his satisfaction with the school.[63] He stated that he 'had great cause to thank God on their behalf'.[64] In May 1768 Wesley further recorded that:

> Among the colliers... the work of God increases greatly; two of the colliers' boys were justified this week. This is the day we have wished for so long, the day we had in view, which has made you go through so much opposition for the good of these poor children.[65]

The Foundery in Moorfields was the first specifically Wesleyan Methodist building in London, adapted for that purpose during the winter of 1739–40. It had seating for fifteen hundred people and sufficient space to permit a wide range of services, including medical dispensary, school, alms houses and accommodation.[66] Wesley's *Arminian Magazine* later recorded 'From the beginning men and women sat apart, as they always did in the Primitive Church. They had no pews, and all the benches for rich and poor, were of the same construction'.[67] Elliott-Binns suggests that society meetings were held in rooms and not in Church so that people who did not possess 'Sunday clothes' could attend.[68] The London Society was the most important Methodist Society in Britain and it was from the Foundery that Wesley planned his movements, and Connexional activities such as publishing and book distribution. By December 1743 the total Methodist membership in the City of London was 2,200; by 1760 it had risen to just over 2,500.[69] The 'Book Room' was set up at the south end of the Foundery for selling Wesley's own publications.[70] The north end was fitted with desks and chairs in order that it could be used as a school room.[71]

By the time Wesley had opened his school at the Foundery, the SPCK already had many charity schools in London parishes. Jacob notes that as early as 1717 there were at least fifty six schools educating about two thousand children; and the London Society of Trustees of Charity Schools raised an estimated ten thousand pounds each year to support these schools.[72] Despite this, unless their offspring attended a charity school, many parents from poorer families could only afford an elementary education for their children before setting them to work. Even attendance at charity schools was likely to be intermittent or irregular, depending on child employment opportunities.[73]

Although Wesley theoretically charged fees for schooling at the Foundery, only a few parents paid. The great majority were extremely poor and their children were taught and clothed gratuitously. The children, the youngest of whom was six years old, began their day by attending preaching at 5am. The school day then ran from 6am to twelve noon and from 1pm to 5pm.[74] It is clear from Silas Told's account of his time at the Foundery school from 1744 to 1751 that girls were significantly outnumbered by boys:

> I was established in the Foundery School and in the space of a few weeks, collected three score boys and six girls; but the society being poor, could

not grant me more than ten shillings per week. This, however, was sufficient for me, as they boarded and clothed my daughter.[75]

Not only were girls in the minority, but, in common with the prevailing sentiments, the instruction boys and girls received was tailored to those subjects deemed 'useful' for their gender. While boys were taught reading, writing and arithmetic, to 'fit them for a trade', girls received instruction in reading, writing and needlework.[76] Silas Told's account of his time at the Foundery referred to the number of boys discharged 'fit for any trade', but made no reference to girls who had left the school:

> Having children under my care from five in the morning till five in the evening, both winter and summer, sparing no pains, with the assistance of an usher and four monitors. I continued in the school seven years and three months, and discharged two hundred and seventy five boys; most of them were fit for any trade.[77]

Predictably perhaps, Wesley's own judgement on the work of the Foundery school was that 'a happy change was soon observed in the children, both with regard to their tempers and behaviour'. Wesley did not differentiate here between the girls and boys; but by adding that 'they learned reading, writing and arithmetic swiftly and at the same time they were diligently instructed in the sound principles of religion', it is evident that Wesley was referring only to the boys at the school.[78]

Wesley may not have differentiated between the 'deserving' and 'undeserving' poor; but, in his desire to keep children from sin, he demanded that 'no days away from school be permitted'.[79] When opportunities for child employment arose, this may have been a commitment that some parents found difficult to maintain. White Kennett advised charity school children to 'Love exercise; Follow your book with an edge and appetite to learning and then divert to thy sports and recreations with activity and all thy strength'.[80] Children at Wesley's day schools, on the other hand, had no 'play-days', and no speaking was allowed other than to the Masters.[81]

Wesley arranged for the Masters and parents of children to meet every Wednesday morning so that the Masters might 'exhort their parents to train them [the children] up at home in the ways of God'.[82] His method of testing pupils was by interviewing them individually. Lloyd suggests that 'it is perhaps too much to say that Susanna's interviews with her young sons were decisive in their promotion of this practice'; but argues that the influence of continental Pietists can be discerned.[83] Wesley was not alone in this practice; at his charity school in Northampton, Philip Doddridge also made a point of examining the proficiency of children personally. He visited the school to support the Master's authority and catechise, instruct and pray with the children. They were taken to public worship regularly and, where necessary, were provided with clothes. An anniversary sermon was preached and a special collection was made for the school. The Northampton Academy also provided six pence per week from the 'fines' box, and benefactors sent money, books and Bibles. The trustees visited weekly by rotation to observe the behaviour and improvement of the children and to receive the Master's report concerning them.[84]

As well as a school for children, there is an account in Wesley's *Journal* on 25 November 1740 that suggests that the Foundery operated a small school for adult poor, to give them skills for future employment:

> To keep them from want and idleness – we took twelve of the poorest, and a teacher, into the Society room, where they were employed for four months till Spring came on, in carding and spinning of cotton, and the design answered; they were employed and maintained with very little more than the produce of their labour.[85]

The work at the Foundery was not without its critics, and Wesley's appeal to the poor aroused suspicion of his motives. The editor of *Weekly Miscellany* remarked on 25 April 1741 that what Wesley was doing at the Foundery was only for selfish gain. He claimed 'the common complaint is that all this is done with an ill design; young servants neglected their Masters' business and in consequence were turned away, only to be received at the Foundery with others of their kind'. The editor added 'John Wesley could only be furthering the system for self-interest with a view to making money. By his preaching, bookselling, workhouse and spinning, he gets £700, and possibly about £1,000 a year'.[86]

In May 1742, Wesley secured a piece of land in Newcastle-on-Tyne, and his original plan for the site was to build an 'Orphan House' modelled on the Moravian orphanage and school he had seen at Halle.[87] The building, when completed, became known as the Orphan House, but there is some doubt as to whether any orphans were ever accommodated there, although it is possible, Milburn suggests, that some abandoned children were offered temporary care.[88] Like the New Room, Kingswood House and the Foundery, the building was multi-functional. Opened on 25 March 1743, it had a chapel on the ground floor and a band room, with four school rooms at either end on the first floor. The second floor contained ten rooms for preachers, with Wesley's study situated at the top of the building. The Orphan House later became the largest Methodist meeting house in England.[89] A day school was established in the eight school rooms on the first floor. The Trust Deed of the Orphan House, dated 5 March 1745, recorded:

> school to be taught in part of the said house and premises from the time of the institution thereof, shall for ever be, and continue, and be kept up, and shall consist of one master and one mistress, and such forty poor children.[90]

It would seem that Wesley's early decision to establish schools for the poor in his preaching houses was not without its difficulties. Stamp, in his history of the

Orphan House noted in 1863 that 'Mr Wesley's purpose as to the establishment of a school for orphans, or others, proved a failure, either from want of funds, or the lack of suitable agent'.[91] The school in the New Room also encountered financial problems. Its first Master, a man named Ramsay, together with an associate called Snoude, fled Bristol taking with them thirty pounds which Wesley had collected for Kingswood School.[92] Wesley recorded in his *Journal* on 23 May 1741:

> At a meeting of the stewards of the Society… it was found needful to retrench the expenses, the contributions not answering thereto. And it was accordingly agreed to discharge two of the schoolmasters at Bristol, the present fund being barely sufficient to keep two masters and a mistress here, and one master and a mistress at Kingswood.[93]

Indeed, Edwards suggests that at the New Room 'gradually the costs became too heavy and the school in time disappeared'.[94] At the Foundery two stewards managed the finances and, Norris comments, surviving London Society's accounts suggest that the costs of running the school were covered by income received.[95]

Wesley's enthusiasm for establishing schools for pauper children in his preaching houses has been thrown into question by what Baker referred to as 'a Hitherto unknown letter' written by John Wesley to Richard Terry of Hull, dated 'Leeds, April 30, 1774'. Wesley's letter, authenticated by Baker, stated:

> The teaching School in a preaching house does it so much hurt, & keep's it so dirty, in spite of all the care which can be taken, that we have made it a rule for several years 'Let no School be taught in any Preaching house'. But I commend your design, if you had a proper place. And a Master might easily be procured.[96]

While Baker suggested that 'Yorkshire was a fruitful ground for experiments in education', he was unable to throw any light on whether Richard Terry's proposed school, of which Wesley approved in principle, ever came to fruition. Rather more significant, Baker commented, was the fact that the ruling to which Wesley referred did not appear to be an official ruling, since there was no record of it coming before Conference. The *Minutes* to which Wesley referred simply gave the following general advice to his assistants: 'Every where insist on decency and cleanliness. Tell them cleanliness is next to godliness'.[97] It is therefore necessary to look at each preaching house individually to discover whether the schools continued. The difficulty in securing 'pious men who would instruct [children] in religion and learning', coupled with his insistence that his preachers be constantly travelling, may in part explain Wesley's comment to Terry about securing a Master for his school.[98]

Methodist preaching houses were of the 'plainest type' for lack of finance; most parents were unable to contribute anything and the expense of lodging and training had to be met from voluntary gifts.[99] In suggesting Terry find a 'proper place' for a school, Wesley's statement might also reflect the difficulties for preaching houses such as the Foundery and the New Room, where financial constraints were compounded by the requirement to support not only the preaching house, society meeting room and school, but lodgings and work for adult poor as well as a book room and dispensary.[100]

As examined further in chapter six, Wesley's emphasis in the closing decades of his life moved from focusing primarily on educating children to a reinforcing of the importance of family in education. That his belief in education in the home did not entirely divert education away from preaching houses is evidenced at the Foundery and Kingswood where the schools continued to operate, albeit somewhat reduced in size and scope. A letter by J. Crowther printed in the *Watchman*, 1852, cited in Hastling's history of Kingswood School records:

> By 1803, only two of the smaller rooms [at Kingswood] were in use as the school, two were used as vestries for class meetings, and the remaining four were added to the gallery of the 'large room' or chapel. The school for the colliers' children was discontinued soon afterwards.[101]

In London, by 1808, the Foundery school had become the Methodist Charity School belonging to the New Chapel, City Road; it accommodated only girls and was by then conducted as a school of industry.[102]

Wesley retained the right to appoint preachers to conduct services in his meeting houses and his travelling preachers, his 'sons in the gospel' were entirely subject to him. He expected them to establish societies in preaching houses for children and advised them 'to see that... schoolmasters... faithfully discharge their several offices'. The structure of the societies was simple; preachers were to use *Instructions for Children*; each society consisted of just ten children, who were required to meet twice a week for instruction.[103] There were occasions when Wesley noted in his *Journal* that meeting with children was, for him, 'the most difficult part of our work'.[104] Nevertheless, he told his preachers 'Gift or no gift, you are to do it, else you are not called to be a Methodist preacher... pray earnestly for the gift and use the means of it'.[105] By the close of the century, both the Foundery and the Orphan House operated thriving Sunday schools.[106]

Wesleyan day schools for the poor

Wesley's Arminian thinking argued that all had the promise of salvation through faith, regardless of status or wealth. In 1748 he wrote to his friend, Evangelical clergyman Vincent Perronet, stating that an abundance of children, whose parents were unable to afford to send them to school, remained 'like a wild ass's colt'.[107] He added 'At length I determined to have them taught in my own house, that they might have an opportunity of learning to read, write and cast accounts (if no more) without being under almost a necessity of learning heathenism at the same time'.[108] Evidence suggests that in addition to his preaching house schools, Wesley encouraged the formation of Methodist schools in private residences and chapels, although this work went largely unrecorded.

In Madeley parish, John Fletcher delighted in instructing children, declaring: 'If I were not a minister, I would be a schoolmaster, to have the pleasure of bringing up children in the fear of the Lord'.[109] As Wilson points out, Fletcher was approached on several occasions with requests from parents to take in children as private scholars. In 1764 he formed a parish 'school' in his home and instructed children on an ad hoc basis, writing to his mother in 1767 that 'it has been about a month since I opened a charity school in my house to instruct the poor children of my parish'. The school initially met in the vicarage, but subsequently in the Church, and was funded by Fletcher himself. As well as receiving instruction during the weekdays, by the 1780s the children of the parish were invited to join Fletcher and his wife Mary (Fletcher née Bosanquet) for a children's society meeting every Thursday evening.[110]

Fletcher, whose role Wilson argues 'was never far from that of a schoolmaster', showed a practical concern and particular compassion, for children and young people.[111] Writing from Switzerland in 1778, he reported meeting every day with 'a parcel of children' to 'sing the praises of God'.[112] Joseph Benson, who witnessed Fletcher's work at Madeley, noted:

> Wherever the smallest religious desire was expressed, he pronounced a blessing upon it, and wherever the weakest endeavour after spiritual attainments was discoverable, he encouraged it with his congratulations, and strengthened it with his prayers.[113]

That is not to suggest that Fletcher did not reprimand pupils in his schools.[114] In prayers written for his Sunday schools, discussed further in chapter seven, Fletcher wrote:

> Thou hast told us although chastisement is for the past grievances it afterwards [brings] the peaceful fruits of righteousness... we pray that the shocks of this rod may be blessed to this poor child, let him not be hardened and discouraged but humbled and reformed thereby. Convince him of the necessity of this correction... let it have the desired effect both on him and on all the children of this school.[115]

Nevertheless, Fletcher's views on child-rearing and education, it would seem, were at odds with that of Wesley. Wesley noted in his *Journal* on 25 March 1779:

> I preached in the new house which Mr Fletcher has built in Madeley Wood. The people here exactly resemble those at Kingswood; only they

are more simple and teachable. But for want of discipline, the immense pains which he has taken with them has not done the good which might have been expected.[116]

Far from a stern breaking of the will, Fletcher's method was to exhort and encourage; he contrasted the softness of heart in children to the hardness of 'grown up people [who] stand fast in their stupidity'.[117]

Fletcher, like most of his contemporaries, saw childhood as a distinct phase of human development and, while drawing on the thinking of Locke to support his theology in defence of human free will, a philosophy fundamental to both his and Wesley's Arminian thought, he believed that praising children for their progress in faith and piety was essential. He was often to be found among children, advocating for their earnestness and spiritual impressionability. One of the children of Madeley parish, John Fennell, described Fletcher's methods:

> [H]e spared no pains to reprove, rebuke, or exhort us, sometimes appearing among us with all the majesty of a judge, minutely examining every part of our conduct, and at other times with all the affection and sympathy of a tender Father, with his eyes brimful of tears, and lips open in blessing and pious admonitions.[118]

Among Wesley's wealthy followers was Lady Darcy Maxwell, who in July 1770 opened a day school for children of the poor in Edinburgh.[119] In June 1782, Wesley noted that the forty children in the school were 'swiftly brought forward in reading and writing, and learn the principles of religion'. It seems, however, that the involvement of an aristocratic patron in the education of the poor was not without its complications. Wesley lamented: 'I observe in them all the *ambitiosa paupertas* [ambitious poverty]. Be they ever so poor, they must have a scrap of finery. Many of them have not a shoe to their foot; but the girl in rags is not without her ruffles'.[120]

Within Methodism, Arminian doctrines of free will and universal salvation were an invitation to self-improvement and self-advancement, and resulted in a conspicuous number of women taking an active role. Wesley made numerous references to women who had established successful boarding and day schools in his *Journal* and *Letters*. Further reference is made to Methodist boarding schools in chapter five. Among the day schools for poor children commended by Wesley was one run by Miss Warren in Wales. In an entry in his *Journal* on 30 April 1781 he stated:

> I met about fifty children; such a company as I have not seen for many years. Miss Warren loves them, and they love her. She has taken true pains with them, and her labour has not been in vain. Several of them are much awakened, and the behaviour of all is so composed that they are a pattern to the whole congregation.[121]

Because Wesley listened to the poor, and created space for them to speak and assume public roles of leadership in Methodist Societies, he opened to the lower orders the opportunity to engage in various activities, and a considerable number of charity day schools were set up. Nevertheless, Baker claims that 'the rise of free schools on Methodist premises is shrouded in obscurity'.[122] Methodism never achieved a large membership during Wesley's lifetime.[123] However successful, Tranter argues, the number of Methodist schools was few in number when set alongside those of the SPCK.[124]

Conclusion

During the eighteenth century many felt a sense of responsibility to help those children whose physical and spiritual interests had previously been neglected. Nevertheless, the provision of an education for children of the poor was marked by tension between piety and a degree of learning that might give pauper children aspirations above their station. Opinions were divided not only on the level of instruction to be given, but to whom. Although Locke believed that children needed to develop reason, for pauper children, the ability to do so was limited by a lack of time to devote to studies. Instead, they were to be taught industriousness; not only how to work, but how to value work. The provision of an education was intended to maintain social order, and to reinforce existing social and gender boundaries, not break them down.

Wesley was undoubtedly sympathetic to the plight of the poor, but there is much in his thinking that accords with sentiments of the day. Giving the poor religious instruction taught them passive obedience; piety was a means of civilising the poor, not ameliorating their condition. Education was gender defined, intended to equip children for their future roles in life; thus while boys were taught reading, writing and arithmetic to 'fit them for trade', girls were instructed in reading, writing and needlework.

Wesley opened day schools for pauper children in his preaching houses. Although this gave Methodists an opportunity to have their children educated, it also allowed Wesley to keep a tight control not only on who they were taught by, but what they were taught. Wesley's Arminian theology argued that salvation and grace were available to all, and this gave Methodists a desire for self-improvement and self-advancement. His followers, many of whom were women, took on active roles, including the instruction of children. Although Methodists opened a number of day schools for the poor, these went largely unrecorded and were few in number when compared with the SPCK.

Although Wesley took a keen interest in the schools opened in Methodist homes and chapels, it seems that children may not have been instructed in the same way. Certainly, John Fletcher appears to have taken a rather softer line than Wesley in his education of children. The apparent demise of schools in preaching houses may have been as a result of several factors, not least a shortage of funds. Wesley's insistence that parents were responsible for instilling an early religious understanding in their offspring brought about a desire to instruct adults as well as children. As chapter six demonstrates, this apparent change of emphasis had implications for Wesley's education programme.

Notes

1. Boswell, James (1799) *The Life of Samuel Johnson* London: Charles Dilly p. 126
2. Mandeville (1723) 'An Essay on Charity and Charity Schools' p. 328
3. Smith (1776) *An Inquiry into the Nature and Causes of the Wealth of Nations* p. 304
4. Both Gregory King's national survey of 1688 and Joseph Massie's of 1760 concluded that the 'labouring poor' had an average income of not more than thirty pounds per year. Among them would be husbandmen, manufacturers, small craftsmen and manual workers of all kinds, who were at the mercy of environmental extremes and market fluctuations. There was essentially no inflation between 1688 and 1760, and while those over the thirty pounds per year line paid poor tax, those under the line benefitted from it. The parish overseers of the poor generally earned about twenty to thirty pounds per year, putting them just within the limits of the poverty level themselves. Heitzenrater, Richard P. (2002) *The Poor and the People called Methodists* Nashville: Kingswood Books p. 20–1
5. Hirschmann (2007) *Feminist Interpretations of John Locke* p. 160–71
6. Telford (1931) *The Letters of the Rev. John Wesley* vol. 3 p. 229
7. Wearmouth (1945) *Methodism and the Common People of the Eighteenth Century* p. 265
8. Scholars are divided over the demographic of a 'typical' Wesleyan congregation. Although statistics can be drawn from circuit membership records, not all those who attended services were members. Heitzenrater claims between 65% and 75% of Methodists in the second half of the eighteenth century were 'poor' earning less than twenty pounds a year, and only a quarter averaged over thirty pounds a year. Heitzenrater (2002) *The Poor and the People called Methodists* p. 27–8
9. Baker (1984) *BCE* vol. 2 p. 228
10. Wesley instructed his preachers to deal kindly with the poor: 'Give none that ask relief either an ill word or an ill look. Do not hurt 'em if you cannot help 'em… put yourself in the place of any poor man, and deal with him as you would God should deal with you'. Baker (1984) *BCE* vol. 10 p. 143
11. Ibid. vol. 21 p. 290
12. cited in Picard (2000) *Dr Johnson's London* p. 184
13. Heitzenrater (2002) *The Poor and the People called Methodists* p. 27–8
14. Payne (2006) 'London's Charity School Children' p. 385
15. Trimmer (1792) *Reflections upon the Education of Children in Charity Schools* p. 8–9
16. cited in Pugh, Gillian (2007) *London's Forgotten Children* Stroud: Tempus Publishing p. 40
17. Watts, Isaac (1728) *An Essay Towards the Encouragement of Charity Schools* London: John Clark and Richard Hett; Emanuel Matthews, and Richard Ford p. 15, 30
18. Hayter, Thomas (1756) *A Sermon Preached in the Parish-Church of Christ-Church* London: J. Oliver p. 21–2
19. A list of the charity schools in England returned in the *Account of Charity Schools* for 1724 revealed that there was a significant effort on behalf of the charity school movement to provide at least limited provision for education across Britain. cited in Jones (1964) *The Charity School Movement* p. 364
20. Kamm, Josephine (1965) *Hope Deferred* London: Methuen & Co. p. 84
21. Trimmer (1792) *Reflections upon the Education of Children in Charity Schools* p. 9
22. 'Profaneness and debauchery are greatly owing to a great ignorance of the Christian religion, especially among the poorer sort', claimed *An Account of Charity Schools Lately Erected* of 1706. 'Nothing is more likely to promote the practice of

Christianity and virtue than an early and pious education of youth' the account stated. Anon (1706) *An Account of Charity Schools Lately Erected* p. 22

23 *The Whole Duty of Man* was published anonymously in 1658. It is generally considered to be the work of Richard Allestree. Relating to the lives of the poor, it provided over four hundred pages of advice about trusting God, observing the Lord's Day, honouring God's Word, reverencing the sacraments, praying and fasting, being humble, sober and temperate, avoiding time-wasting recreation and immodesty in apparel, performing duties towards one's neighbour and abstaining from adultery and fornication. *The Whole Duty of Man* fell out of favour from the 1770s as a result of the proliferation of more specific religious manuals. Tye (2014) 'Religion, The SPCK and the Westminster Workhouses' p. 206, 234
24 Anon (1704) *The Whole Duty of Man* p. 3
25 Payne (2006) 'London's Charity School Children' p. 386–90
26 Gibson, Edmund (1727) *Directions given to the Clergy of the Diocese of London in the Year 1724* London: S. Buckley p. 109
27 *An Account of the Charity Schools Lately Erected* claimed in 1708 that children were made tractable and submissive by being early accustomed to awe and punishment and dutiful subjection. 'From such timely discipline the public may expect honest and industrious servants', it claimed. cited in Cressy, David (1975) *Education in Tudor and Stuart England* London: Edward Arnold p. 24
28 Hayter (1756) *A Sermon Preached in the Parish-Church of Christ-Church* p. 19
29 Dissenter Isaac Watts stated 'The cloths which are bestowed upon them once in a year or two, are of the coarsest kind, and of the plainest form, and thus they are sufficiently distinguished from children of better rank, and they ought always to be so distinguished... there is no ground for these charity children to grow vain and proud of their raiment when 'tis but a sort of livery that publicly declares those who wear it to be educated by charity'. Watts (1728) *An Essay Towards the Encouragement of Charity Schools* p. 42, 37
30 Anon (1706) *An Account of Charity-schools Lately Erected in England* p. 4
    'Plain work is so evidently useful to women in general, but to the poor in particular,' declared Sarah Trimmer, 'that no charity girls can be deemed properly educated who had not attained to a tolerable proficiency at her needle'. Trimmer (1792) *Reflections upon the Education of Children in Charity Schools* p. 22
31 cited in Picard (2000) *Dr Johnson's London* p. 176
32 Sarah Trimmer claimed 'The objection, that education raises children above their station, is completely obviated by making such learning as general as possible, for then it ceases to give pre-eminence, or to be a distinction, and must eventually qualify all better to fit their respective stations in Society'. Trimmer (1792) *Reflections upon the Education of Children in Charity Schools* p. 4
33 Watts (1728) *An Essay Towards the Encouragement of Charity Schools* p. 26
34 Priestley, Joseph (1778) *Miscellaneous Observations Relating to Education* Bath: R. Cuttwell p. 129
35 Stamp, William Wood (1863) *The Orphan-house of Wesley* London: John Mason p. 269
36 Wesley (1755) *Instructions for Children, Fourth Edition* p. 14, 37
37 Walsh suggests that rioting was very common in the eighteenth century, partly because there were very few legal and regular ways for ordinary people to express their grievances; partly because it was difficult to control large crowds. cited in Rack (2002) *Reasonable Enthusiast* p. 271
38 Heath, George (1794) *The New History* Bristol: W. Matthews p. 75
39 In September 1740, the colliers marched to Bristol, along with some weavers, colliers' wives 'and abundance of other women' to complain of the excessive price of wheat: 'The Daily Post Sep 30' reported that on 'hearing of the readiness of the military to meet them, they returned to their homes without doing any damage'.

cited in Wearmouth (1945) *Methodism and the Common People of the Eighteenth Century* p. 22
40 Wesley, John (1773) *Thoughts on the Present Scarcity of Provisions* London: R. Hawes p. 4–17
41 Jason Vickers suggests that alongside conservative High Church doctrines, there is evidence in Wesley's later writings of more liberal, democratic or Whig sentiments. From 1768, he wrote and published twelve political essays, beginning with 'Free Thoughts on the State of Public Affairs' and including 'How Far is it the Duty of a Christian Minister to Preach Politics' in 1782; suggesting a new commitment in the later decades of Wesley's life to limited monarchy, human liberty and natural rights. Vickers, Jason E. (2009) *Wesley: A Guide for the Perplexed* London: T & T Clark p. 60–6
42 Wesley (1773) *Thoughts on the Present Scarcity of Provisions* p. 22
43 Malcolmson, Robert W. (1986) *A Set of Ungovernable People* Bristol: Kingswood District Council p. 7
44 Rack (2011) *BCE* vol. 10 p. 215
45 Dallimore (1980) *George Whitefield* vol. 1 p. 135–207
46 Rack (2002) *Reasonable Enthusiast* p. 192
'Kingswood' covered an area of three or four thousand acres. Edwards (1972) *New Room* p. 1
In May 1753, the Mayor of Bristol said of the colliers: 'the place they come from is very populous, and has in it a great number of under ground workmen, who are but little known and on that account very desperate fellows'. Public Record Office S. P. 36/122, fol, 41, cited in Malcolmson (1986) *A Set of Ungovernable People* p. 4
47 Dallimore (1980) *George Whitefield* vol. 1 p. 206–388
48 Baker (1984) *BCE* vol. 8 p. 25; vol. 7 p. 349
As a letter sent to John Wesley from his brother Samuel in 1739 suggests, these rooms were referred to as 'school': 'It is good news that you have built a charity school and better still that you have a second almost up. I wish you could build not only a school, but a church too, for the colliers, if there is not any place at present for worship where they meet'. cited in Clarke (1832) *Memoirs of the Wesley Family* p. 425
49 Bishop (1996) 'Wesley's Four Schools at Kingswood' p. 48
50 Baker (1984) *BCE* vol. 19 p. 125
51 When Wesley opened his boarding school on the same site seven years later, the Kingswood preaching-house was used by pupils as a chapel. The girl boarders were accommodated in the eight small side rooms during the night, while still being used as classrooms during the day by the colliers' children. Bishop (1977) 'A Detective Story'
52 It had been at Whitefield's suggestion that Wesley place the title to the New Room in his own name, and Wesley later did the same regarding the school. Dallimore (1980) *George Whitefield* vol. 2 p. 71
53 Tudur, Geraint (2000) *Howell Harris* Cardiff: Cardiff University Press p. 55
54 Dallimore (1980) *George Whitefield* vol. 1 p. 299–304; vol. 2 p. 36–9
55 Baker (1984) *BCE* vol. 26 p. 58
56 Rack suggests Cennick was joined by ninety members of the original society, with only fifty two remaining in the Kingswood Society. Rack (2002) *Reasonable Enthusiast* p. 198
57 Gentry (2007) *Bold as a Lion* p. 42
58 Charles Wesley noted in his journal on 4 September 1739 that he 'preached over against the school in Kingswood to some thousands (colliers chiefly)'; and that 'a spirit of contrition and love ran through them. Here the seed has fallen upon good ground... O that our London brethren would come to school to

Kingswood'. In June 1740, he noted that he preached 'Christ, the Way, the Truth and the Life to one thousand little children at Kingswood'. Kimbrough (2008) *The Manuscript Journal of the Reverend Charles Wesley* p. 193–271

59 cited in Ibid. p. 300–1, 329
60 Baker (1984) *BCE* vol. 21 p. 283
61 Ibid. vol. 25 p. 702
62 Graham (1990) *Wesley's Early Experiments in Education* p. 7
63 Wesley (1781) 'A Plain Account of Kingswood School near Bristol' p. 259–63
　Reference is made in Wesley's *Arminian Magazine for 1781* p. 259–63 to a John Woolley, who was 'for some time in [Kingswood] School; but was turned out for his ill behaviour'. Baker notes that 'Woolley, who died on 13 Feb. 1742 aged 13, had been turned out from Kingswood for bad behaviour and then absconded from home. Appearing one night at the New Room, he was converted by a sermon by John Wesley on disobedience to parents and returned home a model child'. Baker (1984) *BCE* vol. 19 p. 251–2
64 Ibid. vol. 20 p. 17
65 Ibid. vol. 22 p. 130
66 Heitzenrater (2002) *The Poor and the People called Methodists* p. 122
67 Wesley, John (1787c) 'Thoughts on Methodism' in *The Arminian Magazine* p. 101
68 Elliott-Binns (1953) *The Early Evangelicals* p. 214
69 Heitzenrater (2002) *The Poor and the People called Methodists* p. 121–2
70 Norris suggests that the Book Room generated significant profits, and may ultimately have saved the Connexion from financial collapse. Norris (2015) 'Prophets and Profits' p. 193
71 Body, Alfred H. (1936) *John Wesley and Education* London: Epworth Press p. 77–8
72 Jacob (2007) *The Clerical Profession in the Long Eighteenth Century* p. 242
73 Muller (2009) *Framing Childhood in Eighteenth-century Periodicals and Prints 1689–1789* p. 70
74 Stevenson, George John (1872) *City Road Chapel* London: George J. Stevenson p. 41
75 Told, Silas (1786) *An Account of the life and Dealings of God with Silas Todd* London: Gilbert and Plummer, and T. Scollick p. 95–6
76 Sangster, Paul (1963) *Pity My Simplicity* London: Epworth Press p. 97
77 Told (1786) *An Account of the life* p. 95–6
78 Baker (1984) *BCE* vol. 9 p. 278–9
79 Stevenson (1872) *City Road Chapel* p. 41
80 Kennett (1746) *The Christian Scholar* p. 40
81 'He who plays when a child, will play when a man'. Wesley (1749b) *A Short Account of the School in Kingswood* p. 5
82 Baker (1984) *BCE* vol. 9 p. 279
83 Lloyd (2007) *Charles Wesley and the Struggle for Methodist Identity* p. 7
84 Deacon (1980) *Philip Doddridge of Northampton* p. 103
85 Baker (1984) *BCE* vol. 19 p. 173
86 cited in Wearmouth (1945) *Methodism and the Common People of the Eighteenth Century* p. 139, 203
87 Heitzenrater (1995) *Wesley and the People called Methodists* p. 138
88 Milburn, Geoffrey (2007) 'The Significance of the Orphan House' in Fisher, Geoffrey & Hurst, Terry *The Orphan House of John Wesley* Newcastle upon Tyne: Wesley Historical Society p. 15
89 'An early description of the Orphan House written on 23 May 1744 by Richard Viney', cited in Ibid. p. 3–8
90 Stamp (1863) *The Orphan-house of Wesley* p. 269
91 Ibid. p. 25
92 Both men became highwaymen in London, a crime for which Ramsay was executed and Snoude deported: J. S. Pawlyn, *Bristol Methodism in John Wesley's*

Day, Bristol: W. C. Hemmons: p. 23–4, cited in Norris, Clive (2014) 'Education, Welfare and Missions', 15 January 2014, Unpublished, Research notes for PhD thesis: Oxford Brookes University p. 8
93 Baker (1984) *BCE* vol. 19 p. 196
94 Edwards, Maldwyn (1972) *New Room* Manchester: Penwick (Leeds) p. 8
95 Norris (2014) 'Education, Welfare and Missions' p. 8
96 Baker noted that Richard Terry was originally a school-master who became a wealthy merchant. Devoted to religion and charity, he was sympathetic to Methodism, although not a full adherent. As a public-spirited citizen of Hull, he became a Governor of the Poor in 1792. Baker, Frank (1943) *Richard Terry and Hull Methodism* Wesley Historical Society p. 1–7
97 cited in Ibid p. 2–3
98 Baker (1984) *BCE* vol. 3 p. 342
99 Wearmouth (1945) *Methodism and the Common People of the Eighteenth Century* p. 189–206
100 Before 1746 Wesley secured the services of an apothecary and an experienced surgeon at the Foundery where, according to his *Journal* entry of 4 December 1746, six hundred patients were treated. An electrical machine for the treatment of a range of ailments was later procured for the Foundery. Ibid. p. 207–9
    As at the Foundery, the New Room had provision for the sale of cheap literature and the distribution of free medicines. Edwards (1972) *New Room* p. 7
101 Hastling (1898) *The History of Kingswood School* p. 23
102 Mathews, Horace Frederick (1949) *Methodism and the Education of the People* London: Epworth Press p. 23
103 Rack (2011) *BCE* vol. 10 p. 139
104 Curnock (1909–1916) *The Journal of the Rev. John Wesley* vol. 6 p. 124; Baker (1984) *BCE* vol. 23 p. 185
105 Rack (2011) *BCE* vol. 10 p. 341
106 Stevenson (1872) *City Road Chapel* p. 153
    John Wesley letter to Charles Atmore 24 Mar. 1790 in Telford (1931) *The Letters of the Rev. John Wesley* vol. 8 p. 207–8
107 White Kennett had similarly referred to the Book of Job when he stated: 'Man is born "like a wild ass's colt", it is education that must reform thee and refine thee; it is learning that must exercise the reason and inspire the understanding… What good will thy life be unto thee if thou were condemned to spend it like a wild beast in ignorance?'. Kennett (1746) *The Christian Scholar* p. 7–8, 29
108 Baker (1984) *BCE* vol. 9 p. 278
109 cited in Wilson, David Robert (2010) 'Church and Chapel: Parish Ministry and Methodism in Madeley c1760–1785' PhD thesis: University of Manchester p. 312
    In an oft quoted incident when he was teaching children, whose attention was waning, a robin flew into the meeting house, exciting them. Fletcher quickly turned their distraction into an opportunity to instruct them on 'the harmlessness of the little creature, and the tender care of its creator'. cited in Ibid. p. 215
110 cited in Ibid. p. 217–8
111 Ibid. p. 312
112 Fletcher, John (1778) Letter to Vincent Perronet, undated but attributed 1778, 'Wesley Family papers' ref. GB 133 DDWes/2/40
113 cited in Wilson (2010) 'Church and Chapel' p. 312
114 John Fletcher's time as a tutor to the Hill family during the 1750s was marked by a constant struggle to decide the right degree of punishment for his pupils with, Streiff states, entries in his notebook indicating his desire not to judge his pupils as strictly as if they were adults. Streiff (2001) *Reluctant Saint?* p. 50
115 Fletcher, John 'Prayers for the use of Sunday schools', 'Fletcher-Tooth Papers' ref. Box 43, folder 3, item 4

116 Baker (1984) *BCE* vol. 23 p. 121
117 cited in Wilson (2010) 'Church and Chapel' p. 312
118 cited in Ibid. p. 309–12
119 Telford (1931) *The Letters of the Rev. John Wesley* vol. 5 p. 181–2
120 Baker (1984) *BCE* vol. 23 p. 241
121 Ibid. p. 201
122 Baker (1943) *Charles Wesley As Revealed by His Letters* p. 3
123 Rack states that membership of Methodist societies represented just 0.35% of the population in 1770; 0.47% in 1790 and 1.04% in 1801 (excluding adherents), although local strength varied considerably. Rack (2002) *Reasonable Enthusiast* p. 427
124 Tranter (1996) 'John Wesley and the Education of Children' p. 21

5 Kingswood boarding school: 1746–1780

John Wesley regarded education as training for a life of holiness as well as academic achievement. For that training to succeed, he believed that the early nurture within the family unit had to be continued at school. Wesley established Kingswood boarding school, alongside the colliers' school that he had opened seven years earlier, because he was particularly concerned for the ongoing nurture of children from Methodist homes. There, he argued, the implementation of, and adherence to, strict rules, upheld by men of piety, would safeguard children from 'all manner of vice'.[1] This chapter focuses on the boarding school during the period from its establishment in 1746 to 1780, examining how questions of piety, gender and class defined its pedagogy. From 1780, the character of the school began to change. The catalyst for this, and the impact on the school, is discussed in chapter six.

Although principally thought of as John Wesley's boarding school, the evidence suggests that Charles Wesley took an interest in Kingswood in its formative years. The chapter discusses his involvement, and provides reasons behind his decision not send his own sons to the school. It examines the work of some of Wesley's contemporaries in the period under review in order to draw comparisons with grammar schools, Dissenting academies and universities of the day. In doing so, this chapter argues that far from offering anything new at Kingswood, there was some convergence of ideas. Nevertheless, while many schools adapted in the face of growing concerns over established forms of education, Wesley appears to have been intransigent in the face of criticism, maintaining his belief in the merits of his educational model.

Wesley's educational 'model' of piety, manliness and academic learning

The *Minutes* of Wesley's Methodist Conference in August 1783 gave a description of Wesley's intentions when founding the boarding school at Kingswood:

> My design in building the house at Kingswood was to have therein a Christian family, every member whereof (children excepted) should be

alive to God, and a pattern of all holiness. Here it was that I proposed to educate a few children according to the accuracy of the Christian model.[2]

From the outset, Wesley was determined to build a strong and rational foundation of religious instruction into his educational programme, declaring to Mary Jones, a prospective parent, that 'it being our view not so much to teach Greek and Latin, as to train up soldiers for Jesus Christ'.[3] Wesley reiterated his intentions in his *Journal* on 12 March 1766, when it appears staff and pupils were failing to uphold the 'Christian model': 'I rode over to Kingswood, and having told my whole mind to the masters and servants, spoke to the children in a far stronger manner than ever I did before. I will kill or cure: I will have one or the other – a Christian school, or none at all'.[4]

Wesley expected places at the school to be filled by offspring of parents known to him, or to others whom he trusted. Indeed, the evidence suggests that Wesley regarded his boarding school as a place where his wealthier followers might send their sons. There was to be no admission of the sort of children who might corrupt their fellows, and Wesley insisted that the pupils, aged between six and twelve, would be 'none but boarders' in an effort to distance them from outside influences.[5] Thompson suggested that when Wesley was planning accommodation for the fifty boys he intended to house at Kingswood, 'there must have crept gratefully into his recollection the image of that adapted duke's tennis court which had housed him among the forty gown-boys'.[6] The 'New House', as Wesley's boarding school became known, opened on 24 June 1748, with twenty eight boys and six Masters.[7] Pupils were boarded, instructed and clothed.[8] They attended the New House by day, and were accommodated there by night, along with Masters and staff.[9] The rectangular three-storey building housed two rooms, a bedroom and a study, set aside for Wesley to use on his frequent visits to the school.[10]

Wesley believed that education was not merely desirable for life in this world, but a preparation for the life to come.[11] Before being accepted into Kingswood, the prospective pupils were expected to display a desire to save their souls and, together with their parents, to agree to abide by the strict rules of the school, which Wesley published in *A Short Account of the School in Kingswood, Near Bristol*, in 1749.[12] Wesley insisted that these rules were 'not [to] be broken in favour of any person whatsoever'; and they remained largely unchanged throughout his life.[13] Writing to Joseph Benson in December 1769, he asserted:

> Every man of sense who reads the rules of the school may easily conclude that a school so conducted by men of piety and understanding will exceed any other school or academy in Great Britain or Ireland. In this sentiment you can never be altered.[14]

Wesley's sermon at the official opening of the New House was based on Proverbs 22:6: 'train up a child in the way he should go and when he is old he will not depart from it'.[15] Charles Wesley composed a hymn especially for the occasion which expressed the spiritual aims of the school; that 'Sacred discipline be given, to train and bring them up for heaven... [by] learning and holiness combined'.[16]

Despite the fact that a small number of girls were admitted to Kingswood School in the early years, and women were among the staff, Wesley made it clear that the boys' upbringing would be 'at the utmost distance from softness and effeminacy'.[17] The manly ideals of endurance and self-reliance were to be built on privation, not softness. Arguing that 'he who plays when a child will play when a man', Wesley contended that childish play, which would be emulated through 'leisure' in manhood, was to be overcome through constant engagement in learning and industry.[18] His attitude was reflected in the hymn written for pupils by Charles Wesley in 1763, which stated:

> Let heathenish boys
> In their pastimes rejoice
> And be foolishly happy at play
> Overstocked if they are
> We have nothing to spare
> Not a moment to trifle away.[19]

Although Olleson describes the regime at Kingswood as one of 'monastic severity' it was not John Wesley's intention to make his pupils miserable.[20] Georgian society regarded effeminacy as the feminisation or weakening of men, and the risk to society of boys unable to mature into men of sterling character was regarded as profound.[21] Wesley considered self-denial, virtue and happiness as congruent: 'True religion or holiness can not be without cheerfulness... true religion has nothing sour, austere, unsociable in it' he stated.[22] Southey claimed that 'Mr Wesley's notions concerning education must have done great evil. No man was ever more thoroughly ignorant of the nature of children'.[23] While this is perhaps an exaggeration, it seems that not all boys were as serious and studious as Wesley had been, and he apparently underestimated the dulling effect for a monotonous routine on young minds. He wrote of the boys following a visit to the school in 1765 'they are all in health; they behave well; they learn well, but alas (two or three excepted) there is no life in them!'.[24]

Wesley's educational model provided training for a life of holiness as well as academic achievement. Nevertheless, in echoing Locke, his 'rules' at Kingswood were written with a specific gender and class bias in mind and, in many respects, accorded with sentiments of the day concerning the fashioning of 'a gentleman'. Indeed, the evidence suggests that up to the 1780s, attendance at the school was largely defined by boundaries of gender and class. Clarke noted in 1833:

> As a religious seminary, and under the direction of one of the greatest men in the world, Mr J. Wesley... the school had a great character, both over

Europe and America, among religious people. Independently of several young gentlemen, the sons of opulent Methodists, there were at that time in it several from the West Indies, Norway, Sweden and Denmark.[25]

A letter from Methodist preacher John Pawson, dated 22 October 1802, addressed to Joseph Benson, indicated that although Wesley may have regarded pupils at his school as 'gentlemen', many of his followers, particularly those from less wealthy backgrounds, had no such aspirations for their sons. Referring to the son of Joseph Cownley, an itinerant preacher between 1744 and 1793, Pawson stated: 'Did not young Cownley tell his blessed father to his face, I am ashamed to be seen walking in the streets with you'.[26] Indeed, Pawson contended: 'I assure you that I saw so much of that School the five years I was stationed in Bristol, that was I blessed with a boy, I would no more send him there, no nor to any boarding school upon earth'. He concluded:

> It would be a thousand times better to teach those children such branches of learning as may fit them for the common life. To make them good English scholars, to write a good hand, to complete them in accompts, and if they can learn French, very well, then by the blessing of God, they may become useful tradesmen... [rather than]... have them made into little gentlemen.[27]

Authority and management in the early years

The primary role of the father in the patriarchal society of the eighteenth century was as the centre of authority, responsible for organising education, training and disciplining of children over the age of seven.[28] Although he had no children of his own, Wesley appears to have conceptualised the schools he established at Kingswood on the lines of a family environment.[29] He frequently referred to staff and children at Kingswood as a 'family', believing this to be the ideal environment in which to provide children with the best possible religious upbringing and education.[30] Mack suggests that Wesley urged his followers to consider themselves members of spiritual families in which leaders were called 'father' and 'mother' and members of the community 'brother' and 'sister', but without the authoritarianism and possessiveness of a biological family.[31] However, that the framework of household–family manifested itself in concepts of authority and possession, and gave childless men paternal roles as well as patriarchal authority, highlights perhaps the significance of Wesley's concept of the household at Kingswood as 'family'.[32]

Wesley assumed a position of patriarchal authority over the school. Although the foundation stone was laid on 7 April 1746, and the school opened on 24 June 1748, he did not appoint a headmaster until 1751. Instead both he and Charles Wesley took responsibility for running Kingswood, even though this was often from a distance.[33] The six Masters taken on when the school opened were all semi-itinerant and liable to be taken off by Wesley at short notice to preach elsewhere. John Jones, the First Master, was not only expected to oversee Kingswood School, but was also in charge of both the Bristol and the Cornwall Methodist Districts.[34]

Up to 1756 the school was largely funded by fees and contributions from Wesley and his followers.[35] In order to boost income, at the ninth Methodist Conference in September 1756, it was agreed that 'a subscription for it [Kingswood School] be begun in every place, and (if need be) a collection made every year'. It was not until the Manchester Conference on 20 August 1765 that a collection was recorded for the school, when an amount of £100–9s-7d was mentioned.[36] Although Wesley remained a Governor of Kingswood School until he died, in August 1766 the burden of management was lightened by the decision to refer matters concerning the operation of the school to Conference: 'so I have cast an [sic] heavy load off my shoulders', Wesley declared.[37] The Conference took responsibility for the approval of the rules and appointed trustees and stewards. It also authorised annual collections and publicised the school to every Methodist Society.

Even before students were enrolled, Wesley made it clear that the discipline at Kingswood would be exact.[38] Pupils were instructed every day of the week except Sunday, when there were two public services and time devoted to learning hymns or poems.[39] Parents were not permitted to take their children out of the school at any time, 'no, not for a day, till they take him for good and all'. Wesley claimed: 'Children may unlearn as much in one week as they have learned in several'.[40] Training for a life of holiness demanded that there were no opportunities for pupils to be idle; they were kept constantly occupied, whether at work or 'leisure'. Periods between lessons, if not engaged in work, were designated as times when they might walk around the grounds, work in the garden or sing. A close watch was kept on the children at all times. Whatever the activity undertaken, Wesley insisted that 'particular care is taken that [the children] never work alone, but always in the presence of a master'.[41]

Wesley stipulated a 'plain and simple' diet at Kingswood, since he was determined to protect his pupils from the dangers of over-indulgence.[42] The diet was not insubstantial, including cold roast beef, hashed meat, boiled mutton and bacon; albeit that Wednesdays and Fridays, as well as the period throughout Lent, were designated as days when only 'vegetable and dumplins' would be served. Wesley also stipulated that on Fridays the boys were to fast until three in the afternoon since, he argued 'experience shows this is so far from impairing health that it greatly conduces to it'.[43] There was no tuck shop at the school; the boys sat together to eat at allotted times during the day. They were to have nothing between meals 'lest they should insensibly contract habits which were neither good for body or mind'.[44]

Rather than the 'small beer' provided for most children at public schools, the boys at Kingswood were to drink water, and only at meals because, Wesley argued, water was 'the best diluter of food which is to be found on earth'.[45] The evidence suggests, however, that this rule was impractical since there was no well at Kingswood.[46] The scarcity of water meant that a large underground cistern, with a pump, supplied the school.[47] This water supply was often inadequate; Clarke recorded having a meal with Masters during his stay at the school in 1782. On being offered beer, he refused and went 'to the vile straining stone behind the kitchen for some of the half-putrid pit water'. Clarke also stated that there was a pond of rain water in the garden, where he occasionally bathed, since 'scanty indeed of water, for there is none in the place but what falls from heaven... I was obliged to contend with frogs, askes, or evets, and vermin of different kinds'.[48]

Self-discipline in the form of early rising meant the boys were expected to rise at 4am both summer and winter and spend an hour in private reading, singing, in meditation or in prayer, before meeting together at 5am for the public service. They were expected to retire early in the evening. Following a public service at 7pm, boys went to bed from 8pm, with the youngest going first. Although the beds had flock mattresses, 'luxuries' such as feather beds were to be avoided.[49] Unlike some public schools where Masters left pupils alone at night, Wesley insisted that the boys lodged in one room with a Master at each end, and a lamp was left burning all night.[50]

As the first boarders came from homes of Wesley's friends and supporters, it was perhaps inevitable that, initially at least, pupils responded to the atmosphere of piety and discipline in which they found themselves.[51] Early in 1749, Charles Wesley's observation was that Kingswood School was: 'very much like a college; twenty one boarders are there and a dozen students (preachers in training), his [John Wesley's] sons in the gospel. I believe he is now laying the foundations of many generations'.[52] Charles's differentiation between 'boarders' and 'students' could be explained by Wesley's *Journal* entry for 22 February 1749: 'My design was to have as many of our preachers here [at Kingswood] during Lent as could possibly be spared; and to read lectures to them every day, as I did to my pupils in Oxford, I had seventeen of them in all...'.[53] It is unclear whether Wesley's 'preachers in training' received their lectures in Wesley's boarding school, or in the adjoining colliers' building.

Wesley's own analysis of the effectiveness of the school was that 'some of the wildest children were struck with deep conviction: all appeared to have some good desires, and two or three began to taste the love of God'.[54] A more detailed analysis of the situation at the school was provided by William Spencer, whose letter to Wesley dated 9 August 1748 was reproduced in *The Arminian Magazine of 1778*. Spencer's 'Account of the Children at Kingswood School' suggested that several named boys were responsible for 'ill behaviour' at Kingswood. Although some were then 'pricked to the heart', Spencer noted that the convictions of Gab Wayne and Robert Jones were soon 'trifled away'.[55]

Although Wesley subsequently recorded 'notwithstanding the strictness of the rules, I had soon as many scholars as I desired; nay, considerably more', evidence suggests that Wesley's 'model' school continued to have its problems.[56] In October 1749, just over a year after its opening, Robert Jones, along with some other boys, ran away from the school. Wesley took a firm line and wrote to his mother Mary Jones, on 7 November 1749, stating:

On Saturday my brother and I were both determined that none of the children should come to the school any more. But the masters interceded so earnestly for them that we were at length induced so far to change our purpose as to take him on trial from week to week. If they behave well they may remain with us. If not, we must put them quite away, that they may not corrupt the rest.[57]

Despite John Wesley's intimation that his brother was in full agreement, Charles Wesley appears to have taken a milder line.[58] Referring to Robert [Robin] in his letter to Mrs Jones of 30 October 1749 as 'our poor fugitive', he stated that 'she should not worry, for in all likelihood her son will have turned up' by the time she had read his letter. Suggesting Robert had been 'seduced by that wicked boy Jacky Williams', Charles advised her to 'treat her son kindly, especially if he admits to wrong'. He advised that as long as Mrs Jones could assure him that her son would behave himself in future, he would stand surety for the boy 'and he shall not be corrected at all'.[59]

A week later, Charles wrote again to Mrs Jones, advising that 'JW has agreed to allow the boys another chance...' but 'if Robin will not be led, he must be driven... I mean whipped through Westminster or some other great school. But I hope he will yet know his true interest'.[60] In January 1750, Charles wrote once more to Mrs Jones stating that he would like to see her, and asking what she was doing about 'poor Robin'.[61] Two days later, Charles Wesley reported having met with her son. It would seem that despite his efforts, Robert Jones could not be persuaded to return to Kingswood since Charles advised his mother that he hoped Robin did not 'forget everything he learnt at Kingswood School'.[62]

By 1751, just three years after Kingswood had opened, either as a result of pupils being dismissed, or withdrawn from the school, the roll had dropped to just two Masters and eleven boys.[63]

Charles Wesley, Kingswood School and new concepts of childhood

Charles Wesley undoubtedly supported John's work at Kingswood, but his response to Robert Jones makes it unclear how committed he was to his brother's regime at the school. He believed a truly Christian school could remedy a child's 'sin-sick mind' and inspire not only academic learning, but a 'spark of heavenly fire, a taste of God, a seed of grace'.[64] He reiterated Puritan thinking in a verse that declared that children were 'conceiv'd and wholly born in sin, the evil principle within'.[65] Referring to children at Kingswood as *our* children,[66] he was a frequent visitor to the school, teaching hymns to the pupils and taking responsibility while his brother was away.[67] Nevertheless, despite living in nearby Bristol, Charles did not send either of his sons to Kingswood.[68] Neither did he send them to be educated under what he considered the corrupting influence of a grammar school. In the unpublished poem *At Sending a Son to School,* he declared:

> V1. His soul from young corrupters save
> And keep him spotless to the end
> V2. From youthful lusts preserve him pure
> Pure in a cage of birds unclean
> In learned nurseries of vice
> Where pride, and dire ambition reign
> And knowing at too dear a price
> They forfeit heaven, a Name to gain.[69]

While Charles's experience at public school may have differed from John's, since he was 'under the protection of a rather indulgent elder brother' at Westminster School, these verses clearly reflected John Wesley's sentiments regarding public schools.[70]

Although Charles and his wife Sally had eight children, five of them died in infancy and this, Best suggests, made the three surviving children particularly precious.[71] When his children were very young, Charles Wesley was frequently away from home, which caused him great anxiety whenever one of them was ill.[72] Once a parent, Charles made every effort to understand his three children, to enter into their world and to bring them up in a way most appropriate to their personalities and talents.[73] Although he did not show his affection for his children in public, Charles Wesley's hymns, poems and letters attest to his deep love for them.[74] He was to reflect in one of his hymns on bringing up children that:

> We would persuade their heart to obey,
> With mildest zeal proceed,
> And never take the harsher way,
> When love will do the deed.[75]

Like John, Charles Wesley was undoubtedly influenced by his upbringing at Epworth. Fearing that his children might be led astray if allowed to mix with other children, he advised his wife Sally in 1766: 'It is superfluous, yet I cannot help cautioning you about Charles, to take care he contracts no acquaintance with other boys. Children are corrupters of each other'. In 1753, when their first child John was only a year old, Charles wrote to Sally advising her that 'The most important of all Locke's rules you will not forget, it is that in which the whole *secret* of education consists – make it your invaluable rule to *cross his will* in some one instance at least every day of your life'. The evidence suggests that his view had mellowed by the time he was advising her concerning their son Charles:

> Charley you *need* not chastise too severely, if he is *indeed* so easy to be managed; but I a little doubt a son of mine [sic]. You will find by and by he has a will of his own, Persuade him, and you need never compel him. If he will lead, 'tis pity he should drive.[76]

In his letter to his seven year old son Samuel on 6 March 1773, Charles advised 'You should now begin to live by reason and religion. There should be sense even in your play and diversions'. However, he did not ban popular children's books and in his letters home referred to *Aesop's Fables, Robinson Crusoe, Gulliver's Travels* and *Don Quixote*. Indeed, while advising Samuel that he should 'every day read one or more chapters of the Bible', he also stated 'I have furnished you with maps and books and harpsichord'.[77] Despite Samuel's prodigious musical talent, Charles referred to learning gained through maps and books before the 'diversion' of the harpsichord. In a fragment of an undated letter from Charles to Samuel, Charles advised his son 'your first business is the grammar, your second finishing lessons. Your kite does not come [before] your study'.[78] Nevertheless, in acknowledging Locke's view that children must play and have play things, Charles reflected a more progressive approach to his children's education than his brother.

Charles felt that the God-given talents of his sons lay in music and, even though he could not afford the best teachers, he estimated that he had spent hundreds of pounds on their musical education. Norris refers to the 'striking aspects' of the Wesleys' budget with regard to expenditure on their children. With around forty pounds a year spent on the musical careers of the Wesley sons and a purchase in 1774 of an organ for Charles junior costing seventy four pounds, Norris calculates that around twenty per cent of the family's annual expenditure comprised investment in the boys' musical endeavours.[79] Charles Wesley's sons had troubled adult lives, and Best suggests that their musical careers suffered because of their father and uncles' involvement in Methodism. Charles, just before he died, mindful of the failure of his sons to become staunch Churchmen, stated 'I have been of little use to my children. But it is too late to attempt it now'.[80]

Although during the 1740s Charles Wesley had travelled widely, by 1756 he took the decision to largely withdraw from itinerancy in favour of a more settled ministry in London and Bristol.[81] This decision, very much against John's wishes, was the result of several factors.[82] His biographer Thomas Jackson claimed it was as a result of disquiet among societies and preachers with regard to their relationship with the Church.[83] Although his health and an increasingly fraught relationship with the Methodist preachers may have had a bearing, there can be little doubt, Lloyd argues, that family responsibilities played a significant part in his decision.[84] In 1771, just as John Wesley was declaring that the learning offered at Kingswood 'would advance the students more in three years than the generality of students at Oxford or Cambridge do in seven', rather than sending his sons to Kingwood, Charles Wesley moved his family from Bristol to London, in order to secure what he considered to be the best possible educational and musical opportunities for his children.[85]

That Charles Wesley did not take a more active role at Kingswood School appears to have been the result of many factors. He had, following his marriage in 1749, begun to mix with gentry and nobility on a more informal basis and his circle of friends began to reflect his wife's privileged background.

Although John Wesley mixed with the same people, their relationships with Charles were more relaxed.[86] The house, in Chesterfield Street, Marylebone, into which the Wesley household moved in 1771, was about three miles from John's London base at the Foundery, and Charles quickly became the acknowledged main pastor to the London societies, regularly visiting the prisons and helping the poor, as well as undertaking preaching.[87]

Charles Wesley was not typical of the lay leadership within Methodism, who, with very few exceptions, came from modest backgrounds and had a limited education.[88] Happily married, Charles had after 1756 largely withdrawn from itinerancy for a settled ministry in London and Bristol. The house into which the Wesley household moved was richly furnished and was offered to Charles by Mrs Gumley, a close friend of the Wesleys and widow of Colonel Samuel Gumley, a wealthy member of the London Methodist Society.[89] Despite the differences between the brothers, Lloyd describes John Wesley as 'one of that rare breed of men who could not only sway people by personality, but inspire devotion even in difficult circumstances'.[90] Although time and again Charles subsumed his own judgement and wishes to John's persuasion, and never entirely shook off his brother's dominance, or indeed his loyalty to him; it would seem that his position regarding Kingswood remained ambivalent.[91] While he was on the one hand prepared to lend support to John's work at the school, this support did not extend to having his own sons educated there.

Comparison with grammar schools, universities and Dissenting academies

When the foundation stone of the boarding school was laid on 7 April 1746, close to the existing site of his preaching house and colliers' school in Kingswood, John Wesley was choosing geographically, as well as educationally, to distance his pupils from the sort of vice he regarded as prevalent in the urban environment. He contended that his Kingswood boarding school would offer an alternative to what he regarded as the anarchic, brutal, godless and Classics-dominated public schools of his day.[92]

Although Wesley believed Kingswood offered something unique, Tompson argues that there was no such thing as a 'typical' grammar school.[93] Eighteenth-century grammar schools were generally situated within or adjoining the Church in a rural market town, or metropolis, but the university connection and personal popularity of the Master were among the factors affecting a school's reputation. The number of boys in these schools varied greatly, from under ten to several hundred. While the 'great' public schools had above a hundred and 'gentlemen's' or large city schools catered for above fifty, smaller town and country schools held up to thirty pupils. The smaller grammar schools were commonly a one-room, one-storey building, divided into an upper and lower 'end' under the Master and Usher respectively. The Master of a grammar school would have been in holy orders, being required to take an oath of conformity to the Thirty Nine Articles of the Church of England.[94]

Wesley criticised the 'great schools', which he condemned both for their curriculum and method of instruction:[95]

> It is not only with regard to instruction in religion, that most of our great schools are defective. In some, the children are taught little or no arithmetic; in others, little care is taken even of their writing. In many, they learn scarce the elements of geography, and as little of chronology. And even as to the languages, there are some schools of note wherein no Hebrew at all is taught; and there are exceeding few wherein the scholars are thoroughly instructed even in the Latin and Greek tongues. They are not likely to be; for there is a capital mistake in their very method of teaching.[96]

Wesley sought to correct this at Kingswood, arguing that it was possible 'with God's assistance to train children in every branch of useful learning'. His 1749 *Short Account of Kingswood School* listed 'reading, writing, arithmetic, English, French, Latin, Greek, Hebrew, history, geography, chronology, rhetoric, logic, ethics, geometry, algebra, physics [and] music' on the syllabus at Kingswood.[97] It seems that by 1751, when the twenty one year old James Rouquet took over as headmaster, the curriculum had widened to include the 'commercial subjects' of 'merchants accounts' and 'surveying and mapping of land'.[98]

Wesley was not alone in his criticism of the teaching and learning experience at grammar and public schools. James Barclay stated in his 1734 *Treatise on Education* 'What can be more ridiculous than the general way of recommending the same task, and expecting the same application and process, from the several children... as if all were precisely of the same genius, and had equally a turn of Greek and Latin'.[99] John Clarke, Master of Hull Grammar School, wrote in 1720 that the common method of grammar schools was:

> So miserably trifling, that any one, who duly considers it, will have much ado to forbear thinking it has been contrived in opposition to all the rules of good method, on purpose to render the learning of the languages more tedious than it need to be.[100]

Indeed, over the course of the eighteenth century, purely classical learning came to be regarded as no longer 'useful' to those in commercial and professional ranks. Grammar schools responded to growing concern among the 'middling sort', anxious to acquire genteel status, useful skills and social graces, and the curriculum at some schools began to change to meet new educational needs.[101] Dissenting academies, with their emphasis on science, modern languages and 'commercial subjects', increasingly offered the 'middling sort' an opportunity to provide their sons with an education away from the classical curricula of grammar schools and universities. While some students entered academies to complete their formal education, others came to pursue a rigorous higher education. Students studying theology stayed for five years and lay students for three.[102]

Dissenter and tutor at Warrington Academy, Joseph Priestley, stated: 'the severe and proper discipline of the grammar school is become a topic of ridicule, and few young gentlemen, especially those who are designed for some of the learned professions, are made to submit to the rigors of it'.[103] He concluded that 'the usual method of educating young gentlemen… [is] remote from the business of civil life', and sought to remedy this by preparing students for a 'civil and active life: rather than the roles of the divine and philosopher only, the Dissenter will be educated for the world rather than the cloister'.[104] Priestley, who had joined Warrington Academy in June 1761 as tutor in languages and *belles lettres*, taught Latin, Greek, French and Italian, gave lectures on the theory of language, oratory and criticism. Observing that many students were intended either for careers in business or for public life, he introduced lectures on history and general policy, the laws and constitutions of England, and the history of England; publishing the syllabus for his lectures in *An Essay on a Course of Liberal Education for Civil and Active Life* in 1765.[105]

In referring to the 'academy at Kingswood', Rack suggests that what Wesley sought to offer was similar to the Dissenting academies, although Wesley himself saw things in a rather different light.[106] Wesley intended Kingswood to train young men in the sort of academic learning that would equip them for the learned professions to which the university students aspired, namely the ministry, the law and medicine, rather than the more 'modern' curriculum of the Dissenting academies.[107] Whether as a result of what he referred to as 'the many and great inconveniences' of his own education, or because of his condemnation of university life, Wesley, it seems, always intended that his school at Kingswood would provide an educational programme for all levels of academic endeavour. Writing in his *Plain Account of Kingswood School* he stated:

> I was indeed thoroughly convinced, ever since I read Milton's admirable Treatise on Education that it was highly expedient for every youth to begin and finish his education at the same place. I was convinced nothing could be more irrational and absurd than to break this off in the middle and to begin it again at a different place and in quite a different method.[108]

As discussed in chapter three, the events surrounding the expulsion of six students from St Edmund Hall, Oxford, in 1768 made the implementation of the academical course at Kingwood 'a necessity'.[109] When Wesley extended Kingswood School's curriculum for older students in 1768–1769, some twenty years after the school was founded, he declared 'whoever carefully goes through this course will be a better scholar than nine in ten of the graduates at Oxford or Cambridge'.[110] Wesley sought to offer, if not improve upon, what was available to students at Oxford; and he outlined in his *Plain Account of Kingswood School* the advantages and disadvantages of his course when compared to that of the University.

Acknowledging the eminent learning of the University, but condemning its manner of delivering that learning; questioning the value of the public exercises, and the choice of company available at Oxford, Wesley set out what he would provide for Kingswood students. If they sought honour, money, preferment in Church or State, let them go to the University for he claimed, if they sought instead 'to know and teach more perfectly the truth which God has revealed to man', 'they can enjoy in as high a degree, in the school or academy at Kingswood as at any College in the universe'.[111]

Wesley's 1768 publication of *A Short Account of the School in Kingswood, near Bristol* represented very much an 'extended' version of the original. The rules and curriculum, like the earlier publication, appear to give little room for flexibility.[112] In practice there may have been some bending of the rules since it appears from details in an old account book at Kingswood dated 1764 to 1770 that at least two pupils were permitted to learn 'painting on glass'.[113]

Locke's thinking undoubtedly influenced Wesley, as indeed it did tutors in Dissenting academies. Philip Doddridge, who always emphasised that his curriculum and teaching methods owed much to his own tutor, John Jennings, wrote that 'a great deal of it [logic] was taken from Mr Locke and we had large references to him and other celebrated authors, almost under every head.[114] It is clear from Doddridge's account of his time with Jennings, that his students were treated as individuals. Doddridge suggested that learning was not confined to 'the study' and 'the lecture room'. In order to 'wear off that ungraceful bashfulness with which young people are frequently oppress'd', Jennings timetabled 'drama' into his curriculum. Doddridge recalled:

> Every Wednesday night we had an entertainment which we call'd a drama. Our groundwork was some diverting story, the hints of which were often taken from the Spectator, Don Quixote, or some other humorous book, at other times from conversation, & sometimes it was a plot of our own invention. A variety of persons were introduced, each had his particular business in the conduct of the affair, & a distinct character which he was to support. We spoke extempore, & when we were a little us'd to it we seldom wanted something to say.[115]

Doddridge also noted that 'Mr Jennings… is sometimes a Calvinist, sometimes an Arminian, – as truth and evidence determine him'; and he upheld the same liberal tradition in his Northampton Academy.[116] While Gibson comments that Dissent in the eighteenth century witnessed theological tension between Calvinism and Arminianism, the majority of Dissenters were Calvinists. Dissenting academies educated students in a liberal theology which might allow ordination in the Church or the Dissenting ministry.[117] There were no tests of religious doctrine exacted on students; the Calvinist Doddridge believed that groups of students at the Academy benefited from each other and from the common core of theological lectures which they all attended.[118]

As discussed in chapter three, Wesley undoubtedly recognised Doddridge's abilities; and used the booklist that Doddridge had sent him as the basis for his *Christian Library*, used extensively at Kingswood.[119] Despite some convergence of thinking, there were some noticeable differences. The sort of free enquiry that allowed Doddridge's students to read texts from both Arminian and Calvinist authors was not available at Kingswood. While Wesley was prescriptive in what was read at his school, Doddridge encouraged his students to read widely. They were also encouraged to make critical annotations as they read, to ask questions during lectures, to voice objections and to present both sides of an argument.[120]

Intellectual freedom encouraged free enquiry and critical reflection; Priestley, who had spent part of his education at Northampton, remarked during his time as tutor at Warrington that 'In my time, the academy was in a state peculiarly favourable to the serious pursuit of truth, as the students were about equally divided upon every question of much importance'.[121] Indeed, Cohen argues that the 'free familiar conversation' at Warrington which took place over group teas was a central part of Priestley's teaching, and was described by him as 'equally instructive and pleasing'.[122]

In its twenty two year existence from 1729 to 1751, Doddridge's Academy in Northampton educated over two hundred students, of which one hundred and twenty became Dissenting ministers.[123] Some Anglican families sent their sons to Northampton Academy in preference to Oxford and Cambridge. Although his son had already attended the University of Edinburgh, a letter which Doddridge received from Sir James Fergusson (Lord Kilkerran) dated 10 November 1743 stated:

> As the education of my children in a right way is what I have much at heart, and that I foresee many dangers in sending young gentlemen to the University, I have long been of opinion, that the better way is to have them taught in an Academy, where they are under the immediate inspection of virtuous people – who will be no less watchful over their morals than over their literature.[124]

It was not only in the style of instruction that the students at the Dissenting academies were given greater freedom. While Wesley's rules for his 'academical' students largely followed the prescriptive regime of his earlier rules, Northampton Academy exercised a degree of democracy. Students were consulted on various matters, and the 'Constitutions, Orders & Rules' of the Academy were 'agreed upon by the tutors and the several members of it…'. Tutors were regarded as mentors and Deacon suggests that there was a strong bond of friendship between Doddridge and his students.[125]

Doddridge insisted that 'children should be instructed in a very tender and affectionate manner'.[126] He was opposed to corporal punishment, arguing that patience should prevail in all of an adults' dealing with children. Nevertheless, he expected rules at the Academy to be adhered to, and fines were an essential part of the Academy's discipline.[127] Neglecting the rules regarding return of library books, lateness at prayers, not pursuing an allotted duty at prayer time, lateness at lectures or failure to prepare a set exercise were all chargeable offences. The small pecuniary fines collected from students over the course of a year were, 'after a weekly deduction towards the support of the Charity School, and excepting only twenty shillings to be reserved in bank... disposed of in books or instruments of the apparatus', according to the vote of the students.[128]

Old account books dated 1764–1771, held in the Kingswood School archive, make reference to 'pocket money'. Since the pupils were not allowed outside the premises, it is unclear what this money was used for.[129] Hastling, in his *The History of Kingswood School* of 1898 suggested it 'found its way as *voluntary* contributions into the collecting plates', but he presented little evidence for this. The account book, together with Hastling's *History*, provide an image of a Kingswood youth, wearing a broad-brimmed hat, a long tail-coat and a pair of knee-breeches fastened round the knee by a ribbon, stockings and shoes with buckles.[130] Joseph Benson's letter of December 1766 rather contradicts this:

> The school is oppressed with debt, and several of the children's parents neglect to send them cloths or procure any for them anyway, especially Mr Hampson [who] seems to have forgot his boys... one wicked boy especially who we know, we sent off yesterday.[131]

Indeed, entries against individual pupils in the account book referring to 'hair cutting', 'shoes mending', 'suit of cloths', 'mending cloths' and 'ribbons' are frequently suffixed by the comment 'he went from this school'.[132] No indication is given as to whether this was an imposed or voluntary decision, but Wesley's letter to Joseph Benson during this period suggesting that he 'Bring the boys into *exact order* and that without delay. Do this at all hazards' might suggest the former.[133]

Although Deacon writes of Doddridge that 'few could emulate him in the use of his time, rising early in the morning and planning carefully every precious moment', his students were not expected to rise until six o'clock in the summer, and seven in the winter, somewhat later than the boys at Kingswood. The 'making of toast and butter and toasting cheese' was allowed for 'parlour boarders', and 'students attacked their meals with relish'. The rules of the Academy stated that 'They that chuse tea in the morning may either breakfast with the tutor in his parlour or at the other tea board in the great parlour, each in that case providing his own tea and sugar in a just proportion as the company shall agree'. Dinner was served in the school hall at two o'clock and supper between 8.30 and nine in the evening; 'neither breakfast, dinner nor supper to be carried into any room except in case of sickness'.[134]

While Wesley sought to ensure the close supervision of students, Doddridge took a gentler approach. Students had 'long vacations', and even when studying at the Academy were permitted to leave the premises provided that they returned by ten in the evening, at which time the gate was locked and fines incurred by anyone returning late. Rules of the Northampton Academy stated:

> No student is to go into a Publick [sic] House to drink there on penalty of a publick censure for the first time, and the forfeiture of a shilling the second… If any one spread reports abroad to the dishonour of the family or any member of it he must expect a publick reproof and to hear a caution given to others to beware of placing any confidence in him.

However, Doddridge did expel students who had persistently failed to take notice of his cautions. On one occasion he wrote 'We had some time spent in fasting and prayer, on account of an unhappy youth, whose folly and wickedness hath obliged me to dismiss him. I pronounced the solemn sentence of expulsion upon him before the whole academy'.[135]

The primary motivation for Wesley in establishing his boarding school at Kingswood was his dissatisfaction with the schools and universities of the day. Nevertheless, new concepts of the individuality of the child and calls for a 'modernization' of the educational curriculum, brought about changes in educational thinking. Educational establishments were able to adapt to meet the changing needs of parents and children.[136] Dissenting academies offered new educational opportunities for students, and many grammar schools took a more progressive approach by adapting in the face of criticism of their Classics driven curricula. Indeed, Hilton argues that most educational ideas and practices in the eighteenth century were ideologically complex and 'saturated with contradictions'. She suggests that educators not only crossed ideological boundaries, but changed their positions while drawing on different, seemingly contradictory, traditions and ideas.[137]

Conclusion

Wesley spoke of his boarding school at Kingswood as a 'Christian model'. He looked upon the staff and pupils as a Christian family to be nurtured in an atmosphere of piety and learning. Pupils were expected to display a desire to save their souls; instruction was designed not only to produce academic learning, but to fit them for life in the world to come. The evidence suggests that despite his desire to protect pupils from harmful influences, Wesley showed little understanding of the effect his strict regime had on some of the adolescent boys. The lack of opportunity for play was not intended to make them miserable. Nevertheless, Wesley seems to have assumed that every child would behave well, and be as serious and studious as he had been.

Although, as chapter three has shown, girls were not prevented from going Kingswood, Wesley only published rules for boys at the school. Not only do these rules resonate with Lockean themes, but they echoed sentiments of the day regarding the fashioning of a gentleman. In the early years at least, most parents were comfortably off, as the fees charged would have discouraged families of lesser means from sending their offspring to the school. Indeed, that Wesley's model was therefore gender and class defined appears to have raised concerns among some of his followers, who had no such aspirations for their sons.

The evidence suggests that Charles Wesley took an interest in Kingswood school and its pupils. Nevertheless, while he seems to have intervened on behalf of Robert Jones, possibly because of his links with the family, it is clear that John Wesley always maintained patriarchal authority over the school. In the case of his own sons, Charles Wesley not only made every effort to understand them but demonstrated a desire to nurture their individuality. At a time when his brother was promoting its merits, Charles was moving his family to London in order to further their musical talents, rather than sending them to Kingswood.

During the eighteenth century, new concepts of the individuality of the child, a growing awareness of the responsibility of parents in decisions regarding children's education, and calls for a 'modernization' of the educational curriculum undoubtedly had an impact on grammar schools as well as Dissenting academies. Any comparison between Kingswood and other educational institutions is, however, fraught with difficulty since their ideologies and pedagogies were adapted to meet the changing needs of parents and children over the period. Indeed, the evidence suggests that there is sufficient convergence of thinking and practice to argue that Wesley's boarding school, rather than offering anything new, in many ways conformed to eighteenth-century norms.

Notes

1. Wesley (1749b) *A Short Account of the School in Kingswood* p. 2
2. Rack (2011) *BCE* vol. 10 p. 539
3. Baker (1984) *BCE* vol. 26 p. 279
4. Ibid. vol. 22 p. 32
5. Wesley (1749b) *A Short Account of the School in Kingswood* p. 2
6. Thompson (1938) *Wesley at Charterhouse* p. 15
7. Bishop, Michael (2002) 'Wesley and his Kingswood Schools' in Lenton, John (ed.) *Vital Piety and Learning: Methodism and Education* Oxford: Wesley Historical Society p. 22
8. Green (1896) *The Works of John & Charles Wesley* p. 61
9. Bishop (1977) 'A Detective Story'
10. Wesley (1781) 'A Plain Account of Kingswood School near Bristol' p. 433
11. Baker (1984) *BCE* vol. 3 p. 341
12. Wesley (1781) 'A Plain Account of Kingswood School near Bristol' p. 434
13. Wesley (1749b) *A Short Account of the School in Kingswood* p. 5–6
14. Telford (1931) *The Letters of the Rev. John Wesley* vol. 5 p. 166
15. Baker (1984) *BCE* vol. 3 p. 347
16. Graham (1990) *Wesley's Early Experiments in Education* p. 9
17. Wesley (1749b) *A Short Account of the School in Kingswood* p. 4
18. Ibid. p. 5

    Wesley was not alone in this view. Lord Chesterfield, whose *Letter to his Son* was published in 1741, advised: 'This is the last letter I shall write to you as a little boy, for tomorrow you will attain your ninth year, so that for the future I shall treat you as a youth. You must now commence a different course of life, a different course of studies. No more levity. Childish toys and playthings must be thrown aside, and your mind directed to serious objects. What was not unbecoming to a child would be disgraceful to a youth'. cited in Pugh (2007) *London's Forgotten Children* p. 64

19 Wesley, Charles (1763) 'Hymns for Children'. cited in Ives (1970) *Kingswood School in Wesley's Day and Since* p. 19
20 cited in Newport, Kenneth G. C. & Campbell, Ted A. (eds.) (2007) *Charles Wesley Life, Literature & Legacy* Peterborough: Epworth Press p. 127
21 Bailey (2012) *Parenting in England c1760–1830* p. 106
22 cited in Best, Gary Martin (1988) *Wesley and Kingswood* Bridgewater: Bigwood and Staple p. 10
23 cited in Wilson (2010) 'Church and Chapel' p. 309
24 Baker (1984) *BCE* vol. 22 p. 23
25 Clarke (1833) *An Account of the Infancy* p. 168
26 Joseph M. Cowley was registered at Kingswood in 1766 – no further details given. Hastling (1898) *The History of Kingswood School* p. 31
27 Bowmer, John C. & Vickers, John A. (eds.) (1995) *The letters of John Pawson* Peterborough: World Methodist Historical Society p. 74–5
28 Bailey (2007) 'Reassessing Parenting' in Berry & Foyster (eds.) *The Family in Early Modern England* p. 219
29 Wesley (1781) 'A Plain Account of Kingswood School near Bristol' p. 382–3
30 The term 'family' was used by both Howell Harris and the Countess Huntingdon to describe their separate communities at Trevecka, and at Doddridge's Academy in Northampton. Schlenther (1997) *Queen of the Methodists* p. 65; Parker (1914) *Dissenting Academies in England* p. 151

 The concept of 'family', consisting of people living under the same roof who were under the authority of the head of the household was well known, and widely understood in the eighteenth century. The 'household-family' was a form of social and familial organisation, the boundaries of which were not those of blood and marriage, but of authority, household management, moral order and obedience. Tadmor (2001) *Family & Friends in Eighteenth-Century England* p. 22–72
31 Mack (2008) *Heart Religion in the British Enlightenment* p. 88
32 Berry, Helen & Foyster, Elizabeth (2007) 'Childless Men in Early Modern England' in Berry & Foyster (eds) *The Family in Early Modern England* p. 183
33 John Wesley noted that 'Mr Grimshaw and Mr Bateman assisted my brother and me at Kingswood': reference is to William Grimshaw and Richard Thomas Bateman [30 July 1749]. Baker (1984) *BCE* vol. 20 p. 293
34 Rack (2011) *BCE* vol. 10 p. 233
35 Norris states that the start-up costs of the school were met by an anonymous private patron; and the running costs, although largely met through fee income, were for many years topped up by subsidies from the Connexion. Thus, he suggests, that while the school may have operated at an annual loss, such losses were modest and 'the basic business model was robust'. Norris (2015) 'Prophets and Profits' p. 284, Annex 9A p. 103; Norris (2014) 'Education, Welfare and Missions' p. 7
36 Rack (2011) *BCE* vol. 10 p. 278, 307
37 Wesley, John (1862) *Minutes of The Methodist Conference 1744–1798 & Large Minutes 1753–1789* London: John Mason p. 61–2
38 Baker (1984) *BCE* vol. 26 p. 35
39 Wesley (1749b) *A Short Account of the School in Kingswood* p. 4
40 Wesley (1781) 'A Plain Account of Kingswood School near Bristol' p. 434
41 Wesley (1749b) *A Short Account of the School in Kingswood* p. 4–5
42 Hastling (1898) *The History of Kingswood School* p. 28
43 Wesley (1749b) *A Short Account of the School in Kingswood* p. 5–6
44 Wesley (1781) 'A Plain Account of Kingswood School near Bristol' p. 435
45 Ibid. p. 435 'Small beer' was a popular drink of the day and mildly alcoholic. Naglee (1987) *From Font to Faith* p. 196
46 Hastling (1898) *The History of Kingswood School* p. 104

Kingswood boarding school: 1746–1780 123

47 Ives (1970) *Kingswood School in Wesley's Day and Since* p. 41
48 Clarke (1833) *An Account of the Infancy* p. 168, 157
49 Locke had likewise contended that 'hard lodging strengthens the parts, whereas being buried every night in feathers melts and dissolves the body, is often the cause of weakness and the forerunner of an early grave'. Locke (1693) *Some Thoughts Concerning Education* p. 23
50 Wesley (1749b) *A Short Account of the School in Kingswood* p. 4–6
51 Ives (1970) *Kingswood School in Wesley's Day and Since* p. 237
52 Sackett, A. Barrett (1972) *James Rouquet and his Part in Early Methodism* Chester: Wesley Historical Society p. 2
53 Baker (1984) *BCE* vol. 20 p. 263
54 Ibid. vol. 20 p. 393
55 Wesley (1778) *The Arminian Magazine* p. 533–4
56 Wesley (1781) 'A Plain Account of Kingswood School near Bristol' p. 433
57 Baker (1984) *BCE* vol. 26 p. 393–4
58 The fact that Charles Wesley had been a friend of Robert's late father, Robert Jones Senior (1706–1742) may have influenced his feelings towards the boy.
59 Wesley, Charles (1749a) Letter to Mrs Mary Jones dated 30 Oct. 1749, John Rylands Library 'Charles Wesley Papers' [copy] reference GB133 DDCW/1/25
60 Wesley, Charles (1749b) Letter to Mrs Mary Jones dated 7 Nov. 1749, John Rylands Library 'Charles Wesley Papers' [copy] reference GB133 DDCW/1/27
61 Wesley, Charles (1750a) Letter to Mrs Mary Jones dated 11 Jan. 1750, 'Charles Wesley Papers' [copy], reference GB133 DDCW/1/28
62 Wesley, Charles (1750b) Letter to Mrs Mary Jones dated 13 Jan. 1750, 'Charles Wesley Papers' [copy] reference GB133 DDCW/1/30

In December 1751, Charles Wesley met with Robert Jones at the home of Samuel Lloyd. In a letter to Mrs Jones dated 29 December 1751 he stated that both he and Lloyd were agreed that 'to send Robin to University would be the ruin of the boy, and at a private school he would not have his full liberty… his temporal ruin I mean, for as to his soul, there is not the slightest chance for that… in the modern way of education'. Wesley, Charles (1751a) Letter to Mrs Mary Jones dated 29 Dec. 1751, 'Charles Wesley Papers' [copy] reference GB133 DDCW/1/42A

Despite the reservations of Mrs Jones, and the Wesleys, Robert was entrusted into the care of John Merton, a Methodist preacher who they did not regard very highly, but whose 'authority over young Robert' meant he 'might be sufficiently tamed for other options to be considered'. Wesley, Charles (1751b) letter to Mrs Mary Jones dated 31 Dec. 1751, 'Charles Wesley Papers' [copy] reference GB133 DDCW/1/42B

63 Baker (1984) *BCE* vol. 20 p. 394
64 Wesley, Charles (1763) Hymn XLVIII in 'Hymns for Children' cited in Best (2006) *Charles Wesley* p. 195
65 Wesley, Charles 'Giver of Nature's Every Gift' cited in Kimbrough, ST Jnr. & Beckerlegge, Oliver, A. (eds.) (1988) *The Unpublished Poetry of Charles Wesley Vol I*. Nashville: Kingswood Books p. 287
66 Charles Wesley's Journal entry dated 22 October 1748 stated: 'Rode over to *our* children in Kingswood and was much comforted by their simplicity and love'. Kimbrough (2008) *The Manuscript Journal of the Reverend Charles Wesley* p. 558
67 Ives (1970) *Kingswood School in Wesley's Day and Since* p. 30–6
68 Charles junior (Charley) who was born in 1757 and Samuel (Sammy), born in 1766, along with their sister Sally (Sarah) who was born in 1759, were educated at home by a combination of their parents and private tutors. Newport (2007) *Charles Wesley Life, Literature and Legacy* p. 124–8

69 Kimbrough (1988) *The Unpublished Poetry of Charles Wesley* p. 291
70 The elder brother being Samuel Jnr.; Charles Wesley's public school experience at Westminster was rather different to John's at Christ Church. Baker (1948) *Charles Wesley As Revealed by His Letters* p. 7
    John Wesley referred to public schools as 'nurseries of all manner of wickedness', and stated that it would be 'better for them [boys] to have been without their knowledge than to have bought it at so dear a price'. Baker (1984) *BCE* vol. 3 p. 341; Baker (1984) *BCE* vol. 9 p. 278
71 John, John James, Martha Maria, Susanna and Selina all died in infancy. Best (2006) *Charles Wesley* p. 313
72 When Sally informed him in a letter that the infant Charles had an undiagnosed sickness, which she hoped was not smallpox, he wrote back expressing 'all my love and concern for our dearest boy'. Baker (1948) *Charles Wesley As Revealed by His Letters* p. 108
73 Newport (2007) *Charles Wesley Life, Literature and Legacy* p. 127
74 Best (2006) *Charles Wesley* p. 313; Newport (2007) *Charles Wesley Life, Literature & Legacy* p. 127
75 Wesley, Charles (1780) *A Collection of Hymns for the Use of the People Called Methodists* Hymn number CCCCLVI verse 6 London: J. Paramore p. 437
76 Baker (1948) *Charles Wesley As Revealed by His Letters* p. 109
77 Ibid. p. 110–11
78 Wesley, Charles (c1776) a fragment of a letter to Samuel Wesley junior, undated but attributed c1776, 'The Wesley Family Papers' ref. GB133 DDWF/27/7
79 Norris, Clive (2013) 'Charles Wesley's Expenditure on Educating his Children', April 2013, Unpublished, Research notes for PhD thesis: Oxford Brookes University
80 Best (2006) *Charles Wesley* p. 314–29
81 Lenton (2009) *John Wesley's Preachers* p. 333
82 When John's engagement to Grace Murray was ended in 1749, principally as a result of Charles's intervention, the relationship between the brothers suffered; this, combined with Charles' outspoken criticism of the growing separation from the Church of England created hostility and resentment, and completed the brothers' partial estrangement. Newport (2007) *Charles Wesley Life, Literature & Legacy* p. 2–7
83 cited in Wearmouth (1945) *Methodism and the Common People of the Eighteenth Century* p. 123
84 Lloyd (2007) *Charles Wesley and the Struggle for Methodist Identity* p. 161
85 Wesley (1781) 'A Plain Account of Kingswood School near Bristol' p. 487; Newport (2007) *Charles Wesley Life, Literature & Legacy* p. 131
86 Lloyd (2007) *Charles Wesley and the Struggle for Methodist Identity* p. 143
87 Best (2006) *Charles Wesley* p. 275–317
88 Mack (2008) *Heart Religion in the British Enlightenment* p. 27
89 Jackson (1862) *Memoirs of the Rev. Charles Wesley* p. 367–8
    Although the Wesleys did not pay the lease on their London home, the property costs were high and the annual expenditure, including heating and lighting etc., was in the region of fifty pounds, some four times that of a typical itinerant preacher and his family. Norris suggests they managed to keep expenditure on such items as clothing and books to around forty pounds a year, as compared to the twenty-four pounds allowance paid for these purposes to the itinerant and his wife. Norris (2013) 'Charles Wesley's Expenditure on Educating his Children'
90 Lloyd (2007) *Charles Wesley and the Struggle for Methodist Identity* p. 30
91 Forsaith, Peter S. (ed.) (2008) *Unexampled Labours* Peterborough: Epworth p. 24
92 Tranter (1996) 'John Wesley and the Education of Children' p. 21

93 Grammar schools catered for the less wealthy gentry, 'middling sort' and well-to-do tradesmen. Speck, W. A. (1977) *Stability and Strife* London: Edward Arnold p. 82
94 Tompson (1971) *Classics or Charity?* p. 28–33
95 The 'great' public schools of Eton, Harrow, Westminster and Winchester catered for those who could afford them, which included wealthy farmers, lawyers and merchants as well as the aristocracy and gentry. Ibid. p. 29
96 Wesley (1781) 'A Plain Account of Kingswood School near Bristol' p. 383–4
97 Wesley (1749b) *A Short Account of the School in Kingswood* p. 2–4
    Thompson suggests that inclusion in the Kingswood syllabus of subjects which had long been on offer in Dissenting academies, such as algebra, geometry, the natural sciences and what were referred to as 'philosophical experiments', owed much to Wesley's time at Charterhouse under the influence of Andrew Tooke, who was not only a classical scholar but a mathematician and scientist. Thompson (1938) *Wesley at Charterhouse* p. 6
98 Sackett (1972) *James Rouquet and his part in Early Methodism* p. 3
    James Rouquet was educated at Merchant Taylors' School in London (where he was converted under George Whitefield) and at St John's College, Oxford; he went on to be an Evangelical clergyman and close friend of John Wesley. Lenton (2009) *John Wesley's Preachers* p. 319
99 Barclay (1743) *Treatise on Education* p. 39–40
100 Clarke, John (1720) *An Essay Upon the Education of Youth in Grammar-schools* London: John Wyat p. 9
101 That is not to suggest that changes to the grammar school curriculum went unopposed. George Huntingford of Winchester College commented: 'I am convinced that an early habit of applying grammar-rules leads to accuracy and precision in reasoning at a more advanced age. The fashion of the day is superficial and unnatural prematurity; it is the bane of real knowledge and substantial ability'. cited in Mather (1992) *High Church Prophet* p. 305
102 Parker (1914) *Dissenting Academies in England* p. 24, 97, 102–32
103 Priestley, Joseph (1765) *An Essay on a Course of Liberal Education*, London: C. Henderson, T. Becket, De Hondt, J. Johnson and Davenport p. 6–7
    Warrington Academy (1757–1786) is described by Cohen as the most famous and successful Dissenting institute of education. Joseph Priestly was appointed as a tutor there in 1761. Cohen (2009) 'Familiar Conversation' p. 109
104 cited in Bygrave (2009) *Uses of Education* p. 142–3
105 Wykes, David L. (2008) 'Joseph Priestley, Minister, and Teacher' in Rivers, Isabel & Wykes, David L. (eds.), *Joseph Priestley, Scientist, Philosopher and Theologian* Oxford: Oxford University Press p. 30–1
106 Rack (2002) *Reasonable Enthusiast* p. 357
107 Although the Register of boys educated at Kingswood School between 1768 and 1793 lists few professions, among those shown is an Attorney (William Clulow 1768–1769); a Magistrate (James Wood 1789); a Doctor (Thomas Warwick 1780); a surgeon (Richard Summers 1791–1793), as well as several Wesleyan Ministers. Hastling (1898) *The History of Kingswood School* p. 1–182
108 Wesley (1781) 'A Plain Account of Kingswood School near Bristol' p. 487
109 Ibid. p. 487–8
110 Wesley, John (1768a) *A Short Account of the School in Kingswood Near Bristol*, Bristol: William Pine p. 12
111 Wesley (1781) 'A Plain Account of Kingswood School near Bristol' p. 492
112 Wesley (1768a) *A Short Account of the School in Kingswood* p. 10–2
113 Kingswood School archive: Account book dated 1764–1770
114 cited in Whitehouse, Tessa (ed.) (2011) *Dissenting Education and the Legacy of John Jennings, c.1720–c.1729* Dr Williams' Centre for Dissenting Studies p. 1
115 cited in Ibid. p. 5

116 cited in Porter (2000) *Enlightenment* p. 347
117 Gibson, William (2007) *Religion and the Enlightenment 1600–1800* Oxford: Peter Lang p. 250, 355
118 Deacon (1980) *Philip Doddridge of Northampton 1702–1751* p. 24, 77, 93–6
119 Humphreys (1803) *The Correspondence and Diary of Philip Doddridge* p. 484
120 Deacon (1980) *Philip Doddridge of Northampton 1702–1751* p. 97–9
121 Wykes (2008) 'Joseph Priestley, Minister, and Teacher' p. 25–7
122 Cohen (2009) 'Familiar Conversation' p. 109
123 Wykes (2008) 'Joseph Priestley, Minister, and Teacher' p. 93
124 cited in Humphreys (1830) *The Correspondence and Diary of Philip Doddridge* p. 285–6
125 Deacon (1980) *Philip Doddridge of Northampton 1702–1751* p. 24, 191, 94
126 Doddridge, Philip (1790) *Sermons on the Religious Education of Children* London: George Jerry Osborne Jun'r p. 56
127 Laqueur, Thomas Walter (1976) *Religion and Respectability* London: Yale University Press p. 18
128 Deacon (1980) *Philip Doddridge of Northampton 1702–1751* p. 94–5
129 Kingswood School archive: Account book dated 1764–1770
130 Hastling (1898) *The History of Kingswood School* p. 52–3
131 Benson, Joseph (1766) Letter from Kingswood School to unnamed correspondent, dated 22 Dec. 1766, John Rylands Library 'Joseph Benson Papers' ref. GB 133PLP 7/6/1
132 Kingswood School archive: Account book dated 1764–1770
133 Wesley, John (1769) 'Letter to Joseph Benson' (undated) but attributed 1769: Kingswood School Archive
134 Deacon (1980) *Philip Doddridge of Northampton 1702–1751* p. 94, 144, 193
135 Ibid. p. 191–4, 94–5
136 Bygrave (2009) *Uses of Education* p. 26
137 Hilton (2009) *Educating the Child in Enlightenment Britain* p. 5

6 Growing tension between education and Evangelism: 1760–1791

This chapter argues that in the closing decades of Wesley's life there was a growing tension between education and Evangelism which saw him moving away from the education of children in favour of the Evangelism of their parents. Amid a desire to 'form' the child, and a drive to 'reform' their parents, Wesley increasingly looked to his preachers to promote family worship and religious education in the home. Many of Wesley's preachers were from humble backgrounds, with little education. This chapter examines the steps Wesley took to encourage their self-improvement through reading and study. It suggests that it is something of a contradiction that while he stressed the importance of family in raising pious and virtuous children, Wesley expected his preachers to leave their wives and children to travel where he sent them. That is not to suggest that he was insensitive to their children's upbringing and education. As far as Wesley was concerned, Kingswood School provided the perfect 'family' environment that the preachers' sons were missing.

The 1760s marked a crucial period for the emerging Methodist movement. Amid a growing call for more, better educated and trained preachers, Lady Huntingdon resolved to open a 'nursery for preachers'. In 1764 she began to formulate plans for a theological College in Trevecka, South Wales. Shortly after Trevecka opened its doors to students, the expulsion of six students from St Edmund Hall prompted the implementation of Wesley's academical course at Kingswood School. When tension between the Arminian and Calvinist factions of the Methodist movement resurfaced in 1770 Wesley's preachers, no longer welcome at Trevecka, were once again invited to attend Kingswood to advance their learning. As a consequence, there was increasing pressure on the school. By the time of Wesley's death in 1791 the boarding school, having opened for fee-paying pupils who were primarily offspring of Wesley's wealthy followers, increasing became a place not only where his preachers might advance their learning, but where their sons, who were in the main from a very different demographic to the early boarders, might be educated.

Importance of family

Throughout the eighteenth century, the family was regarded as the seat of virtue and piety. *The Whole Duty of Man* advised parents that they should improve their children's minds 'with sound principles of religion and good morality, and bring them up to learning'.[1] Mandeville argued that 'It is precept, and the example of parents and those they eat, drink and converse with that have an influence upon the minds of children'.[2] Describing Christian families as 'nurseries of piety', Doddridge reminded parents of the importance of 'the good influence which a proper discharge of family duty [had] by impressing your children and servants with a sense of religion'.[3] Stating that children were 'the soft clay, easily fashioned into what form you please...', Doddridge concluded that 'if they are not pressed into the service of religion, they will be employed as dangerous artillery against it'.[4]

Wesley's own upbringing at Epworth had convinced him that Christian education had to begin in the home. Children were to be instructed in Christian values in order that they might seek salvation; parents were the first instructors, whose duty it was to instruct children early, plainly, frequently and patiently. Wesley's sermon *On Family Religion*, delivered on 25 May 1783, asserted that the wickedness of children was generally due to the fault or neglect of their parents.[5] Not all parents were willing, or able, to instruct their offspring. Whitefield stated in 1738: 'The only reason why so many neglect to read the words of scripture diligently to their children is because the words of scripture are not in their hearts, for if they were, out of the abundance of their heart their mouth would speak'.[6]

In the spring of 1741, Lady Huntingdon wrote to John Wesley concerning a school she had supported at Markfield, Leicestershire, advising him that she had 'dismissed all its masters'. She argued, 'a school will never answer the end of bringing forth any of the Gospel fruits of holiness till the parents are first made Christians. The parents must lay up for the children, not the children for the parents'.[7] Indeed, Wesley became increasingly aware that if family religion was to be strengthened, there was a need to first evangelise parents. At the Methodist Conference in 1766 he declared 'Family religion is shamefully wanting, and almost in every branch... we must instruct them *from house to house*. Till this is done, and that in good earnest, the Methodists will be little better than other people'.[8]

Wesley was not alone in asserting that family worship played an important part in religious instruction. Doddridge contended that it was 'a most proper way of teaching children religion'; he added 'it is the greatest cruelty to your children to neglect giving them those advantages which no other attention in education, exclusive of these can afford'.[9] Wesley told his preachers to strongly recommend family prayer both morning and evening. They were to encourage parents to work with children on memorising parts of his *Instructions for Children*, and by so doing they could also gain greater religious understanding themselves. Preachers were to encourage the head of the family to call everyone together every Sunday evening so that the children could repeat what they had learnt.[10]

As the Methodist movement expanded, there was a growing need for itinerant preachers prepared to leave their families to travel wherever Wesley directed. He was especially concerned that itinerant preachers identified with the communities they served rather than their own families, and that they were single-minded about their vocation as Evangelists.[11] It would seem something of a contradiction that while Wesley stressed the importance of the family in raising pious and virtuous children, he nevertheless expected his preachers to be indifferent to their own families, to abandon their wives and children to travel wherever he sent them.

Wesley believed that preachers could only sustain their spiritual energy by constant travel.[12] Although he claimed that 'Persons may be as holy in a married, as it is possible to be in a single state', he contended that single people 'enjoy a blessed liberty from the trouble in the flesh... from a thousand nameless domestic trials... especially... disobedient children'. He told single people: 'You have leisure to improve yourself in every kind, to wait upon God in public and private, and to do good to your neighbour'.[13] Wesley may have preferred itinerants who had no family, but the need for preachers meant that he often settled for older men, bringing with them a wife and family. For the majority of Wesley's preachers the travelling expected of them made family life difficult enough; and this was compounded by the lack of financial provision for wives and widows.[14] At the Conference in Bristol in 1774 the question was asked 'What can be done, in order to pay for the clothes of the preachers' children?'. It appears that some financial provision was available since the answer was recorded: 'If their parents can pay for them, in whole or in part, they should, if they cannot, all is well'.[15]

Wesley recognised that, with the father absent, the families of his itinerant preachers were affected by more than just financial difficulties:

> Boys, when they grow too big to be under their mother's direction, having no father to govern and instruct them, are exposed to a thousand temptations. To remedy this, we have a School on purpose for them, wherein they have all the instruction they are capable of, together with all things necessary for the body... The parent eased of his weight, can the more cheerfully go on in his labour.[16]

In addition, the Connexion agreed to pay towards an education for some preachers' daughters, albeit that funding provided for them was less than that for boys not able to attend Kingswood.[17] Although precise details are unclear, Curnock noted under Wesley's *Journal* for December 1778 that 'Mr Edward's widow at Lambeth maintained and educated more than 12 preacher's daughters'.[18] It is known that by 1780, girls aged between eight and eleven were receiving money towards their education.[19] Lenton suggests that the education some preachers' daughters received allowed them to work in small schools, or as governesses.[20] Nevertheless, this decision by the Connexion, Mack argues, may have been based less on a desire to support the education of girls than a commitment to offer financial support to itinerant preachers and their families.[21]

For Wesley, Kingswood School provided the perfect 'family' environment that his preachers' sons were missing. Although some may have joined the school earlier, the first record of preachers' sons going to Kingswood is in the 1773 *Minutes*.[22] With the Conference taking a collection for the school, it was possible to admit an increasing number. Wesley declared in 1779:

> It is well known that the children want nothing, that they scarce know what sickness means; that they are well instructed in whatever they are capable of learning; that they are carefully, and tenderly governed, and that constant care is taken that the behaviour of all belonging to the house is such as becometh the Gospel of Christ.[23]

That the move to accept an increasing number of preachers' sons did not happen more quickly appears to be based on financial constraints. Clarke recorded that in 1782 the school 'consisted of the sons of itinerant preachers and parlour boarders; the parlour borders taken in because the public collections were not sufficient to support the institution'.[24]

Wesley's preachers' children tended to have more education than the majority of the population since their parents laid more stress on it; but their acceptance into the school alongside the sons of wealthier families was not without difficulty.[25] Clarke was enrolled as an 'academical' student, and attended Kingswood for a brief time in 1782, when there were both fee-paying parlour boarders and preachers' sons at the school. His account of what he witnessed during his short stay presented an image far removed from the family model of nurture that Wesley intended:

> ... it was the worst school I have ever seen, and though the teachers were men of adequate learning; yet as the school was perfectly *disorganised* and in several respects each did what was right in his own eyes, and there was no efficient plan pursued, they mocked at religion, and trampled under foot all the laws. The little children of the preachers suffered great indignities; and it is to be feared, their treatment there gave many of them a rooted enmity against piety and religion of life. The parlour boarders had every kind of respect paid to them and the others were shamefully neglected. Had this most gross mismanagement been known to the Methodist preachers, they would have suffered their sons to die in ignorance, rather than have sent them to a place where there was scarcely any care taken either of their bodies or souls.[26]

Wesley recognised that there were problems at the school around this time. Perhaps unsurprisingly, his own analysis was that they had arisen because his rules were not being observed. At the Methodist Conference in Bristol on 29 July 1783 he declared:

> But at present the school does not in anywise answer the design of its institution, either with regard to religion or learning. The children are not

religious; they have not the power, and hardly the form, of religion. Neither do they improve in learning better than at other schools; no, nor yet so well. Insomuch that some of our friends have been obliged to remove their children to other schools. And no wonder they improve so little either in religion or learning, for the rules of the school are not observed at all. All in the house ought to rise; take their three meals, and go to bed at a fixed hour. But they do not. The children ought never to be alone; but always in the presence of a master. This is totally neglected; in consequence of which they run up and down the road, and mix, yea, fight, with the colliers' children.

'How may these events be remedied, and the school reduced to its original plan?' Wesley asked. 'It must be mended or ended; for no school, is better than the present school'.[27]

The problems at the school were apparently remedied by the appointment of Thomas McGeary, an energetic young man of twenty two, as headmaster in 1783. Kingswood prospered under his guidance.[28] Wesley was able to declare in March 1784: 'I talked at large with our masters at Kingswood School who are now just such as I wished for. At length the rules of the House are punctually observed, and the children are all in good order'.[29] Ives contends that this success laid not in the application of the rules themselves, but in the choice by Wesley of a headmaster who was not only pious, but who had a real ability as a schoolmaster. McGeary remained head until after Wesley's death in 1791.[30] Whatever his abilities, Wesley was adamant that success lay in the observance of his rules, and his *Journal* of July 1786 stated:

I walked over to Kingswood, now one of the pleasantest spots in England. I found all things just according to my desire, the rules being well observed, and the whole burden of the children showing that they were now managed with the wisdom that cometh from above.[31]

Whether on McGeary's suggestion, or as a result of circumstance, in the closing decade of Wesley's life, the Conference resolved that the number of preachers' sons at the school be raised to thirty and the number of boarders reduced to ten.[32] By 1787, Hastling claimed, preachers' sons 'were, by force of numbers and the justice of their silent claims, usurping the lay boarders'.[33] The last entry concerning Kingswood School of any significance was made by Wesley in his *Journal* on Friday 11 September 1789 when he wrote: 'I went over to Kingswood; Sweet recess! where everything is now just as I wish'.[34]

The evidence suggests that the decision to open up Wesley's boarding school to sons of his itinerant preachers had unwelcome consequences. In a letter from Methodist itinerant preacher John Pawson to Joseph Benson dated 22 October 1802, Pawson described as 'too easy to give terrible examples in proof...' of the implications of raising the aspirations of preachers' sons above their class. Pawson, who had spent five years stationed in Bristol noted: 'In my opinion the time allowed for the boys at Kingswood is not sufficient to render it necessary for us to procure a Classical Master... and if the time was longer, perhaps not more than one in ten of the boys would make much of that sort of learning'.[35] Of the son of Thomas Brisco, an itinerant from 1751–1798, Pawson suggested: 'Never did I hear a letter from a child express such supreme contempt of his parents as that lad did in a letter to Mr Clulow'.[36] Pawson's damning view of Kingswood: 'I should much rather a child of mine was an honest shoemaker than that he should be exalted so far above his parents with contempt and despise the whole Methodist Connection'.[37]

Drive to train preachers

Many of the preachers within the Methodist Connexion, although men of piety came from humble backgrounds, and lacked the educational advantages of Anglican clergy.[38] They filled a large number of jobs before becoming preachers, and often had similar backgrounds to those who made up a majority of their congregations.[39] As a result, Wesley's travelling preachers were mocked in person, and in print, by the privileged classes who were more accustomed to clergymen educated at Oxford or Cambridge.[40]

Although Wesley encouraged his preachers' self-improvement through reading and study, not all Evangelicals supported anything broader than an education beyond learning the 'doctrines of the Gospel'. There was a belief that intellectual ability was irrelevant to the development of a personal commitment of faith; some Evangelicals shunned intellectual pursuits, believing that they were called to make better use of their short and accountable time on earth. Richard Cecil stated:

> However desirable and useful in various respects learning may be, it is not essential to the Christian... I have met with poor and illiterate men, who having the grace of God in their hearts, could state the doctrines of the Gospel with admirable distinction and accuracy.[41]

Wesley did not expect his preachers to have a university education, but stated at the Conference in 1746 that preachers should consider themselves 'as young students at the University, for whom therefore a method of study is expedient in the highest degree'.[42] That Wesley continued to regard his preachers in the same way as he had done his students at Oxford is confirmed by an entry in his *Journal* on 13 January 1777: 'I took the opportunity of spending an hour every morning with the preachers, as I did with my pupils at Oxford, And we endeavoured not only to increase each other's knowledge but to provoke one another to love and to good works'.[43]

Methodism was, during Wesley's lifetime, autocratic and managed by him through the annual Methodist Conference. Each year, from the first Conference in 1744, Wesley met with his lay preachers to discuss their practice and doctrine, to promote training and to receive reports on the preachers' success, or otherwise.[44] The question of a 'Seminary' for the preachers was raised at the Conference in 1744. When asked 'Can we have a Seminary for labourers?' Wesley answered 'If God spare us to another Conference'; then in 1745 the question was raised again, and the reply, 'Not till God gives a proper tutor'.[45] The idea of putting ministers through a dedicated course of training was unique,[46] but Wesley increasingly saw Kingswood as a place where preachers could be trained, writing in his *Journal* of February 1749: 'My design was to have as many as possible of our preachers here during Lent as could possibly be spared and to read lectures to them every day as I did to my pupils at Oxford, I had 17 in all divided in 2 classes...'.[47] With an estimated fifty preachers in total in 1748, Lenton suggests that the number attending Kingswood represented a high proportion of the preachers at that time.[48] Wesley continued to recommend Kingswood as a centre where his preachers might be accommodated in order to improve their knowledge. Unfortunately, as Peter Jaco discovered in 1753, there were not always places available for them to study at the school.[49]

Wesley corresponded with his preachers at length, and urged them to improve their education by constant study. He expected them to write an account of their own spiritual experience.[50] They learned scripture and doctrine by reading the Bible, Wesley's printed sermons and his *Notes on the New Testament*; they were instructed in Christian tradition through reading his *Christian Library*.[51] He cautioned: 'If we read nothing but the Bible, we should hear nothing but the Bible; and then what becomes of preaching?'.[52] Wesley expected his preachers to distribute his publications wherever they went. He complained in 1763 that 'The Societies are not half supplied with books, not even with Kempis, *Instructions for Children* and *Primitive Physic*, which ought to be in every house'.[53]

Wesley advised his preachers to read 'the most useful books, regularly and constantly'; to rise at 4am and to study for five hours a day. In order to assist their study, he recommended books contained within the curriculum of Kingswood School.[54] He told his preachers that he would give them: 'as fast as you will read them, books to the value of five pounds'. When at the 1766 Conference in Leeds he was asked 'Why are we not more knowing?' Wesley's reply was characteristically robust: 'Because we are idle... which of you spends as many hours a day in God's work, as you did formerly in man's work?... We talk, or read history, or what comes to hand. We must, absolutely must, cure this evil, or give up the whole work'.[55] Indeed, Brantley suggests that Methodists, advised by Wesley not to waste time in idleness, committed time to reading and the difference in degree of knowledge between the poor Methodists and the poor in general was, as a result, 'very remarkable'.[56]

Although Wesley reaffirmed Kingswood as 'a place of reserve for preachers' at the Conference in 1770, Joseph Benson expressed concern over the standard of education and training available for Methodist preachers. In order to remedy this, he formulated a plan which included not only the testing of all preachers, but the recommendation that a greater number of the less well educated should receive additional training at Kingswood.[57] Benson first submitted his proposals to John Fletcher, who forwarded them to Wesley. In a letter from Fletcher to Wesley, dated 1 August 1775, Fletcher suggested that:

> Kingswood School was entirely appropriate to the reception and improvement of the candidates for Methodist orders; to the education of the children of the preachers; and to the keeping of the worn-out Methodist preachers, whose employment shall be to preserve the spirit of faith and primitive Christianity in the place, by which means alone the curse of a little unsanctified learning may be kept out.[58]

Benson had the opportunity to present his concerns at the Conference in 1775. It would seem that Wesley noted the advice of Fletcher and Benson, and increasingly regarding Kingswood as a place where preachers could receive training prior to starting their itinerancy.[59] Although not poorly educated, Wesley offered Adam Clarke a place at Kingswood, that he might improve his knowledge of the Classics and at the same time have the opportunity to preach in the various local societies.[60] Clarke, who was later to become three times President of the Wesleyan Conference, stayed at Kingswood for a short period when he was twenty two, and recalled:

> ... the impressions made upon my mind by the bad usage I received there, have never been erased; a sight of the place has ever filled me with distressing sensations, and the bare recollection of the *same* never fails to bring with it associations both unpleasant and painful. Those who were instruments of my tribulation are gone to another tribunal and against them I never made any complaint.[61]

Clarke, who had been led to consider that Kingswood offered students an education akin to a university but much better conducted, travelled from Ireland and on his way stayed at the home of Joseph Brettell in Birmingham. Brettell's statement 'I hope you may not be disappointed: I question whether you will meet there with anything you expect', surprised Clarke, who referred him to Wesley's *Arminian Magazine*, 'where such an account was given of this seminary, as quite justified all his expectations'. Leaving Birmingham early on 24 August 1782, Clarke reached Bristol that evening. The next morning he walked to Kingswood, arriving at seven in the morning, when the preaching in the chapel was about to take place. When the preaching ended he delivered Wesley's letter of introduction to Thomas Simpson the headmaster. Simpson, stating that Wesley was in Cornwall and unlikely to be back for a fortnight, said he had heard nothing of Clarke's coming, and as there was no room for him at the school, he should go back to Bristol and await Wesley's return. Simpson added that as the school was 'only for preachers' children, or for such preachers as cannot read their Bible' and, as Clarke had already 'been at a classical school, and [had] read both Greek and Latin authors', he should, rather than stay at Kingswood, 'go out into the work at large'.[62]

Clarke was eventually offered a spare room at the end of the chapel in the colliers' school, a room he referred to as his 'prison-house', where he declared he felt 'a stranger in a strange land, and alas! among strange people: utterly friendless and penniless'. The room contained 'scanty bedclothes' on a bed 'not worth ten shillings'; and Clarke stated, 'it is utterly impossible for me to describe the feelings, may I justly say the agony of my mind… there was no book, not even a Bible in the place'.[63] These inadequacies presumably arose because children had not been boarded in the Old House since girls were enrolled at Kingswood in its early years.[64] He recorded being brought '*bread and milk* for breakfast – for dinner – and for supper, for generally I had nothing else, and not enough of that'; and being denied clean bedsheets, a change of clothes, or a fire he stated that 'for more than three weeks no soul performed any kind act for me… '. Although Clarke's account suggests that he was, in the early days of his brief stay at Kingswood, denied access to the New House, he was allowed to work in the garden. He also attended preaching and public band meetings at the chapel in the Old House, which he declared were 'often sources of spiritual refreshment to me'. After speaking at a band meeting, Clarke was invited to preach at a local meeting, where he was well received.[65]

By early September, Wesley had returned to Bristol. Clarke met him for the first time on 6 September in 'Mr Wesley's study, off the great lobby of the rooms over the chapel in Broadmead'. After a 'short conversation', Clarke was advised by Wesley to hold himself in readiness to go to the Bradford circuit in Wiltshire. Although he made no mention of Wesley visiting the school, following their meeting, Clarke was assigned a bed in the New House. He joined 'about forty' boys in the large room where each had 'a separate cot, with a flock bed'. He was also permitted to dine 'with the family'. Less than three weeks later, Clarke received instructions from Wesley to fill a preaching vacancy in Trowbridge, Wiltshire. Clarke declared on leaving the school on 26 September 1782, 'I left Kingswood without a sigh or a groan. It had been to me a place of unworthy treatment, not to say torment'.[66]

It is impossible to say how representative Clarke's three week stay in the New House was; although when Simpson left Kingswood in 1783, he set up a classical school at Keynesham 'which he managed for many years with considerable credit'. Following the appointment of Thomas McGeary, Clarke was able to concluded a few months after his visit that:

> The school has certainly been 'mended' since; and is now stated at be in a progressive state of greater improvement than ever. May it ever answer in every respect, the great end which its most excellent founder proposed when he laid its first stone, and drew up its rules.[67]

The evidence suggests that Wesley's intention that Kingswood might become not only a seminary for training preachers, but a place where their sons would be inspired to follow them into preaching was not fulfilled. While the register of pupils at the school is incomplete, details for the 1770s and 1780s suggest that only a small number of them went on to become Methodist preachers, although by the 1790s this number had begun to increase.[68]

Trevecka College

Writing in 1764 that she wished to have a 'nursery for preachers', Lady Huntingdon began to formulate plans for a theological College in the Calvinist stronghold of Trevecka, South Wales.[69] She had lengthy conversations with George Whitefield, and appointed him as one of her chaplains.[70] Although he preached at Trevecka's opening ceremony, Whitefield had within a year of its opening left for America, where he died on 30 September 1770. Charles Wesley visited the College in the weeks that followed the opening ceremony, and was able to maintain a close friendship with Lady Huntingdon. John Wesley, on the other hand, only visited Trevecka on one occasion, to preach at the first anniversary celebrations in 1769.[71]

Although some Methodist leaders were willing to mix with Calvinist Dissenters, John Wesley rarely preached inside a Dissenters' meeting house.[72] He declared 'I am afraid Lady Huntingdon's preachers will do little good wherever they go. They are wholly swallowed up in that detestable doctrine of predestination and can talk of nothing else'.[73] Indeed, although Ives suggests Lady Huntingdon is likely, during her frequent visits to Bristol, to have taken an interest in Kingswood School in its early years,[74] Wesley appears to have become increasingly suspicious of her work at Trevecka. Welch suggests that with a temperament similar to hers, he was always uneasy in her company and even unwilling to meet her.[75] Nevertheless, Trevecka held out the prospect of a united venture that would supply trained ministers for the expanding Methodist movement.[76]

Trevecka was Lady Huntingdon's most significant undertaking; she sustained the entire cost of the College and rarely accepted donations.[77] Trevecka was intended as a training centre for the education of young men of piety who, when prepared, would uniquely be at liberty to enter into the ministry either by seeking ordination in the Church of England or among the Dissenters.[78] Although the remoteness of the site may have been seen by the Countess as a means of shielding students from outside temptations, John Berridge, vicar of Everton, Bedfordshire, wrote to her on 26 December 1767 warning: 'Welsh mountains afford a brisk air for a student; and the rules are excellent, but I doubt the success of the project and fear it will occasion you more trouble than all your other undertakings besides'.[79] Nevertheless, work began on the College buildings in December 1767 and Trevecka opened eight months later.[80] In an attempt to give Trevecka the aura of a university, not only did Lady Huntingdon use the title 'College', but supplied caps and gowns for her students.[81] She was especially maternal towards her students who received their room, board and clothes from her benevolence.[82] Indeed, Welch argues that she lavished care and affection on her students in a way that Wesley never had the time or the inclination to do.[83]

Although she read widely in later life, Lady Huntingdon's own education had been very limited.[84] Prior to the College opening, she sought, not the advice of Wesley, but of John Fletcher, in selecting appropriate books for the students to study. Fletcher, who stated that he had studied and taught abroad and had not used 'English' books with his pupils, suggested in a letter dated 3 January 1768 that she first draw up a plan of studies. Advising the Countess that 'grammar, logic, rhetoric, ecclesiastical history, a little natural philosophy, geography, with a great deal of practical divinity, will be sufficient for those who do not care to dive into languages', Fletcher then went on to suggest several titles, among them Wesley's *Christian Library*. He further commended Wesley by adding: 'With regard to those who propose to learn Latin and Greek, the master your Ladyship will appoint may choose to follow his particular method. Mr Wesley's books, printed for the use of Christian youths, seem to me short and proper'.[85] Most of the students came from humble backgrounds, which necessitated that they receive both a rudimentary general education as well as extensive theological training.[86] The teaching of English was also important because many of the students only spoke Welsh.[87]

Despite the Countess's efforts, only seventeen students were enrolled at the College in its first nine months, and they were of very mixed abilities.[88] They were not subject to the 'constant supervision' Wesley insisted upon at Kingswood, but Lady Huntingdon believed that any spare time which they might have was to be spent in 'wholesome bodily exercise', and 'profitable conversation'. The students rose at five and after private and communal prayer, breakfasted, studied between eight and twelve and again between two and five. They had evening private prayers, supper and family prayer and retired to bed at ten o'clock.[89]

Students at Trevecka travelled as preachers in Lady Huntingdon's Connection, being sent out as temporary assistants to both Church of England and Dissenting ministers as the need arose.[90] This made a thorough education almost impossible and meant that there was no formal understanding of how long the course of study was, or what constituted the standard curriculum.[91] As early as October 1768 students were making preaching excursions into the neighbourhood, and before long a pattern of weekend preaching tours emerged with selected students leaving on a Friday or Saturday and returning on the Monday. Over time, although on average there might be eight to twelve students resident at Trevecka, there were between a dozen to fifteen itinerant preachers, many spending years on end away from the College, who were nevertheless treated as students of Trevecka.[92] Some students disliked the interruption to their studies and pleaded to be allowed to return to College.[93]

Lady Huntingdon invited John Fletcher to take up the post of superintendent at Trevecka. Writing to her on 24 November 1767, he stated 'with regard to the superintendency of the college... I am ready to throw in my mite into the treasury that your Ladyship may find in other persons'.[94] Benson's *Memoirs* record that Fletcher 'took the post of superintendence of this Seminary without fee or reward'.[95] Although acceptance of the Presidency meant that Fletcher took on the oversight of Trevecka, he did not relinquish his responsibilities in his parish of Madeley, Shropshire. Instead, he travelled to Trevecka several times a year to carry out his duties as Visitor.[96] Wesley followed the plan for the College from a distance; and wrote to his brother Charles on 14 May 1768 stating; 'Did you ever see anything more queer than their plan of institution? Pray who penned it, man or woman? I am afraid the Visitor too will fail'.[97] His early impression of the school is evident from a letter to Joseph Benson dated 2 January 1769, in which he declared 'I will have another kind of school than that at Trevecka or none at all…'.[98]

In April 1769, Fletcher visited Trevecka and wrote a report for Lady Huntingdon of his observations of staff and students there. Although, Streiff suggests, he would have preferred to be found among the students rather than the leaders,[99] Fletcher reported that he 'found things here upon a tolerable footing', and suggested that some students had 'made some progress in general both as to their preaching and studies'. Fletcher's report went on to identify seventeen students by name; James Glazebrook, a twenty three year old miner from Madeley, who had been recommended for Trevecka by Fletcher, was described by him as 'one of the most sensible of them'.[100] Fletcher suggested that Masters needed to be 'a grave, steady, experienced, zealous person who hath parts, activity and devotedness to God and his cause'. Of one of the Masters, John Williams, Fletcher reported:

> [He] did well for the first months, but now he do but very middling, because not taking care to improve himself or not having time for it, he is likely to be outstrip'd soon by the most forward [students]. I spoke very close to him this evening and told him I must absolutely beg of your Ladyship to procure another master… [he] promises… he will bestir himself more for the public good.[101]

It was on Fletcher's advice that Joseph Benson was selected by Lady Huntingdon as Master of the College; and in September 1769 the Countess visited Kingswood with Wesley when, presumably under his recommendation, Benson was invited to take up the post at Trevecka.[102] Benson did not take up this offer immediately. In fact by November 1769 Wesley was complaining to his friend Mary Bishop of Lady Huntingdon's 'narrowness of spirit'.[103] From his letter to Benson dated 26 December 1769, it seems that he had become increasingly unhappy with Lady Huntingdon's attitude towards her College, contending that:

> Trevecka is much more to Lady Huntingdon than Kingswood to me. It mixes with everything. It is *my* college, *my* masters, *my* students I do not speak so of this school. It is not mine, but the Lord's. I look for no more honour than money from it… I am glad you defer your journey.[104]

Nevertheless, Benson paid a short visit to Trevecka in January 1770, and moved from Kingswood to the College in the spring of 1770.[105]

Initially at least the work at Trevecka seemed to be sound since both Fletcher and Benson were academically able men.[106] Although Fletcher's letter to Walter Sellon on 7 October 1769 suggested that 'the Calvinists are three to one', in an effort to promote harmony, men of both Calvinist and Arminian inclination served on the staff at Trevecka.[107] In the early days, only those doctrines that were otherwise held in common formed the chief body of instruction.[108] Benson's *Memoirs* recorded that under the care of these two men, 'the young men were serious and made considerable progress in learning, and many of them seemed to have talents for the ministry'.[109]

The activities of the Wesley brothers, George Whitefield and Lady Huntingdon were regarded by the majority of clergy as eccentric, and by many with suspicion. Although in areas remote from the universities, such as Wales, there were a high proportion of non-graduate clergy,[110] Lady Huntingdon's hopes that her students would become candidates for ordination in the Church were dashed as suspicion of Trevecka caused the religious establishment to close ranks against the 'irregularity' of her innovations.[111] That Lady Huntingdon was able to secure Anglican ordination for twenty of her Trevecka students, Brown-Lawson argues, was due in part to her position as a peeress of the realm.[112] Anglican Evangelical John Berridge told her 'The bishops look on your students as the worst kind of Dissenters; [they] manifest this by refusing that ordination to your preachers which would be readily granted to other teachers among the Dissenters'.[113]

Although Dissenting ministers lacked national institutions to educate, admit or monitor them, acceptance into Dissenting ministry was not easy for students from Trevecka to obtain either.[114] Harding comments that Dissenting ministers could be just as suspicious as Anglican bishops of the Evangelical theology and low academic standards they associated with Trevecka.[115] Lady Huntingdon's Connection was less well organised than Wesley's; there was no annual conference, and there are no surviving definitive records of its membership or preachers.[116] In the absence of a complete list of students and details about their origin or social background, Welch argues that it is difficult to draw any conclusions about students trained at Trevecka.[117] Over the College's twenty four-year history more than two hundred students were enrolled and most found employment in the Countess's Connection or served among Dissenters.[118] Lady Huntingdon's Connection eventually chose to separate from the Church of England and her leading preachers and most prominent chapels were listed among the Dissenters.[119]

'Minutes Controversy' of 1770

Although Lady Huntingdon had intended Trevecka as a training centre for the entire Methodist movement, the 'Minutes Controversy', which erupted over the publication of the *Minutes* of the 1770 Wesleyan Conference, drove a wedge between the Calvinist and Arminian sections of the movement. The Wesleys saw the *Minutes* as an attempt to recapture the Anglican synthesis of faith and works. The Calvinist Methodists read the Wesleyan *Minutes* as a repudiation of justification by faith alone. To Lady Huntingdon, the *Minutes* implied a move towards Arminian thinking and the disagreement that had divided Whitefield and Wesley over predestination at Kingswood over twenty years earlier was now reignited between Wesley and the Countess at Trevecka.[120] Had none of the students been permitted to preach during the course of their education, MacDonald argued that 'they might have lived together in harmony and love'. Instead, by the autumn of 1770 Lady Huntingdon had decided 'to censure as heretical the doctrines held by Mr Fletcher, Mr Benson and Mr Wesley [and] at length determined to exclude from her College all anti-predestinarians'.[121]

Perhaps because teaching at the College had not been specifically inclined towards Arminianism or Calvinism, it seems that despite the Countess's directive, none of the students were in fact excluded from Trevecka.[122] For Benson and Fletcher, the situation was rather more complex. MacDonald contended in his *Memoirs* of 1822 that Benson, who had been at Trevecka for less than a year, believed that 'the points still at issue betwixt Calvinists and orthodox Arminians, having long appeared matters of mere opinion, on which the wise and good may safely differ'.[123] Nevertheless, he refused to write a disavowal of the *Minutes* and as a result was dismissed by Lady Huntingdon.[124] She was, however, prepared to provide him with a reference. Her letter dated 17 January 1771 stated:

> This is to certify that Mr Joseph Benson was master for the languages in my College at Talgarth for nine months, and that during that time, from his capacity, sobriety, and diligence, he acquitted himself properly in that character, and I am ready at any time to testify this in his behalf whenever required.[125]

Hearing of Benson's dismissal, Wesley responded by writing to him four days later, stating 'I know not why you should not keep the rest of your terms at Oxford and take a Bachelor's degree'.[126]

Benson, who had on 15 March 1769 entered his name at St Edmund Hall, decided to return to his studies at Oxford. Unfortunately, when he recounted to his tutor, Mr Bowerbank, the Vice-Principal of St Edmund Hall, his connection with Wesley at Kingswood, and with Lady Huntingdon at Trevecka, Bowerbank promptly refused Benson permission to complete his studies; and refused to sign his testimonial for ordination. Thus Benson, MacDonald stated, 'On account of these irregularities, and without his ever having been admonished to relinquish them, was subject to censure more severe than he would have incurred, had his conduct been proved immoral'.[127] Although he went down without a degree, Benson joined Wesley's band of itinerant preachers, where his qualities, Ives contends, were later to carry him far.[128]

Following Benson's dismissal, Fletcher wrote to Wesley stating '… if every Arminian must quit the College I am discharg'd for one, for I cannot give up the possibility of the salvation of all, any more than I can give up the truth and love of God'.[129] Fletcher's lengthy letter to the Countess, dated 7 March 1771, which concluded with his resignation for 'this seminary of pious learning', was significant, Forsaith argues, since it defined his position within the ensuing theological controversy. Stating that he believed that the 1770 *Minutes* were intended 'to guard against antinomianism', Fletcher advised that he was, nonetheless, ready to disavow 'every tenet maintain'd by Mr Wesley, or any man, which is contrary to scripture, and inconsistent with the grand fundamental doctrine of salvation by grace, through faith in Jesus Christ'.[130] Suggesting that 'the College appears to me rather in danger of running into the antinomian than the legal extreme', Fletcher declared 'abhorrence from the sense some persons… do absolutely fix to Mr Wesley's *Minutes*'.[131] While not holding with Wesley per se, Fletcher wrote 'I cannot disavow the doctrines they fairly contain, any more than I dare reject some parts of St James's Epistles, and our Lord's discourses, which in my humble judgement contain the same sentiments'.[132] In endeavouring perhaps to bring some balance to the situation which he regarded as having 'a spirit of prejudice and needless division', Fletcher wrote: 'I shall declare Mr Wesley shall be welcome to my pulpit, and I shall think myself honor'd in giving him & every Gospel minister (whether an Arminian or a Calvinist) the right hand of fellowship'.[133]

Fletcher valued peace and freedom of thought, and believed there ought to be freedom of conscience among Methodists over all that went beyond the generally accepted basic doctrines. He became more and more concerned to find a theologically acceptable consensus even on disputed questions. Fletcher's relationship with Lady Huntingdon was interrupted only briefly. In 1773 he was permitted to preach again in one of her chapels, and at the beginning of 1774 he reported that they had reached agreement on doctrinal questions. Fletcher's longing for reconciliation and agreement between Calvinist and Arminian Methodists come to nothing, though in a narrow circle around Fletcher, an understanding was reached between some leading exponents who were able to pick up the threads of their former friendship and mutual respect.[134]

Lady Huntingdon took control at Trevecka and charged Wesley with 'establishing another foundation repugnant to the whole plan of man's salvation'.[135] Wesley now saw Trevecka as a direct threat to his own educational enterprises and claimed that the prime purpose of the College was constantly to send out preachers to challenge his own men.[136] Trevecka continued to flourish, despite Wesley's ongoing complaints about the students.[137] Indeed, Best comments that this may partly explain why Wesley's interest in Kingswood School resurfaced, and suggests that he appointed the talented McGeary to develop the school so that it had the potential to become a 'Wesleyan Trevecka'.[138]

Conclusion

There is little doubt that Wesley maintained an interest in child-rearing and education throughout his life. Along with other Evangelicals, he believed that the family was the seat of virtue and piety. Tension between the desire to 'form' the child and a drive to 'reform' their parents saw Wesley increasingly looking to his preachers to promote family worship and religious education in the home. He contended that family religion was 'shamefully wanting' and sought to strengthen this, built not only on the education of children, but the Evangelism of their parents.

Wesley recognised that, as his preachers travelled in his Connexion, their sons were being deprived of nurture in the family unit. Although he believed that Kingswood School provided the perfect 'family' environment that the preachers' sons were missing, it seems that the 'parlour boarders' were less than welcoming. At the same time, it appears that the small number of boys who did settle in to life at the school were elevated to a level of learning not enjoyed by their preacher fathers; leading some to treat their parents with derision.

Amid growing tension between education and Evangelism, Wesley sought men who would not only preach, but also teach. Although men of piety, many of Wesley's preachers were from humble backgrounds, with little education. Wesley encouraged their self-improvement through reading and study. He also looked upon Kingswood as a place where preachers, however well educated, might go to improve their learning. Clarke's experience suggests that this was not always practical. At the time of his brief stay Kingswood the school was inadequately staffed and lacking in facilities. Even if Kingswood had been able to offer the learning Clarke expected, the shortage of preachers curtailed any lengthy stay at the school.

The evidence suggests that in the absence of Masters willing, or able, to enforce Wesley's strict rules, Kingswood School appears to have experienced many of the problems that blighted other educational establishments of the day. Through force of circumstance, during the final decades of Wesley's life, Kingswood witnessed an at times uncomfortable transition across social and cultural distinctions as sons of wealthy Methodist supporters were joined first by Wesley's 'academical' students and, second, gradually replaced by sons of his itinerant preachers, whose place at the school was generally funded by the Connexion.

Although Trevecka held out the prospect of a united venture that would supply trained ministers for the expanding Methodist movement, the theological differences between the Calvinist and Arminian wings of the Methodist movement took a toll on educational endeavours on both sides of the divide. That both Wesley and Lady Huntingdon were able to inspire young men to join their Connections is undeniable; that some even secured Anglican ordination is unquestionable. Wesley's claim that Kingswood could be said to rival Oxford University is harder to argue. Nor indeed, despite the evidence of training offered to some of Wesley's preachers, can Kingswood be claimed to be the 'Wesleyan Trevecka' to which Best alludes. Similarly, Lady Huntingdon's efforts to give her College at Trevecka the aura of a university seem overambitious, if only for the reason that, in their haste to send out preachers to strengthen their own Connections, neither Wesley nor Lady Huntingdon appear to have kept students in the colleges long enough to satisfy the claims they had made about the potential of their individual ventures.

Notes

1. Anon (1734) *The New Whole Duty of Man* London: Edward Wichsteed, p. 364
2. Mandeville (1723) 'An Essay on Charity and Charity Schools' p. 305
3. Doddridge, Philip (1761) *A Plain and Serious Address to the Master of a Family* London: C. Hitch and L. Hawes, et al. p. 15–18
4. Doddridge (1790) *Sermons on the Religious Education of Children* p. 35
5. Baker (1984) *BCE* vol. 3 p. 335–40
6. Whitefield, George (1738) *The Great Duty of Family Religion* London: W. Bowyer p. 9
7. Schlenther (1997) *Queen of the Methodists* p. 22–3
8. Rack (2011) *BCE* vol. 10 p. 332
9. Doddridge (1761) *A Plain and Serious Address to the Master of a Family* p. 13–16
10. Rack (2011) *BCE* vol. 10 p. 313, 339, 366
11. Mack (2008) *Heart Religion in the British Enlightenment* p. 85–9
12. John Fletcher's desire to remain at Madeley was incomprehensible to Wesley. In 1785, he wrote to his brother Charles 'About once a quarter I hear from Mr and Mrs Fletcher. I grudge his sitting still; but who can help it? I love ease as well as he does, but I dare not take it while I believe there is another world'. Letter John Wesley to Charles Wesley dated 2 Jun. 1785 in Telford (1931) *The Letters of the Rev. John Wesley* vol. 7 p. 272
13. Wesley, John (1765) *Thoughts on a Single Life* J. Paramore: London p. 2–5
    Wesley's own marriage to Mary Vazeille was a difficult and fractured one; she appears to have preferred to take care of herself and her children without much assistance or support from, or even the presence of her husband. Burton (2008) *Spiritual Literacy in John Wesley's Methodism* p. 193
14. The Church of England had a large number of curacies and poor livings: The Corporation of the Sons of the Clergy was established 'To remedy the distress and to ease the struggles of the clergy, their widows, their unmarried daughters, and, perhaps above all, their boys and girls who are starting out to make their way in life'. Cox, Nicholas (1978) *Bridging the Gap* Oxford: Becket Publications p. xiii
15. Rack (2011) *BCE* vol. 10 p. 432
16. Wesley, John (1779) *Minutes of Several Conversations* London: G. Whitfield p. 35
17. Wesley confirmed: 'if any preacher can give a sufficient reason why his boy should not go to the school he shall be allowed twelve pounds a year from the Kingswood Collection. That the daughters of travelling preachers from the time that they are nine years of age, shall receive from the said Collection eight guineas a year for four years'. Ibid. p. 66
18. Curnock (1909–1916) *The Journal of the Rev. John Wesley* vol. 6 p. 218
19. Norris notes that in 1780 there were four payments of £6 for four preachers' daughters; in 1785, three payments; and in 1790, eight preachers' daughters received the subsidy. Norris (2015) 'Prophets and Profits' Annex 9c p. 106
20. Lenton (2009) *John Wesley's Preachers* p. 118
21. Mack (2008) *Heart Religion in the British Enlightenment* p. 85–9
22. Rack (2011) *BCE* vol. 10 p. 420
23. Wesley (1779) *Minutes of Several Conversations* p. 65–6
24. Clarke (1833) *An Account of the Infancy* p. 159
25. Lenton (2009) *John Wesley's Preachers* p. 113

144   *Education and Evangelism: 1760–1791*

26   Clarke (1833) *An Account of the Infancy* p. 162
27   Rack (2011) *BCE* vol. 10 p. 539–40
28   Mathews (1949) *Methodism and the Education of the People* p. 28
29   Baker (1984) *BCE* vol. 23 p. 297
30   Ives (1970) *Kingswood School in Wesley's Day and Since* p. 103–7
31   Baker (1984) *BCE* vol. 23 p. 410
32   Rack (2011) *BCE* vol. 10 p. 639
33   Hastling (1898) *The History of Kingswood School* p. 81
     By 1796 Kingswood was exclusively for preachers' sons, who boarded at the school for around three years, and were then apprenticed, often to a fellow Methodist. Lenton (2009) *John Wesley's Preachers* p. 113–15
34   Baker (1984) *BCE* vol. 24 p. 155
35   Bowmer (1995) *The letters of John Pawson* p. 75
36   Hastling (1898) *The History of Kingswood School* p. 31, 20: Thomas Brisco (Jnr.) attended Kingswood 1781–1789
37   Bowmer (1995) *The letters of John Pawson* p. 75
38   Although Walsh suggests 'the Church remained a career open to the talent of the humbly born', clergy were generally a distinctive professional group whose pervasive presence both geographically and socially was monitored and supervised. Walsh, John, Haydon, Colin and Taylor, Stephen (eds.) (1993) *The Church of England c.1689-c.1833* Cambridge: Cambridge University Press p. 4; Jacob (2007) *The Clerical Profession in the Long Eighteenth Century* p. 6
39   Lenton (2009) *John Wesley's Preachers* p. 46–55
40   Laurence Sterne sneered that Methodist preachers were 'much fitter to make a pulpit than to get into one'. cited in Himmelfarb, Gertrude (2008) *The Roads to Modernity* London: Vintage Books p. 128
41   Rosman states that the 'prejudice that operated against learning was deeply rooted in the fundamental tenets of evangelicalism, and as such influenced the thinking of even the most able men'. Rosman (2010) *Evangelicals & Culture* p. 151–2
42   Rack (2011) *BCE* vol. 10 p. 179
43   Baker (1984) *BCE* vol. 23 p. 40
44   Rack (2011) *BCE* vol. 10 p. 124
45   Ibid. p. 144, 159
46   Most men destined for ordination into the Church of England received a classical education at Oxford or Cambridge. Although they read theology, studied handbooks on preaching and studied the published sermons of famous preachers, they were not expressly trained for parish ministry. Burton (2008) *Spiritual Literacy in John Wesley's Methodism* p. 11
     Harding suggests that they were expected to learn these skills as their ministry developed. Harding (2007) *Selina* p. 90
47   Baker (1984) *BCE* vol. 20 p. 263
48   Lenton (2009) *John Wesley's Preachers* p. 63
49   In a letter to Wesley dated 4 October 1778, Jaco expressed his great disappointment that in 1753, although it was proposed by Wesley that he should go to Kingswood, he found the school full. *The Arminian Magazine 1778* p. 543
50   Rack (2011) *BCE* vol. 10 p. 340
51   Wesley advised preachers to 'contract a taste for [reading] by use, or return to [their] trade'. Rack (2011) *BCE* vol. 10 p. 340
52   Telford (1931) *The Letters of the Rev. John Wesley* vol. 6. p. 130
53   Wesley (1862) *Minutes of The Methodist Conference* p. 867
     Wesley advised one of his preachers, Christopher Hopper, in a letter dated 20 November 1769: 'If you love the souls or bodies of men, recommend everywhere the *Primitive Physic* and the small tracts'; adding that however poor Methodists

were they should 'lay out a penny to buy a book every other week'. Telford (1931) *The Letters of the Rev. John Wesley* vol. 5 p. 161

54 Wesley's desire to train preachers in basic medicine was reflected by the presence of books by Cheyne in the Kingswood library. Maddox (2002) 'Kingswood School Library Holdings' p. 343

55 Rack (2011) *BCE* vol. 10 p. 340-2

56 Brantley (1984) *Locke, Wesley, and the Method of English Romanticism* p. 120

57 Streiff (2001) *Reluctant Saint?* p. 221-2

58 cited in Forsaith (2008) *Unexampled Labours* p. 329

59 Lenton identifies preachers Jeremiah Brettell, William Baynes, John Pritchard, John Catermole, Joseph Pilmore and others, who like Adam Clarke stayed at Kingswood before commencing their itinerancy. Lenton (2009) *John Wesley's Preachers* p. 63

60 Clarke (1833) *An Account of the Infancy* p. 121

61 Ibid. p. 169

62 Ibid. p. 150-3

63 Ibid p. 154

64 The main school room of the old colliers' school became the chapel both for the boarding school and for the local Methodist Society, and remained so until the building of a Wesleyan Chapel in the village in 1844. Its eight side rooms were used, among other things, for the accommodation of the girl boarders. Bishop, Michael (1983) *The Wesley Pulpit and its Background* Bath: Kingswood School, unpaginated

65 Clarke (1833) *An Account of the Infancy* p. 155-8

66 Ibid. p. 165-9

67 Ibid. p. 160-2

68 Hastling (1898) *The History of Kingswood School* p. 7-127

69 Schlenther (1997) *Queen of the Methodists* p. 65-75

As a Calvinist, Lady Huntingdon was able to add to her circle of friends an increasing number of Evangelical Dissenting ministers. She regularly corresponded with Philip Doddridge; in 1747, she offered to support a student at his Northampton Academy; and presented Archbishop Leighton's *Selected Works* to the Academy Library there. Welch (1995) *Spiritual Pilgrim* p. 70-1

70 Gibson suggests that chaplains played an increasingly significant role in this period. He argues that 'the relationship between women of high social status and their chaplains enabled women to scale heights in religious life that had previously been closed to them'. Not only did they take responsibility for the religious life and spiritual health of the household, enabling the nobility to be self-sufficient in religious matters, but chaplains were also used to advance their patron's religious opinions. Gibson, William (1997) *A Social History of the Domestic Chaplain* London: Leicester University Press p. 2, 56-64, 86

71 Dallimore (1980) *George Whitefield* vol. 2 p. 473-4

72 Welch (1995) *Spiritual Pilgrim* p. 117, 51-2

73 cited in Ibid. p. 123

74 Ives (1970) *Kingswood School in Wesley's Day and Since* p. 4

75 Welch (1995) *Spiritual Pilgrim* p. 45

76 Tyson, John R. & Schlenther, B. S. (2006) *In the Midst of Early Methodism* Plymouth: The Scarecrow Press Inc. p. 1-11

77 Welch (1995) *Spiritual Pilgrim* p. 184

John Fletcher referred to the 'expensive housekeeping' of Trevecka, namely the cost of building works, together with furnishing and equipping the College, costing £1,000. cited in Forsaith (2008) *Unexampled Labours* p. 238

78 MacDonald (1822) *Memoirs of the Rev. Joseph Benson* p. 15

79 Tyson (2006) *In the Midst of Early Methodism* p. 159

80 Welch (1995) *Spiritual Pilgrim* p. 114
81 Harding (2007) *Selina* p. 94
82 Tyson (2006) *In the Midst of Early Methodism* p. 2
83 Welch (1995) *Spiritual Pilgrim* p. 124
84 Ibid. p. 45
85 cited in Tyson (2006) *In the Midst of Early Methodism* p. 161
86 Ibid. p. 157
87 Welch (1995) *Spiritual Pilgrim* p. 185
88 Forsaith (2008) *Unexampled Labours* p. 240–2
    Among them were James Matthews and Joseph Shipman, two of the students expelled from St Edmund Hall, who were, Schlenther suggests, the least qualified of the six. Within a year of enrolling, Matthews had left and Shipman had declared himself dissatisfied, and keen to leave. Schlenther (1997) *Queen of the Methodists* p. 76–8
89 Welch (1995) *Spiritual Pilgrim* p. 185
90 Ibid. p. 180
91 Tyson (2006) *In the Midst of Early Methodism* p. 13, 157
92 Harding (2007) *Selina* p. 98–168
93 Welch (1995) *Spiritual Pilgrim* p. 179
94 cited in Tyson (2006) *In the Midst of Early Methodism* p. 160
95 MacDonald (1822) *Memoirs of the Rev. Joseph Benson* p. 15
96 Streiff (2001) *Reluctant Saint?* p. 143
97 Telford (1931) *The Letters of the Rev. John Wesley* vol. 5 p. 88
98 Ibid. p. 123
99 Streiff (2001) *Reluctant Saint?* p. 143
100 cited in Forsaith (2008) *Unexampled Labours* p. 239–42
101 cited in Ibid. p. 239
102 MacDonald (1822) *Memoirs of the Rev. Joseph Benson* p. 15
103 Tyson (2006) *In the Midst of Early Methodism* p. 11
104 Telford (1931) *The Letters of the Rev. John Wesley* vol. 5 p. 166
105 Ives (1970) *Kingswood School in Wesley's Day and Since* p. 68
106 Tyson (2006) *In the Midst of Early Methodism* p. 11
107 cited in Ibid. p. 166
108 Dallimore (1980) *George Whitefield* vol. 2 p. 473–4
109 MacDonald (1822) *Memoirs of the Rev. Joseph Benson* p. 16
110 Jacob (2007) *The Clerical Profession in the Long Eighteenth Century* p. 304–6
111 Tyson (2006) *In the Midst of Early Methodism* p. 158
112 Brown-Lawson (1994) *John Wesley and the Anglican Evangelicals of the Eighteenth Century* p. 122
    Harding suggests that twenty Trevecka students, after much effort and often rigorous examination, were successful in securing ordination in the Church of England. Others were only successful in securing ordination because they went on from Trevecka to Oxford or Cambridge. Harding (2007) *Selina* p. 172–3
113 cited in Elliott-Binns (1953) *The Early Evangelicals* p. 177
114 It was not until 1806 that *The Evangelical Magazine* recorded the establishment by Dissenters of societies to finance the education of ministers' children. Rosman (2010) *Evangelicals and Culture* p. 160
115 Harding (2007) *Selina* p. 173–4
116 Norris (2015) 'Prophets and Profits' p. 67
117 Welch (1995) *Spiritual Pilgrim* p. 177–8
118 Harding (2007) *Selina* p. 172
119 Tyson (2006) *In the Midst of Early Methodism* p. 158
120 Question #3 of the *1770 Minutes* explained: 'We have received it as a maxim, that "a man is to do nothing in order to [receive] justification". Nothing can be

more false. Whoever desires to find favour with God, should "cease from evil, and learn to do well…" Is not this salvation by works? Not by the merit of works, but as works as a condition'. Ibid. p. 157–8
121 MacDonald (1822) *Memoirs of the Rev. Joseph Benson* p. 16
122 Welch (1995) *Spiritual Pilgrim* p. 191
123 MacDonald (1822) *Memoirs of the Rev. Joseph Benson* p. vi
124 Forsaith (2008) *Unexampled Labours* p. 15
125 'No. 228: To Joseph Benson (Jan. 17, 1771)' cited in Tyson (2006) *In the Midst of Early Methodism* p. 168
126 cited in Ibid. p. 168
127 MacDonald (1822) *Memoirs of the Rev. Joseph Benson* p. 21–5, v
128 Ives (1970) *Kingswood School in Wesley's Day and Since* p. 74
129 Fletcher to John Wesley letter dated 20 Feb. 1771 cited in Forsaith (2008) *Unexampled Labours* p. 239
130 Ibid. p. 260–1
131 cited in Ibid. p. 262
132 One of the central teachings in the epistle of James is that faith without works is dead (James 2.17). This epistle is thus a key scriptural source for the argument against antinomianism, and it supports the *1770 Minutes* in which God is said to grant salvation 'not by the merit of works, but by works as a condition'. Ibid. p. 262
133 cited in Ibid. p. 269–70
134 Streiff (2001) *Reluctant Saint?* p. 175, 215–16
135 Tyson (2006) *In the Midst of Early Methodism* p. 11–13
136 John Wesley letter to Mary Bishop 22 Nov 1769 cited in Schlenther (1997) *Queen of the Methodists* p. 76–8
137 Welch (1995) *Spiritual Pilgrim* p. 191
138 Best (2006) *Charles Wesley* p. 322

7 Educating pauper children after 1780

Throughout the eighteenth century education initiatives were designed primarily to regulate and reform the poor rather than ameliorate their condition. The combined pressures of a concern for the religious welfare of the young and the growing need for child labour modified the original idea of day school instruction. In the closing decades of the eighteenth century Sunday charity schools, organised and financed by the same methods as the older charity schools, came into prominence. The emergence of the Sunday school movement was to have far-reaching consequences for the religious and social life of the poor. Although John Wesley died in 1791, he witnessed the beginnings of the Sunday school movement at a time when it was a product of the religious and philanthropic sentiment of the day.

Evangelicals were concerned with reforming the character of the individual, not bringing about social change. Wesley was not alone among Evangelicals in believing that a stable home with parents eager and competent to instruct their children was the ideal. Despite this, he promoted Sunday schools among Methodist Societies. Drawing on previously unpublished material, this chapter examines the work of John Fletcher in his Sunday schools in Madeley, and demonstrates that there were different approaches to the way pauper children were instructed, even among early Methodists.

The eighteenth century expectation that mothers foster intellectual growth in children not only empowered female educators with an authoritative voice but, Davis argues, challenged the patriarchal domination of educational discourse by Locke and Rousseau.[1] This chapter looks at two women who were influential figures in the field of education in the late eighteenth century. Sarah Trimmer was a prolific and influential writer, publishing over twenty five works, many of which were designed for use in the Sunday, or charity schools that she founded. Although Hannah More contributed to the debate regarding education of elite girls, this chapter considers her involvement in the education of pauper children, which began in 1789 with the established of her Sunday schools in the Mendip hills. More published a series of tracts for use in these schools, which featured a female protagonist, and advanced the notion of the Sunday school as beneficial not only for pauper children, but as a means by which values learned could be passed on to their parents.

The closing decades of the century saw anxieties about the perceived fecklessness of the poor expose growing fears about problems arising from the expanding and unsustainable population. This chapter argues that thinking concerning the poor hardened following the French Revolution of 1789, and events in France contributed to the growing suspicion among Churchmen of the work of non-Anglican Evangelicals.

Emergence of the Sunday school movement

It was largely due to the enthusiasm of Anglican Robert Raikes, that the Sunday school movement reignited the tradition of popular education associated with the Church. Sunday schools were a development of charity schools and accommodated the growing requirement for child labour by providing a cheaper form of education on just one day a week. In allowing children to remain at their jobs, poor families ceased to be penalised by the loss of their children's earnings, and employers by the loss of children's labour. By his efforts in *The Gloucester Journal*, of which he was owner and publisher, and later by articles and letters in *The Gentleman's Magazine*, Raikes transformed what started as a local system into a national institution.[2]

During the 1770s and 1780s, clergy became enthusiastic promoters of Sunday schools as a means of educating children of the poor in the catechism, as well as in reading, and in some cases, writing.[3] Nevertheless, the education provided in Sunday schools was not intended to give children aspirations above their station. In a view commonly held by the English Establishment, Bishop Pretyman-Tomline of Lincoln declared in January 1789: 'subordination of ranks, and the relation of magistrates and subjects, are indispensably necessary in the state of society for which our Creator has evidently intended the human species'.[4]

Raikes had, for over twenty years, visited the two prisons in Gloucester in an effort to teach adult inmates to read. He became convinced of the link between idleness, ignorance, vice and crime.[5] He recognised that Sunday was a day when the incidence of crime increased, noting in *The Gloucester Journal* on 3 November 1783 that 'Farmers and other inhabitants of the towns and villages complain that they receive more injury in their property on the Sabbath than all the week besides'.[6] William Jesse, Rector of Dowles and chaplain to the Earl of Glasgow, contended that 'idleness among uninstructed youth' was 'filling the land with villains, render[ing] property insecure, crowding our jails with felons, and bringing poverty, distress and ruin upon families'.[7]

Raikes was prompted into action when, in 1780, he reported seeing 'a group of little miserable wretches' in the street:

> I was expressing my concern to one, at their forlorn and neglected state, and was told, that if I were to pass through that street on Sundays, it would shock me indeed, to see the crowds of children who were spending that sacred day in noise and riot; to the extreme annoyance of all decent people.[8]

Along with Thomas Stock, curate of St John the Baptist, Gloucester, Raikes decided to take action against 'this deplorable profanation of the Sabbath'.[9] He sought the help of four local women and 'engaged to pay the sum they required for receiving and instructing such children as I should send to them every Sunday'.[10] Raikes's schools were open to all children aged between six and fourteen, not just those from religious families. Both he and Stock visited parents, urging them to send their children to school. 'With regard to the parents', wrote Raikes:

> I went round to remonstrate with them on the melancholy consequences that must ensue from so fatal a neglect of their children's morals. They alleged that their poverty rendered them incapable of cleaning and clothing their children fit to appear either at school or at church… All that I required were clean faces, clean hands, and the hair combed – in all other respects they were to come as their circumstances would admit.[11]

Raikes's reputation as the founder of the Sunday school movement owes much to the fact that his account of the establishment of schools in Gloucester found its way, via Colonel Richard Townley of Bolton, to *The Gentleman's Magazine*; where it was published in 1784.[12] From there it was disseminated across the country by the extensive network of magazines and newspapers available to the wealthy and 'middling sort' in the late eighteenth century.[13] Sunday schools rapidly became the favourite charity of hundreds of provincial philanthropists, prompted by testimonials published by Raikes:

> The farmers etc. declare that they can now leave their houses, gardens etc. and frequent the public worship without danger of depredation… a man upwards of eighty years of age who seemed about the rank of yeomanry declared 'Oh that I should live to see this day, when poor children are thus befriended, and are taught the road to peace and comfort here, and happiness and heaven hereafter'.[14]

Raikes's first Sunday school was opened in Sooty Alley, Gloucester, in 1780.[15] The children attended the Sunday school from ten in the morning until noon, when they were allowed to go home for an hour. Returning at one, they read a lesson, attended Church and learned the catechism. When dismissed at five, they were instructed 'to go home without making a noise; and by no means to play in the street'.[16] Raikes gave his 'experiment' a three year trial, and during that time set up seven or eight Sunday schools with an average of thirty pupils in each; initially with an intake of boys, but later a mix of segregated boys and girls.[17] Raikes's own view of Sunday schools was that:

> This mode of treatment has produced a wonderful change in the manners of these little savages… they have been transformed from the shape of wolves and tigers to that of men. In temper, disposition, and manners, they

could hardly be said to differ from the brute creation – but since the establishment of the Sunday schools they have shown that they are not the ignorant creatures they were before... they are become more tractable and obedient, and less quarrelsome and revengeful.[18]

So successful was the venture that by 1785 a national society, the Society for the Support and Encouragement of Sunday Schools, was established in London.[19] Among its founders was Anglican philanthropist and reformer Jonas Hanway, who declared 'Among the lower classes, Sunday schools seem to be well calculated to remedy the evil, not only for communicating the rudiments of Christianity, but that the whole system of relative duties may be gradually taught'.[20] The Society had the support of both the Established and Nonconformist Churches.[21] Dissenter William Turner declared:

> May we not hope that the opening of the first Sunday school at Gloucester, will hereafter be considered as an important epocha in the history of the practical religion of mankind, and that the name of Raikes will be gratefully remembered for it by future generations?[22]

Sunday schools were financed by funds raised through subscriptions and donations, largely from the 'middling sort', and by collections in churches on Sundays.[23] Supporters recognised that not only did children learn to read so that they could read the Bible, but they helped sustain their families' contact with the Church.[24] Children might also be a means by which Christian values were passed on to their parents.

The Society for the Support and Encouragement of Sunday Schools had among its contributors many eminent bankers and merchants and several Evangelical members of Parliament. William Morton Pitt stated: 'On the one hand these schools extend religious knowledge among the ignorant, on the other they instil into the lower classes of the community the principles of industry, decency, sobriety [and] subordination'.[25] The Society offered financial support to laymen and clergy so that they could set up and maintain schools.[26] Like the earlier charity schools, the Society was sponsored and supported by the SPCK, and some of the ablest ministers of the day, among them Bishop Samuel Horsley, preached sermons on their behalf.[27] Raikes then published these sermons, and copies were sold in support of the movement.[28]

Anglican Sunday school instruction was overwhelmingly religious in character. The school began and ended with prayer and, like the earlier charity school, used the Bible, the Book of Common Prayer, catechism and biblical commentaries as text-books for instruction.[29] Writing to a Society in London on 7 October 1786, Raikes commended the Sunday school in Painswick, Gloucestershire by declaring 'Young people lately more neglected than the cattle in the field, ignorant, profane, filthy, clamorous, impatient of every restraint, were here seen clean, quiet, observant of order, submissive, courteous in behaviour, and in conversation free from the vileness which marks our wretched vulgar'.[30] Sunday schools were encouraged by Adam Smith, who claimed that 'no plan promised to effect a change of manners with equal ease and simplicity since the days of the Apostles'.[31] William Romaine, a prominent Evangelical and one-time chaplain to Lady Huntingdon, wrote to a friend in 1784 stating that 'the Lord God has marvellously favoured the plan. He has inclined vast numbers of children to come; the parents in general are thankful, and the schoolmasters and mistresses have given great satisfaction'.[32]

Despite some local opposition from farmers who feared increased literacy would deter the poor from working on the land, Sunday schools were, initially at least, welcomed by the rural and urban middle class. The zeal of the clergy, and their lay helpers, appears to have been matched by that of the children: 'Many have their books at their loom, to seize any vacant minute, when their work is retarded by the breaking of threads' stated Raikes in 1786.[33] The children learned hymns and Bible passages by heart; 'But what is yet more extraordinary', wrote Raikes in 1784 was that:

> These little ragga-muffins have in great numbers taken it into their heads to frequent the early morning prayers, which are held every morning at the cathedral at seven o'clock. They assemble at the house of one of the mistresses, and walk before her to church, two and two, in as much order as a company of soldiers.[34]

Diligent children were given 'little rewards' of 'books, combs, shoes, or some article of apparel'; and 'certain boys, who are distinguished by their decent behaviour, were appointed to superintend the conduct of the rest, and make a report of those that swear, call names &c...'.[35] The *Gloucester Journal* published the following 'extract of a letter from Cheltenham' dated 9 January 1789:

> After church a dinner was given to the poor children, which was served to them by the ladies and gentlemen, the directors of the charity... After their comfortable meal, the children gave such specimens of their advancement in reading, and a sense of their duty, as afforded the highest satisfaction. The improvement in general civility and decency of behaviour, was also extremely gratifying to those, who remembered their former state when they were totally neglected![36]

Attendance at Sunday schools was recorded meticulously for each student and teacher. Estimates of the average length of attendance range from one to four years per student. Reports from the Sunday School Society detailed the growth of schools, numbers enrolled and their geographical spread. Jones concludes that the details recorded suggested that few working class children, except in London, escaped at least some exposure to Sunday school education.[37]

Despite the huge level of support for Sunday schools, there were those who were opposed to their non-denominational nature, arguing that they should instead be completely under the control of the Church.[38] Critics also argued that attendance at Sunday school rendered the poor proud and idle, and undermined family life by removing children from their families on the day they might otherwise be together.[39] Even among supporters of the schools there was disagreement over the level of instruction that should be given. Jonas Hanway, though not in principle opposed to teaching some of the poor to write and do arithmetic, did not support the teaching of writing for all. While he maintained that 'the better condition the labourers' children are put in, the less they will turn their thoughts to pilfering and beggary', he argued that 'as to writing, if one in twenty acquires this part of learning, it may answer for the other nineteen'.[40]

While the average charity school of the eighteenth century contained no more than twenty to twenty five children, the earliest Sunday schools of Northamptonshire had average enrolments of over eighty; and those aided by the Sunday School Society had between ninety and one hundred children. Indeed, rural schools run by the parish priest, drawing instructors from ordinary weekday school teachers, were soon replaced by larger concerns, where children were taught by unpaid working class laymen and women. This raised serious concerns among those who believed that such a move encouraged itinerant preaching with its panoply of levelling tendencies that caused men and women to regard themselves as equivalent to the clergy of the Established Church.[41] Discussed later in this chapter, this was to have serious ramifications after the French Revolution in 1789.

John Wesley and Methodist Sunday schools

Wesley's relationship to the Sunday school movement was ambivalent. An entry in his *Journal* in 1784 stated: 'I find these schools springing up wherever I go. Perhaps God may have some deeper end therein than men are aware of. Who knows but some of them may become nurseries for Christians?'.[42] The evidence suggests that the central contradictions for Wesley were three-fold. First, time spent away from the family on Sundays broke down his favoured family model. Second, while the question of children's behaviour was central to the purpose for Sunday schools, salvation of the child's soul was Wesley's priority. Third, the non-denominational approach of many Sunday schools, where children might come under 'dangerous' influences of other children, fell short of Wesley's 'nurture–educational' model. Wesley seems, nevertheless, to have recognised that there was a place for Sunday schools for those children whose families could not, or would not provide this education themselves.

Wesley first encountered the work of Sunday schools in High Wycombe, where Methodist Hannah Ball founded her school in 1769. Ball was a frequent correspondent of Wesley's and, in the preface to her *Memorials*, Thomas Jackson wrote: 'Her talent for Christian training of children was considerable… that she enjoyed in high degree the respect and confidence of Mr Wesley is very manifest from the general tenor of his correspondence with her'.[43] Hannah Ball wrote to Wesley on 16 December 1770, advising him that: 'the children meet twice a week, every Sunday and Monday. They are a wild little company, but seem willing to be instructed. I labour among them, earnestly desiring to promote the interest of the Church of Christ'.[44] Wesley continued to take an interest in Ball's work and wrote to her in March 1782 enquiring of her 'little maidens':

> I trust some of them will bring forth fruit to perfection. As you have a peculiar love for children, and a talent for assisting them, see that you stir up the gift of God which is in you. If you gain but one of them in ten, you have a good reward for your labour.[45]

While Raikes was later to champion the Sunday school as a way of moulding children to be 'tractable and obedient, and less quarrelsome and revengeful',[46] Ball was clear on the purpose of the instruction she was providing: 'I desire to spend the remaining part of my life… instructing a few of the rising generation in the principles of religion, and in every possible way I am capable, ministering to them that shall be heirs to salvation'. Indeed, in May 1775 she wrote that 'In the meeting of the children one, about fourteen years of age, said she had found the love of Jesus shed abroad in her heart'.[47]

Both John Wesley and George Whitefield were known to the Raikes family, and Wesley visited them when he was in Gloucester.[48] As Raikes's non-denominational Sunday school movement gathered pace, Wesley endorsed the establishment of Sunday schools where Methodists, like Dissenters and Anglicans, offered instruction to pauper children on the Sabbath.[49] When invited to preach in the parish Church in Bingley on 18 July 1784, Wesley witnessed the work of the Sunday school, and commented:

> I stepped into the Sunday-school, which contains two hundred and forty children, taught every Sunday by several masters, and superintended by the Curate. So, many children in one parish are restrained from open sin, and taught a little good manners, at least, as well as to read the Bible.[50]

In 1785 Wesley published an article written by Raikes in *The Arminian Magazine* and urged his followers to set up Sunday schools in their local societies.[51] When members of the Methodist Society in Bolton proposed opening a Sunday school it was initially opposed by the superintendent minister, who objected to its non-denominational enrolment. His objection failed and the school opened to all on 16 April 1786. Wesley noted in his *Journal* that: 'The house was crowded the more because of five hundred and fifty children, who are taught in our Sunday schools. Such an army of them got about me when I came out of the chapel that I could scarce disengage myself from them'.[52]

On 27 July 1787, Wesley returned to Bolton, and recorded in his *Journal* that 'Here are eight hundred poor children taught in our Sunday schools by about eighty Masters, who receive no pay but what they are to receive from their

General Master'.[53] The venture at Bolton was evidently successful since Wesley noted in his *Journal* following a further visit nine months later:

> About three I met between 900 and a thousand of the children belonging to our Sunday schools; I never saw such a sight before. They were all exactly clean, as well as plain in their apparel. All were serious and well-behaved. Many, both boys and girls, had as beautiful faces as, I believe, England or Europe can afford. When they all sung together, and none of them out of tune, the melody was beyond that of any theatre; and what is the best of all, many of them truly fear God, and some rejoice in his salvation.[54]

Wesley included a report on the Bolton Sunday school in his *Arminian Magazine* the same year. It concluded that 'the masters love the children and delight to instruct them; the children love their masters, and cheerfully receive instruction'. The report suggested:

> We see at present the prospect of a glorious reformation. Among many who attend... there is already a great change in their manners, morals and learning. They are taught to read and write by persons who are very well qualified for the work... their natural rusticity is greatly worn off and their behaviour is modest and decent... The principles of religion are instilled into their minds.[55]

Records from the City Road Chapel indicated, Stevenson suggested, that following Wesley's recommendation, Sunday schools were 'taken up with determination and energy by Mr William Marriott and Mr Thomas Tegg, among others'; with the result that in March 1798 the Methodist Sunday School Society was established in London. Teachers were unpaid; and by way of rewarding children, Mr Marriott noted: 'in May 1799, bonnets and tippets were distributed for regular attendance, and shoes in November. This was to ensure a good attendance in the winter season; but the finances did not allow its continuance'. Whether influenced by these 'rewards' or not, the City Road Sunday school recorded six hundred and thirteen children in attendance in August 1799.[56]

Although the day school at Wesley's Orphan House in Newcastle had long-since closed, it would seem from a letter written by Wesley to Charles Atmore on 24 March 1790, that a thriving Sunday school had replaced it:

> I am glad you have set up Sunday schools at Newcastle. This is one of the noblest institutions which have been seen in Europe for some centuries and will increase more and more, provided the teachers and inspectors do their duties. Nothing can prevent the success of this blessed work but the neglect of the instruments. Therefore be sure to watch over these with all care that they may not grow weary of well-doing.[57]

Indeed, Stamp recorded that subscriptions and donations 'quickly promised', and amounting to thirty eight pounds and fifteen shillings, enabled the Sunday school at the Orphan House to open on 28 February 1790, when nearly three hundred and fifty children were enrolled as students. By 21 March 1790 the number of children had risen to eight hundred, taught in thirty two classes.[58]

The idea of Sunday schools was seized upon by Methodists in many other places.[59] Cornelius Bayley, an English teacher at Kingswood School between 1773 and 1781 and curate at Madeley during 1782, was by 1784 a Methodist preacher and prominent member of the interdenominational committee set up in Manchester to promote Sunday schools.[60] In *An Address to the Public* dated 1 August 1784, he stated: 'The hardest heart must melt at the melancholy sight of such a multitude of children, both male and female, in this town, who live in gross ignorance, infidelity, and habitual profanation of the Lord's Day'.[61]

In June 1784 Quaker Abiah Darby, having read about the success of Sunday schools in Gloucester, wrote to John Fletcher recommending that he take up Raikes's plan in Madeley. Stating that she 'was much pleased with the humane benevolent act to restrain and instruct these poor neglected children', Darby suggested that Fletcher consider the foundation of a Sunday school 'to inculcate into the minds of the poor children the holy fear of almighty God, and their duty to parents and one another'. Lamenting 'the great neglect of children, and their rioting in play upon that solemn day', she suggested Fletcher propose the plan in Church, and encouraged him to raise a subscription, to which she herself agreed to contribute.[62]

Unpublished manuscript notes held in the John Rylands Library provide an outline of Fletcher's 'Proposals towards the Sunday Schools' in Madeley, Madeley Wood and Coalbrookdale:

> It is proposed that Sunday schools be set up in this parish for such children as are employed all the week, and for those whose education has been neglected… That in these schools children shall be taught to read and write, and shall be instructed in the principles of morality and piety… That in the Dale, in Madeley, and in Madeley Wood, there shall be a school for boys and another for girls, six schools in all… That £20 shall be paid by subscription for this charity, namely £15 for the salary of six teachers… and £5 shall be laid out in tables, benches, books, pens and ink… That three or four inspectors shall be appointed to visit the schools to see that the children attend regularly and that the masters do their duty by the children and to make their report to the Director.[63]

By February 1785 Fletcher had enlisted a subscription 'for building a meeting-place and Sunday school in Coalbrookdale', and even before all the meeting houses were prepared, and Masters found, three hundred children had gathered as willing scholars.[64]

Children were welcomed to Fletcher's Sunday schools based not on their religious affiliation, but on their residency within the parish.[65] According to an account written by Fletcher's wife, Mary Bosanquet, music was used to teach the children to read. Each of them was given a little hymn book and assigned to a Methodist friend or neighbour in the community who would teach them to sing. Mary Fletcher observed: 'The little creatures were greatly taken with this new employment and would many of them scarce allow themselves to sleep or dine for the desire they had of learning their lesson'. The venture was so successful that the number of children continued to rise and 'Numbers both of the rich and the trading people cheerfully lent their helping hand not only to defray the expense of teachers but to [build] a very convenient school in Coalbrookdale for the teaching of a great number of children on that side of the parish'.[66]

In Madeley, a school room had already been built close to the Church and in Madeley Wood, Fletcher's school, already in use on weekdays and Thursday evenings for the instruction of children, was brought into use for the Sunday school.[67] Although never published, Fletcher drafted 'A Moral and Evangelical Catechism for the use of Sunday Schools'. The children were taught to love God, the 'infinitely good and the great author of all good in heaven and earth'. In a statement reflective perhaps of the environment in which some of the children were being raised, Fletcher told them 'Conscience proves God just as the constable who serves a warrant proves the existence of a magistrate. Godliness proves God just as sunshine proves there is a sun'.[68]

Fletcher prepared a list of 'School Questions' in which children were asked: 'Do you love to come to Sunday School?'; 'Do you wish to be instructed?'; 'Do you wish to learn to read well?'. Presumably when answered to the affirmative, the children were told:

> Reading may teach many things, are all good who read or only them who mind to do as their Book teaches? What does it teach – that we are sinners, must come to God for pardon, and to be made like himself or we cannot be happy in heaven. Beasts have no reason to understand the will of God, therefore no duty – we have scripture.[69]

In a practice widespread in Sunday schools, children who distinguished themselves were awarded books, in Fletcher's case hymn books. Such awards served a dual purpose; not only did they encourage diligence, but by taking books home, children became an instrument through which parents could be encouraged in literacy and piety.[70]

Female educators and role models

Throughout her life, High Church Anglican Sarah Trimmer was a prolific and influential writer, publishing over twenty five works. Many of her publications were designed for use in the Sunday schools or charity schools that she founded. Her overriding concern was that education should always be religious in nature, and in strict conformity to the Church of England.[71] She regarded the discipline of religion, combined with the discipline of labour, as the only cure for the evils of the age.[72]

Trimmer's most substantial work, read and acted upon throughout the late eighteenth and early nineteenth century was her *The Oeconomy of Charity*.[73] First published in 1786, Hilton describes the treatise as 'a handbook on Sunday schools' and suggests that it was one of the first attempts by a woman educationalist to construct a whole functional moral and social economy. Precise details of charitable activity and the responsibilities of the wealthy towards the poor were discussed at length. Trimmer's rationale was that by establishing charity institutions for the poor, wealthy young ladies might reform the unruly behaviour of children, so that they might grow up to be docile and grateful servants of the charitable rich.[74]

Trimmer understood the necessity of poor children's weekly industrial labour to the family economy. But she wrote: 'I cannot think of the children who work in the manufactures without the utmost commiseration'.[75] She argued that it would be an act of charity to instead place children into industrial schools, where the national interest could be served by teachers who took care not only of the health, but of the morals of children in their care.[76] She reflected:

> Day schools of industry have as yet made but little progress among us, but from the happy success of an experiment at this time in one of the most populous parishes in London, we may reasonably hope to see, in the course of a few years, parochial schools of industry in every parish of the metropolis, and in every town in England.[77]

The education provided at schools of industry was basic. Boys were taught 'to put heads upon pins, and close shoes and boots intended for exportation'. Girls were taught 'to spin wool for blanket manufacture, to spin flax, and to knit their own stockings'. They were taught to read and write only 'for the common purposes of life'. 'A great part of the business of religious instruction', noted Trimmer 'might be carried on while girls were occupied at their needles'. In some cases, children attended a school of industry during the week and a Sunday school. Like charity and Sunday schools, schools of industry relied largely for their existence on wealthy benefactors. Writing concerning a local girl's school for industry, Trimmer argued:

> The annual subscriptions towards the school are in general half a guinea, the price of an opera ticket, as the benevolent foundress observed when she proposed its establishment… can a public entertainment… be ever so enchanting, afford such zeal, heart-felt satisfaction, as the exercise of benevolence like this produces?[78]

Trimmer reasoned in *The Oeconomy of Charity*:

> If, for instance, there was a school for spinning flax, girls of five years of age might be employed at it, and the yarn might easily be manufactured

into white or striped linen and checks; and by the time each little spinstress had worn out the clothes with which the parish or private benefactors should at first furnish her, she might earn sufficient to entitle her to linen and other necessaries.[79]

In practice, by the close of the century many schools were in debt and unable to support themselves and the scheme was in decline.[80] This decline may have arisen for several reasons. Certainly, lack of funds was one issue; children were unskilled workers and, with a lack of competent teachers, there was little market for defective goods.[81] Moreover, although parish children in manufacturing towns might have benefited from training received in this type of school, it would have been of little use in country parishes where agricultural skills were needed. Similarly, in large towns, including London, the demand was more likely to be for boys who could write and keep accounts, that they might be placed with shop-keepers.[82]

Trimmer began her own Sunday school in 1786, and with interested patrons including Queen Caroline, exerted a significant High Church influence upon the early development of the Sunday school movement.[83] Despite her reputation as an education reformer, Trimmer did not regard Sunday schools as an appropriate place for instructing children beyond learning to read. She argued: 'Sunday schools, while they hold out religious instruction suitable to all degrees of poor children furnish a sufficient portion of learning to fit the poor... the Sabbath is not the proper time to acquire the articles of writing and account'.[84]

Rescuing the poor from habits of vice and indolence, inuring children to early habits of going to Church and spending leisure hours on Sunday decently and virtuously, did not require intensive or advanced instruction.[85] Some Sunday schools taught writing, but the advantage of providing only a basic level of instruction was that it did not require educated teachers. Trimmer contended:

> It is not intended that the children of the poor should be instructed in languages, geography, history and other articles that constitute a polite education, but merely in such a knowledge of the English language as shall enable them to read the Scriptures; in the plain duties of Christianity; and in those modes of conduct which their station requires.[86]

Mathews wrote 'Among Evangelicals who bear honoured names in the history of the Sunday school movement were Hannah More and her sisters'.[87] While the More sisters were, on the one hand, concerned about the poor and generous in their support of them, the motivation behind their work was not altogether altruistic. In common with many supporters of the Sunday school movement, their work was poised between a desire to make life more pleasant for people in hard circumstances and a wish to keep them 'in their place'.[88] More, like Wesley, reacted to the problem of poverty in a manner characteristic of reformers throughout the eighteenth century; their concern being for the spiritual and moral welfare of the poor, not their state of poverty.[89]

Nevertheless, the importance of More's contribution to Sunday school education in Somerset at the end of the eighteenth century merits consideration on several counts. First, it is witness to the difficulties faced by those involved in establishing Sunday schools. Second, it highlights the way in which the convictions of their founders shaped the pedagogy of the schools they established. Third, and perhaps most importantly, it demonstrates how More advanced the notion that the Sunday school was a means by which religious values could be transmitted to parents via their children.

Although she lived for some time in Bristol, More had no contact with, or sympathy for, Methodism. Wesley's only reference to Hannah More was in a letter to his niece Sarah Wesley dated 31 July 1790.[90] In it Wesley suggested that he regarded the interests of the More sisters to be with 'earthly' rather than 'heavenly' matters: 'I should be glad to meet any of the Miss Mores', he wrote, 'but I doubt my conversation would suit them, I have little relish for anything which does not [concern] the upper world'.[91] Nor did More have any contact with Lady Huntingdon's chapel in Bath, contending that the Anglican Church provided the spiritual piety she required.[92] Although tolerant of Nonconformity, Mathews argued, she regarded anything approaching 'enthusiasm' as suspect.[93] Despite her suspicion of Methodism, More, like Wesley, regarded family religion as being of 'unspeakable importance' and stressed the importance of scripture and the necessity of living a Christian life.[94]

Writing to her friend, the Non-juror and High Church barrister John Bowdler, More stated 'The grand object of instruction is the Bible... the great thing is to get it faithfully explained, in such a way as shall be, likely to touch the heart, and influence the conduct'.[95] Like Wesley, she regarded education as a means of producing a piety that was both sober and heartfelt; a religion of the heart that also recognised the importance of reason.[96] Where More's thinking and practice differed from Wesley's was in her belief that the poor need not be taught to write:

> My object has not been to teach dogmas and opinions, but to form the lower class to habits of industry and virtue... to make good members of society (and this can only be done by making good Christians) has been my aim... principles not opinions are what I labour to give them.[97]

Hannah More's involvement in the education of pauper children began in 1789, when, at a meeting with her friend William Wilberforce, concerns were expressed over the immorality of the age. Although this meeting has historically taken on huge significance, Stott argues that a venture as ambitious, expensive and time-consuming as the Mendip schools could not have owed its existence to a single incident.[98] Nevertheless, More, who had moved into a cottage she had had built three years earlier in Somerset in order to find 'quiet and leisure', quickly responded to Wilberforce's plea 'to do something for Cheddar'. Before he left, Hannah and her sisters had drafted a plan for the moral reformation of the neighbourhood by the establishment of schools for the poor.[99] The Mores knew of Raikes's work in Gloucester; and, with Wilberforce supplying the greater part of the required funds, Hannah More set about organising the work in the Mendips in a manner that Wilberforce pronounced as 'truly magnificent'.[100]

More's scheme was on a far larger scale than similar efforts by her friend, Sarah Trimmer, at Brentford. The ambitious plan proposed by the sisters was to mark out a ten-mile circuit in which to establish schools, incorporating both agricultural and industrial areas. The problem of securing adequate facilities for school buildings and the difficulties in finding teachers for the schools were formidable. In seeking the co-operation of parents, the More sisters came in direct contact with the poor in their homes, causing Hannah to write 'I believe I see more misery in a week than some people believe exists in the whole world'. Just as Wesley had done, More quickly realised that she needed not only to educate children, but adults: 'We were struck', she recorded in 1791 'with an idea of at least attempting to teach the parents of these children, by reading a chapter, and a sermon to them on Sunday evenings, to sing a psalm and read a prayer'.[101]

In recognising that poverty often led families to go hungry, and in order to encourage attendance at their schools during the summer, the children were given treats, including fruit, gingerbread or gooseberry tarts.[102] The More sisters organised school feasts for children and their parents.[103] Modelled on feasts given by Raikes at Painswick, this annual event was attended by visiting gentry in an attempt, Stott argues, both to promote solidarity between classes and neighbours, and to help people identify with the parish Church.[104] More wrote:

> On May-day all the school attend her church, each in a gown of their own earning, and a cap and white apron of her giving. After church there was an examination made into the learning and behaviour of the schools; those who were most perfect in their chapters and brought the best character for industry, humility, and sobriety, received a Bible or some other good book.[105]

Like Wesley, More challenged the new prevalence towards treating children as if they were innocent, arguing that the primary purpose of education was to rectify their corrupt nature and evil disposition. Her *Historical Questions from the Bible, with Answers Written for the Mendip Schools,* taught children that they were 'all born in sin, and should be lost for ever, if Jesus Christ, the Son of God, had not died to redeem us from the bad effects of the transgressions of our first parents'.[106] Nevertheless, More tried to practise kindness, and outlaw physical punishment in her Mendip schools.[107] The grading of learning in order of difficulty, attempts to vary routine and the use of rewards were all typical of the methods used in Sunday schools, and More also sought to avoid over-tiring the children, and to teach through question and answer rather than rote learning.[108] Her teaching methods were intended to encourage children by associating learning with pleasure rather than pain.[109] The teachers in her schools were not to be 'merely moral', but were to possess vital religion; and be capable of conveying it to others. 'Unless the Bible is laid open to the understanding', she declared, 'children may read from Genesis to the Revelation, without any other improvement than barely learning how to pronounce words'.[110]

Like Wesley, the More sisters quickly discovered that men and women with enough education to teach children to read, and with the ability to keep order among large numbers of undisciplined children were not easy to find. They also needed their teachers to be able to withstand interference and criticism from local opponents of the schools.[111] When suitable recruits could not be found, the More sisters sought out the most educated person in the area; who they proceeded to instruct in how they should teach.[112] To assist teachers in their task of imparting religion to their pupils, More drew up the *Mendip School Questions and Catechism*. In a letter to William Wilberforce in 1801, Hannah More set out her Sunday school *modus operandi*:

> In the morning I open school with one of the Sunday school prayers... I have a Bible Class – Testament Class – Psalter Class. Those who cannot read at all are questioned out of the first little *Question Book for the Mendip Schools*... Those who attend four Sundays without intermission, and come in time for Morning Prayer [at Church] receive a penny every fourth Sunday, but if they fail once, the other three Sundays go for nothing. They must begin again. Once in every six weeks I give a little gingerbread. Once a year I distribute little books according to merit – those who deserve most get a Bible, a second rate merit gets a Prayer Book, the rest, Cheap Repository Tracts.[113]

More promoted the effectiveness of Sunday schools through a series of anecdotal tracts. Her *Cheap Repository Tracts* offered spiritual and moral guidance for unsophisticated readers, with recognisable working class characters illustrated in a fictional framework.[114] Many women writers, including More, employed the implicit authority of the maternal educative role in their writing.[115] More's tracts, taken direct from everyday circumstances of people for whom they were intended, left the reader in no doubt that the hardship of this world would be compensated for in the next, and that it paid to be good.[116] *The Sunday School*, printed in 1796 provided an account of a Sunday school run by More, in the guise of 'Mrs Jones'. It declared:

> It is something gained to rescue children from idling the Sabbath away in the fields or the streets. It is no small thing to keep them from those tricks to which a day of leisure tempts an idle and the ignorant. It is something for them to be taught to read; and it is much to be taught to read the Bible, and much indeed to be carried regularly to church.[117]

Confident that she could raise the money to open the school, 'Mrs Jones' sought someone of 'good sense, activity and piety' to direct it. Mrs Betty Crew was appointed as teacher not only for her promotion of Christian knowledge and piety, but because she demonstrated compassion for the poor and a practical sense of how to help them clothe and feed their families. Mrs Jones visited mothers to invite them to send their children to the school, warning them that if their children did not attend regularly they would: 'have to answer for it at the Day of Judgment'.[118] Mothers were advised to go home and set about providing their children with decent apparel for school; and parents were told that younger children would only be taken if older children were also sent.[119]

The impact of Sunday schools on working class families was illustrated in two tracts which followed *The Sunday School*, in which More recounted *The History of Hester Wilmot*. The anecdotal accounts of the female protagonist served as a salutary tale for those who doubted the effectiveness, and usefulness, of Sunday schools. Born of 'ungodly parents', the eldest of five children, Hester was by the age of fourteen unable to 'tell a letter, nor had she ever been taught to bow her knee at him who made her'. Hester's father, the tract claimed, had, on account of his drinking, lost his affection for his family through 'self-indulgence'. Hester's mother saw 'no good in learning', and claimed that religion 'made folks proud, lazy, and dirty'. Nevertheless, Mrs Jones was able to convince her parents that Hester should attend the Sunday school. Betty Crew not only instructed her in how to spell and read, but loaned Hester books. She quickly learned the catechism and gained an understanding of the Christian life.[120] In part II of the *History of Hester Wilmot*, Hester was portrayed as a role model for daughters, having maintained her humility and obedience to her parents in difficult circumstances.[121] Hester not only excelled in school; she went on to teach both her parents how to pray and her father how to read.[122]

Thus, importantly for Evangelicals like More, her tract advanced the notion of Sunday school as beneficial not only for pauper children, but as a means by which the values learned there could be passed on to parents. Wesley similarly acknowledged that children could be a vehicle through which parents might come to faith. Writing in his *Journal* on 8 June 1784 he suggested: 'Is not this a new thing in the earth? God begins His work in children. Thus the flame spreads to those of riper years, till at length they all know Him'.[123]

More's plan was to make her schools the centre of village life. Before the end of the century, she had established a dozen schools, some day working schools, some Sunday schools and several women's benefit clubs in association with them. In Cheddar, a successful school of industry operated alongside a Sunday school, which opened in 1791 with 100 children and had doubled four years later.[124] Indeed, three of the schools, at Cheddar, Shipham and Nailsea, survived More's death, finally to be absorbed into the state system in the twentieth century.[125]

Sunday schools in a post-revolutionary age

By the late summer of 1789 the British newspapers were giving extensive coverage to what was already being called the French Revolution. Although initially the papers welcomed the fall of the Bastille as symbolic of the triumph of freedom over tyranny,[126] by November 1790 Edmund Burke was warning in *Reflections on Revolution in France* that the radicalism of the French Revolution represented a fundamental assault on Christian civilisation.[127] Most members of the Church hierarchy responded slowly and cautiously to the Revolution.[128] Bishop Samuel Horsley, however, regarded French republicanism as catastrophic, declaring in his *Rochester Charge* of 1800: '… they openly renounce the first principles of morality… to wean men from Christianity they have introduced something like the old pagan idolatry… '.[129]

Controversy was ignited by Thomas Paine's *Rights of Man*, published in 1791, which attacked Burke's traditionalist arguments of the ancient authorities ingrained in Church and State, and declared that the British constitution was founded on the injustice and irrationality of inherited privilege.[130] Paine described religion as a trade, extracting money 'even from the pockets of the poor, instead of contributing to their relief'.[131] Paine's publication, and his call for a republic in Britain, shook the political establishment to its core, and within a week of the publication of part II, Paine's *Rights of Man* was condemned as a seditious libel.[132] Although the ramifications were far-reaching, of significance here was an apparent hardening of attitudes towards the poor. Although not published until after John Wesley's death, Horsley's *Rochester Charge* of 1800 provides a useful insight into the anxieties of the Established Church, and the implications this had for the education of children of the poor in the closing decades of the eighteenth century.

Bishop Horsley was, and indeed remained, a firm advocate of education, particularly religious education. He defended charity and Sunday schools, but in his *Rochester Charge* made a clear distinction between those schools which he considered beneficial as long as they were in 'proper hands', and those which, in 'improper hands' were 'very pernicious'. Horsley advised his fellow Churchmen that they 'should by all means in your power, promote the establishment of Sunday-schools in your respective parishes, and take the trouble to superintend the management of them'.[133] Mather suggests that 'superintendence' meant leaving nothing to the discretion of a Master or Mistress, allowing no books to be introduced which they had not previously vetted and confining the selection of reading material to expositions of the Church catechism, Psalters, prayer-books, Testaments and Bibles, using the SPCK lists as a guide.[134]

Although Mather argues that serious political engagement is hard to find in Sunday schools during this period, Churchmen, and particularly High Churchmen, were fearful of itinerant Evangelism 'which had spread as a wave through the English villages in 1797–8'.[135] In 1800 a report was published based on statistics gathered in seventy nine of the more than twelve hundred parishes in Lincoln, the largest diocese in Britain, which concluded that family religion had largely disintegrated. Although Dissenters were not considered a problem, Methodists were singled out for particular condemnation.[136] The *Report of the Clergy of a District in the Diocese of Lincoln*, described their itinerant preachers as:

> A wandering tribe of fanatical teachers, mostly taken from the lowest and most illiterate classes of society; among whom are to be found raving

enthusiasts, pretending to divine impulses of various and extra-ordinary kinds, practising exorcisms, and many other sorts of impostures and delusions, and obtaining thereby an unlimited sway over the minds of the ignorant multitude.[137]

The remedy, the report claimed, was the restoration of Church and family religion guided by devoted clergy who were themselves to be perfect Christian examples; 'avoiding levity, unbecoming dress and common discourse'.[138]

Speaking out against non-Anglican institutions, among them the non-denominational Sunday schools, Horsley claimed 'A circumstance which gives much ground for suspicion that sedition and atheism are the real objects of these institutions... the teachers... abuse the Established clergy, neglect their flock, are cold in their preaching and destitute of Spirit'.[139] Referring to teachers as the 'illiterate peasant or mechanic', Horsley declared: 'It is very remarkable that these new congregations of non-descripts have been mostly formed, since the Jacobins have laid under the restraint of two salutary statutes, commonly known by the names of the Seditious [meetings] and the Treason Bill'.[140] While Methodist itinerant preachers came in for particular criticism for their 'sway over the minds of the ignorant multitude', Hannah More's schools in the Mendips provided Anglicans with an example of how, by Horsley's definition, a 'proper' Sunday school was to operate.

Conclusion

Although John Wesley died in 1791, he witnessed the beginnings of the Sunday school movement at a time when it was a product of the religious and philanthropic sentiment of the day. In the closing decades of the eighteenth century Sunday charity schools had come into prominence as a means by which children of the poor might be inculcated in Christian values, and the morally beneficial principles of industriousness and submission to authority. Sunday schools were intended for both boys and girls; many of whom were employed all week, so were not receiving an education. Although the early Sunday schools were non-denominational, they reignited the tradition of popular education associated with the Church. At the same time as teaching children to read, enabling them to read the Bible, they also acted as a way that Christian values learned might be passed on to parents.

Although Sunday schools brought families into contact with the Church, critics argued that they undermined family religion by removing children on the one day when they might otherwise be together. Instruction at Sunday schools was limited and basic; it was not intended to give children aspirations above their station or diminish class distinctions. Nevertheless, the Sunday school movement was to have far-reaching consequences for the religious and social life of the poor, as rural schools run by the parish priest were replaced by larger concerns. Not only were more children receiving an education, but they were increasingly taught by working class laymen and women.

Wesley was not alone among Evangelicals in believing that a stable home with parents eager and competent to instruct their children was the ideal; and that the salvation of the child's soul was the primary purpose of such education. Despite his concerns over their non-denominational approach and the moral contamination from mixing children, Wesley recognised that there was a case for opening Sunday schools. Although not directly involved himself, he published articles in support of Raikes in *The Arminian Magazine* and promoted Sunday schools among Methodist Societies. The idea of Sunday schools was seized upon by Methodists in many places, including at Wesley's preaching houses in London and Newcastle. Here, Sunday schools appear to have flourished where day schools had long-since reduced in size, or closed altogether. In Madeley, John and Mary Fletcher welcomed children into their Sunday schools where they were taught morality and piety, alongside learning how to read and write.

Among authoritative female educators in the late eighteenth century were Sarah Trimmer and Hannah More. Trimmer was a prolific writer and education reformer who championed schools of industry and Sunday schools. The education these schools provided for children of the poor was intentionally basic, limited to reading, and in conformity to the Anglican Church. Hannah More's concern was for the spiritual and moral welfare of the poor, not their state of poverty. While not her primary purpose, a by-product of her desire to train women of the labouring classes to teach in Sunday schools gave them an opportunity for social mobility. Although she shared many of Wesley's values, her schools in the Mendips were intended to instruct children in how to be good members of society, which in More's view only necessitated teaching them to read. Through her series of *Cheap Repository Tracts*, More offered spiritual and moral guidance to unsophisticated readers; and in her tales of Hester Wilmot, More not only offered girls a female role model, but illustrated the benefits of Sunday school as a means of reaching parents as well as children.

Events in revolutionary France in 1789 harden thinking towards the poor, and the level of education deemed appropriate to their needs. Amid growing suspicion of the work of non-Anglicans, pressure intensified to ensure that instruction in Sunday schools was limited, and confined to practices and values espoused by the Established Church. While Anglican Sunday schools like those established by Hannah More were considered appropriate, growing fears over Methodists and their 'sway over the minds of the ignorant multitude' saw the Established Church close ranks against 'the wandering tribe of fanatical teachers' who, they claimed, taught atheism and sedition.

Notes

1 Davis (2014) *Written Maternal Authority and Eighteenth-Century Education in Britain* p. 1–5
2 Jones (1964) *The Charity School Movement* p. 142–3
3 Jacob (2007) *The Clerical Profession in the Long Eighteenth Century* p. 18

4   cited in Soloway (1969) *Prelates and People* p. 26
5   Peters, Michael (2008) *Robert Raikes* Enumclaw: Pleasant Word p. 23
6   cited in Briggs (1981) 'Innovation and Adaption' p. 18
7   Jesse, William (1785) *The Importance of Education* Kidderminster: N. Rollason p. 19
8   Raikes, Robert (1785) 'An Account of the Sunday-Charity Schools, Lately Begun in Various Parts of England' published in *The Arminian Magazine* p. 41
9   *The Gentleman's Magazine* (1784) London: John Nichols p. 411
10 Raikes (1785) 'An Account of the Sunday-Charity Schools' p. 41
11 Ibid. p. 42
    Sophie Cooke was one of the first teachers who, along with Raikes, 'conducted the first company of Sunday scholars to church' and was 'exposed to comments and laughter of the populace, as they passed along with their ragged procession'. Mathews (1949) *Methodism and the Education of the People* p. 37
12 Richard Townley (1726–1802) was the son of a Rochdale cloth merchant and a regular correspondent to the Manchester papers and *The Gentleman's Magazine*
13 Laqueur (1976) *Religion and Respectability* p. 25
14 Raikes, Robert (1787) Letter to the 'Society Established in London for the Support and Encouragement of Sunday Schools' in *The Gentleman's Magazine* London: John Nichols p. 73
15 Ferguson, John (1981) 'Robert Raikes's First Sunday School' in Ferguson, John (ed.) *Christianity, Society and Education* London: SPCK p. 2
16 Raikes (1785) 'An Account of the Sunday-Charity Schools' p. 41–2
17 Peters (2008) *Robert Raikes* p. 30
18 Raikes (1785) 'An Account of the Sunday-Charity Schools' p. 43
19 Andrew (1989) *Philanthropy and Police* p. 171
20 Hanway, Jonas (1786) *A Comprehensive View of Sunday Schools* London: Dodsley and Sewel p. vii
21 'The Plan of a Society…' stated 'persons of all denominations of the protestant faith will be induced to unite'. First Circular Letter of the Sunday School Society, 1784: cited in Jones (1964) *The Charity School Movement* p. 152
22 Turner, William (1793) *Sermons on Various Subjects* London: Joseph Johnson p. 268
    Turner was an associate of Joseph Priestley and ran a school in Cheshire during the 1740s and 1750s.
23 Jones (1964) *The Charity School Movement* p. 143–8
24 Burton (2008) *Spiritual Literacy in John Wesley's Methodism* p. 269
25 Pitt, William Morton (1789) *A Plan for the Extension and Regulation of Sunday Schools* London: The Sunday School Society p. 5
26 Jones (1964) *The Charity School Movement* p. 152
27 Horsley is described by Mather as the ablest bishop on the bench in the late eighteenth century and a firm advocate of education. Mather (1992) *High Church Prophet* p. 280–3
28 Booth, Frank (1981) 'Robert Raikes' in Ferguson *Christianity, Society and Education* p. 31
29 Sangster (1963) *Pity My Simplicity* p. 114
30 Raikes (1787) Letter to the 'Society Established in London' p. 73
31 Ferguson (1981) 'Robert Raikes's First Sunday School' p. 3
32 Elliott-Binns (1953) *The Early Evangelicals* p. 379
33 Raikes (1787) Letter to the 'Society Established in London' p. 74
34 *The Gentleman's Magazine* (1784) p. 411
35 Raikes (1785) 'An Account of the Sunday-Charity Schools' p. 42
36 *The Gloucester Journal of 12 January 1789* Gloucester: R. Raikes

37 In 1787 Raikes claimed that a quarter of a million children had attended Sunday Schools. While Jones suggests that the number cannot be substantiated, the rapid progress of the movement was attested by the reports of the Sunday School Society. There were 201 affiliated schools with 10,232 children returned in 1787, and 1,086 schools with 69,000 pupils in 1797. cited in Jones (1964) *The Charity School Movement* p. 153
38 Laqueur (1976) *Religion and Respectability* p. 66–7
39 Jacob (2007) *The Clerical Profession in the Long Eighteenth Century* p. 247
40 Hanway, Jonas (1786) A Comprehensive View of Sunday Schools p. iii, vi; Hanway, Jonas (1767) *Letters on the Importance of the Rising Generation* London: A Millar and T. Cadell; et al. p. 38
41 Laqueur (1976) *Religion and Respectability* p. 63–125
42 Baker (1984) *BCE* vol. 23 p. 323
43 Ball, Hannah (1880) *Memorials of Miss Hannah Ball* London: Wesleyan Conference Office p. vii–viii
44 Ibid. p. 67
45 Morrow, Thomas M. (1967) *Early Methodist Women* London: Epworth Press p. 38–9
46 Raikes (1785) 'An Account of the Sunday-Charity Schools' p. 43
47 Ball (1880) *Memorials of Miss Hannah Ball* p. 57, 100
48 Elliott, Shirley (1981) 'Raikes and Reform' in Ferguson *Christianity, Society and Education* p. 35
49 Burton (2008) *Spiritual Literacy in John Wesley's Methodism* p. 22
50 Baker (1984) *BCE* vol. 23 p. 323
51 Raikes (1785) 'An Account of the Sunday-Charity Schools' p. 41–3
52 Baker (1984) *BCE* vol. 23 p. 390
53 Ibid. vol. 24 p. 46
54 Ibid. vol. 24 p. 77
55 Wesley, John (1788a) 'An Account of a Sunday School' in *The Arminian Magazine* p. 489–90
56 Stevenson (1872) *City Road Chapel* p. 153–4
57 Telford (1931) *The Letters of the Rev. John Wesley* vol. 8 p. 207–8
58 Stamp, William Wood (1863) *The Orphan-house of Wesley* London: John Mason p. 148–9
59 Streiff (2001) *Reluctant Saint?* p. 296
60 Bowmer, John C. (ed.) (1963–4) *Proceedings of the Wesley Historical Society* Leicester: Alfred A. Taberer p. 153–4
61 Bayley, Cornelius (attributed to 1790) *An Address to the Public on Sunday Schools* Manchester: publisher unknown p. 1
62 Darby, Abiah (1784) Letter to John Fletcher, 22 Jun. 1784, 'Fletcher-Tooth Papers' ref. GB 135MAM/FL/2/7/1
63 Fletcher, John (23/8) 'Proposals Towards the Sunday Schools', 'Fletcher-Tooth Papers' ref. Box 23, folder 8 p. 15
64 Wilson (2010) 'Church and Chapel' p. 218–21
65 Ibid. p. 220
66 cited in Burton (2008) *Spiritual Literacy in John Wesley's Methodism* p. 273
67 Wilson (2010) 'Church and Chapel' p. 219
68 Fletcher, John (17/9) 'A Moral and Evangelical Catechism for the Use of Sunday Schools', 'Fletcher-Tooth Papers' ref. Box 17, folder 9
69 Fletcher, John (43/3/8) 'School Questions' for the Use of Sunday schools, 'Fletcher-Tooth Papers' ref. Box 43, folder 3, item 8
70 Wilson (2010) 'Church and Chapel' p. 215
71 Andrews (2015) 'Women of the Seventeenth and Eighteenth-century High Church Tradition' p. 49–64

72　Sarah Trimmer had twelve children, nine of whom survived to maturity. Gill (1994) *Women and the Church of England* p. 49
73　Oeconomy, meaning 'the management of the household'. Hilton (2007) *Women and the Shaping of the Nation's Young* p. 146
74　Ibid. p. 147
75　Trimmer, Sarah (1787) *The Economy of Charity* London: T. Bensley; for T. Longman; et al. p. 200
76　Jones (1964) *The Charity School Movement* p. 156
77　Trimmer (1792) *Reflections upon the Education of Children in Charity Schools* p. 13
78　Ibid. p. 23–4, 14
79　Trimmer (1787) *The Economy of Charity* p. 69–70
80　Kamm (1965) *Hope Deferred* p. 90
81　Payne (2006) 'London's Charity School Children' p. 391
82　Bernard, Thomas (1799) *Account of the Foundling Hospital* London: Thomas Jones p. 66–7
83　Andrews (2015) 'Women of the Seventeenth and Eighteenth-century High Church Tradition' p. 61
84　Trimmer (1792) *Reflections upon the Education of Children in Charity Schools* p. 11
　　In 1787 Trimmer published *The Servant's Friend: An Exemplary Tale, Designed to Enforce the Religious Instructions Given at Sunday and other Charity Schools*
85　Laqueur (1976) *Religion and Respectability* p. 127
86　Trimmer (1787) *The Economy of Charity* p. 37
87　Mathews (1949) *Methodism and the Education of the People* p. 38
88　Tomkins, Stephen (2010) *The Clapham Sect* Oxford: Lion Hudson p. 79
89　Jones, M. G. (1968) *Hannah More* New York: Greenwood Press p. 153
90　Wesley, John (1788c) 'An Extract from a Poem on Slavery by Hannah More' in *The Arminian Magazine* p. 558–60, 612–16
91　Telford (1931) *The Letters of the Rev. John Wesley* vol. 8 p. 230
92　Jones (1968) *Hannah More* p. 79
93　Despite distancing herself from Methodism itself, it was in Hannah More's house that Charles Wesley first met William Wilberforce. Mathews (1949) *Methodism and the Education of the People* p. 38
94　Jones (1968) *Hannah More* p. 97–152
　　More claimed she 'knew no way of teaching morals but by infusing principles of Christianity, nor of teaching Christianity without a thorough knowledge of scripture'. cited in Jones (1968) *Hannah More* p. 152
95　cited in Ibid. p. 159
96　Stott, Anne (2009) 'Evangelicalism and Enlightenment' in Hilton *Educating the Child in Enlightenment Britain* p. 55
97　Hannah More letter to John Bowdler the Younger. cited in Jones (1968) *Hannah More* p. 152
98　Stott (2003) *Hannah More* p. 105
99　Hannah More had four sisters: Mary, Elizabeth (Betty), Sarah (Sally) and Martha (Patty). They were, in 1789, living in Bristol, but moved to Bath in 1790. Jones (1968) *Hannah More* p. 151–2
100　cited in Ibid. p. 92
　　Sympathetic to Evangelism, the Bishop of Bath & Wells, Charles Moss, granted More a license to go up to twenty eight miles to instruct the poor; and supported her when a local clergyman, Thomas Bere, prosecuted her for doing so. Gibson, William (1986) 'Somerset Evangelical Clergy' in *The Proceedings of the Somerset Archaeological and Natural History Society* p. 135–40
101　Jones (1968) *Hannah More* p. 153–9, 181
102　Stott (2003) *Hannah More* p. 115

170 Educating pauper children after 1780

103 The annual feast days began in 1791 when 517 children and 300 elders picnicked together. Jones (1968) *Hannah More* p. 157
104 Stott (2003) *Hannah More* p. 114, 165
105 More, Hannah (1796c) *The History of Hester Wilmot; or, the New Gown Part II* London: Cheap Repository for Moral and Religious Tracts p. 5
106 More, Hannah (1798) *Historical Questions from the Bible* Bath: S. Hazard p. 2
107 Hilton (2009) *Educating the Child in Enlightenment Britain* p. 12
108 Stott (2009) 'Evangelicalism and Enlightenment' p. 53
109 Hilton (2009) *Educating the Child in Enlightenment Britain* p. 12
110 More, Hannah, (1796b) *The History of Hester Wilmot* London: Cheap Repository for Moral and Religious Tracts p. 10
111 Jones (1968) *Hannah More* p. 159
112 At Shipham, near Cheddar, a young dairymaid was recruited and 'under instruction in our manner of teaching' the More sisters enabled her to open and maintain a successful school for the children in the area. Ibid. p. 164
113 cited in Ibid. p. 160
114 Neuburg (1971) *Popular Education in 18th Century England* p. 128
   The tracts were intended as safe and cheap alternatives to the 'dangerous' literature of the 'school of Paine'. Soloway (1969) *Prelates and People* p. 57
115 Davis (2014) *Written Maternal Authority* p. 3
116 Jones (1968) *Hannah More* p. 138–48
117 More, Hannah (1796a) *The Sunday School* London: Cheap Repository for Moral and Religious Tracts p. 1–16
118 Ibid. p. 3–9
119 Mrs Jones stated: 'I have not set up a nursery but a school… it ought to be a rule in all schools not to take the troublesome young children unless the mother will try to spare the elder ones, who are capable of learning'. More, Hannah (1796b) *The History of Hester Wilmot* p. 7
120 Ibid. p. 2–10
121 Having saved diligently for a year to buy a gown for the May-day feast, Hester's father gambled the money away. Hester, who attended the feast in an old dress, declared 'God looks not at the gown, but at the heart'. Mrs Jones, who stated 'meekness and an humble spirit is of more value in the sight of God and good men than the gayest cotton gown, or the brightest pink ribbon in the parish' awarded Hester the Bible not only for her excellence at school but for displaying Christian understanding. More (1796c) *The History of Hester Wilmot; or, the New Gown Part II* p. 7–11
122 Ibid. p. 13–16
123 Baker (1984) *BCE* vol. 23 p. 315
124 Jones (1968) *Hannah More* p. 152, 161
125 Stott (2009) 'Evangelicalism and Enlightenment' p. 41
126 Gibson points out that one of the subjects for the Latin prize at Cambridge in 1790 was whether the French Revolution might prove 'advantageous' to Britain. Gibson, William (1994) *Church, State and Society, 1760–1850* Basingstoke: MacMillan p. 48
127 Stott (2003) *Hannah More* p. 126–30
128 Soloway (1969) *Prelates and People* p. 29–31
129 Mather (1992) *High Church Prophet* p. 267
130 Paine stated 'The idea of hereditary legislation is as inconsistent as that of an hereditary mathematician, or an hereditary wise man, and as ridiculous as an hereditary poet laureate'. Paine, Thomas (1791) *Rights of Man* p. 83 cited in Stott (2003) *Hannah More* p. 132
131 Paine, Thomas (1859) 'Letter to Camille Jordan 1797' in *The Theological Works of Thomas Paine* p. 204 cited in Soloway (1969) *Prelates and People* p. 57

132 Stott (2003) *Hannah More* p. 136–7
133 cited in Mather (1992) *High Church Prophet* p. 280–3
134 Ibid. p. 283
135 Ibid. p. 282
136 Soloway (1969) *Prelates and People* p. 51
137 cited in Mather (1992) *High Church Prophet* p. 282
138 Soloway (1969) *Prelates and People* p. 52
139 cited in Mather (1992) *High Church Prophet* p. 282
140 Ibid. p. 281–2

Conclusion

The eighteenth century marked a period of considerable change in how children were raised and educated. While questions of gender, class and religious affiliation defined and contained educational practice, changing concepts of childhood influenced the way children were regarded, and impacted upon parental decisions regarding the upbringing of their offspring. John Wesley lived in an age when the political, religious and ideological backdrop to his work was neither static nor consistent. Despite this, the evidence supports Porter's claims that in the educational free market of the eighteenth century 'the instruction children got, determined by parental choice and pocket, tended to reinforce existing social, cultural, and gender distinctions, rather than break them down and make new ones'.[1] Wesley's educational thinking and practice did little to redress this.

Nevertheless, from the extensive catalogue of literature left by Wesley it is evident that he maintained an interest in how children were to be raised and educated through his life. His legacy was not insignificant. Although his education practice was not unique, it is hard to justify Plumb's claim that Methodism 'was at its worst in its attitude to education'.[2] Indeed, education and literacy, combined with Wesley's Arminian doctrine of self-advancement, often led to upward social mobility and gave the adult poor within Methodist Societies opportunities to become involved, either within the Society or as preachers and teachers of the young. Nor does the evidence support E. P. Thompson's claim that 'Methodism was a strongly anti-intellectual influence'.[3] Although Wesley encouraged learning which conformed to Christian values of virtue, morality and piety, by exposing followers to the practice of frequent reading, Methodism ignited an urge for self-improvement, which was supported through association with preachers and fellow Methodists. In spite of that, it is clear that Wesley's educational practice was more strongly Evangelical than intellectual, more pious than academic.

That Wesley's educational programme was more Evangelical than academic is hardly surprising; he was a prominent figure at the heart of the spiritual revival in England in the eighteenth century. Wesley frequently claimed that he would 'live and die a member of the Church of England'.[4] The Church was not complacent in its attitude towards education. Anglican charity schools provided the poor with an opportunity to have their children educated. While public schools and universities have frequently been portrayed as anarchic and brutal, the education they provide did not fail all, or even a majority of students. Religious instruction formed an important part of what was taught in these institutions. Nevertheless, while not all Evangelicals were Anglican, what united them was a desire to reinvigorate Christianity, and one way of doing that was through promoting a more pious education for the young.

Evangelicals were concerned with reforming the individual; for some this required nothing more than learning the 'doctrines of the Gospel'.[5] Wesley, on the other hand, regarded scholarship as a Christian virtue, and championed education as an aid to piety. His Arminian theology argued that salvation through faith was available to all; hence education should be available to all. He argued that the sole end of life, and consequently of education, was to prepare for eternity; 'for this and no other purpose is our life either given or continued', he stated.[6] Yet salvation through faith required not only a change of 'mind', but a change of 'heart'; therefore, education represented just one aspect of what Wesley considered necessary for an individual to live a Christian life of holiness.

Wesley's early upbringing at Epworth was in an atmosphere of piety and learning. His experience of public school and university, on the other hand, convinced him that these institutions, although offering sound academic learning, neither nurtured their students in a way that protected their virtue, or enhanced their piety. His condemnation of public schools was based not on their academic prowess, but on their failure to protect pupils from 'all kinds of vice'.[7] His condemnation of Oxford University was not of the institution itself, but the failure of those within it to conduct themselves in accordance with its Statutes.[8] Acknowledging the eminent learning of the University, Wesley spoke out against the manner in which this learning was delivered. In 1768, he declared that his newly instigated academical course at Kingswood 'would advance the students more in three years than the generality of students at Oxford or Cambridge do in seven'. He claimed this not on the grounds of high academic achievement, but because Kingswood's educational programme was grounded on 'the truth which God has revealed to man'.[9]

Wesley's academical course at Kingswood was to be taught in an atmosphere of piety and virtue. It offered students an intellectual alternative to Oxford, and at the same time gave Wesley an opportunity to expand the school into a training college for his preachers. The theological divisions within the early Methodist movement, brought to a head over the 'Minutes Controversy' of 1770, not only polarised Arminian and Calvinist supporters, but hampered the ambitious claims that both Wesley and Lady Huntingdon had made for their colleges. While purporting to offer academic advancement, it is clear that, because of the urgent need to fill preaching appointments, neither Wesley nor the Countess kept their students at Kingswood or Trevecka long enough to achieve the academic results they had hoped for.

It has frequently been argued that Susanna Wesley's education letter of 24 July 1732 was the model on which John Wesley based his thinking on how children should be raised and educated. Building on the work of Elizabeth Lynch, chapter two demonstrated that Susanna Wesley was not only an early reader of Locke, but her education practices were, in no small way influenced by him. Although she upheld Puritan values of industry, sobriety, frugality and temperance, her practices have been shown to be less austere than many commentators have hitherto suggested. Indeed, Susanna Wesley not only acknowledged the individuality of her children, but held them in affection and respect.[10] But, while new concepts of childhood were increasingly moving towards a more affectionate relationship with children, John Wesley saw no place for a 'softening' in the relationship between parents and their offspring.[11]

Wesley's Christian upbringing undoubtedly influenced his belief in the importance of family in the early religious nurture of children. Piety learned with and by example of parents from an early age was a frequent theme of his writing on children. His early years in a predominantly female household may well have influenced his later thinking on the education of young women. Despite his sisters being lively and literate, public school and university education was only available to young men, and then only those in the higher echelons of society. Wesley's condemnation of these institutions did not arise from their class or gender bias, but a belief that they were failing to educate pupils for 'the world to come'. Referring to large public schools as 'nurseries of all manner of wickedness', he told parents that sending their sons to them was little better than sending them to the devil.[12]

Although he was not prepared to compromise his strongly held Christian principles, Wesley was comfortable to build upon philosophies and practices that in no small measure matched his own firmly held views. While there are discernible Puritan influences, there is much in Wesley's educational thinking that echoed Locke's *Some Thoughts Concerning Education*. His association with the German Pietists, most notably the heart religion of the Moravians, was significant not only to his understanding of the importance of introspection and emotional experience, but in helping to broaden his educational philosophy. Although suspicious of Dissent, Wesley recognised the abilities of Philip Doddridge and sought his advice when drawing up a catalogue of books for Kingswood School. Nevertheless, Wesley's close scrutiny of texts and heavy editing ensured that those books not written by him had any reference to Calvinist theology omitted. While Doddridge argued that all knowledge was interrelated, Wesley limited his student's theological 'free enquiry' to those works that accorded with his Arminian thinking.

In assessing Wesley's significance in the field of education, scholars have most often associated his work with Kingswood boarding school, primarily because of the significance he himself placed on it. But, as this book has shown, his interest extended well beyond the confines of its walls. Although he had great sympathy for the poor, Wesley's motivation for opening schools for their children was based on a desire to save their souls, rather than an attempt to ameliorate their condition. Indeed, he promoted passive obedience among the poor, telling them they should await the time when God would 'arise and maintain his own cause'.[13] Claiming that poor children who were not receiving an education were 'like a wild ass's colt', he desired not only to teach them to read and write, but to cast accounts. While these skills elevated them above their uneducated peers, Christian values of obedience and submission to authority ensured that they had no aspirations above their station.[14]

Invited by George Whitefield to build a school at Kingswood, Wesley's schools for sons and daughters of the 'barbarous and savage' colliers were not the 'little schools' that Whitefield had envisaged.[15] Instead, in a pattern he repeated elsewhere, Wesley's schools for children of the poor were incorporated into his preaching houses. By doing so, Wesley and his preachers were not only able to instruct children, but to evangelise their parents. As chapter four demonstrated, although Wesley's enthusiasm for preaching house schools was thrown into question by his letter to Richard Terry, the evidence suggests that their decline was likely to have resulted for several reasons.[16] Among the most likely causes were financial pressures, and the need for 'school rooms' to become multi-functional. Despite this, that preachers were advised by Wesley to bring together ten children in a society for instruction twice a week suggests that offspring from Methodist homes continued to receive religious instruction in his preaching houses.[17]

Wesley spoke of his boarding school at Kingswood as a 'Christian model'. He looked upon staff and pupils as a Christian family. He believed that pupils there would flourish in an atmosphere of piety and learning. In constantly employing Masters for their piety rather than their academic credentials, Wesley, by his own admission, frequently encountered problems at the school.[18] He appears to have assumed that every child would behave well, and be as serious and studious as he had been; but the evidence suggests that this was far from the case. He also appears to have shown little understanding of the effect that his strict regime had on adolescent boys. The lack of opportunity for play was not intended to make pupils miserable, but, as demonstrated in chapter three, Wesley underestimated the dulling effect that a monotonous routine based on self-denial and introspection had on the juvenile mind and body.

Despite constantly elevating piety over academic achievement, Wesley had a broad curriculum of study at Kingswood, and this became more so when he extended the school to include his 'academical course'.[19] His claim that the academical course would advance the students 'more in three years than the generality of students at Oxford or Cambridge do in seven', was innovative, but ultimately impractical.[20] With too few students, and a lack of Masters able to teach at the required level, and at the same time uphold the strict regime that Wesley demanded, his claim was never fully tested. Nor is it possible to quantify the benefits gained by Wesley's preachers from instruction received at Kingswood. Although Adam Clarke's experience, discussed in chapter six, may not be representative, it is likely that any period of study at the school would have been short, curtained by the shortage of preachers to fulfil Wesley's appointments.

During the final decades of Wesley's life, Kingswood School witnessed an at times uncomfortable transition as sons of wealthy Methodist supporters were joined first by Wesley's 'academical' students and, second, by sons of his itinerant preachers. His decision to allow the Methodist Conference to take responsibility for approving rules and appointing trustees and stewards, as well as authorising annual collections and publicising the school to every Methodist Society, ensured that the boarding school did not close on his death. Nevertheless, any comparison between Kingswood and other educational institutions is complicated by the fact that not only was Wesley's boarding school changing to meet the needs of the emerging Methodist movement, but grammar schools and Dissenting academies were also adapting to suit the changing requirements of parents.

Wesley was not directly involved in opening Sunday schools, but in recognising their usefulness, he recommended them among his followers. The idea was seized upon by Methodists in many places, including at Wesley's preaching houses in London and Newcastle. Unpublished material included in chapter seven, held in the 'Fletcher-Tooth papers' at the John Rylands Library, provides a useful insight into the work of John Fletcher at Madeley. The children who attended Fletcher's Sunday schools did not have to be from Methodist homes, and were welcomed not because of their parents' religious affiliation, but on their residency within the parish. Fletcher's 'Proposals towards the Sunday Schools' suggest that along with learning to read and write, poor children were instructed in 'the principles of morality and piety'.[21] They were taught to love God the 'infinitely good and the great author of all good in heaven and earth'.[22] Although Fletcher's teaching methods were designed to encourage rather than intimidate his pupils, he, like many of his fellow Evangelicals, continued to reiterate the doctrine of original sin. Fletcher told his Sunday school children that they were 'sinners' who 'must come to God for pardon.[23]

As this book has demonstrated, although new concepts of childhood became increasingly influential through the eighteenth century, there remained clear gender distinctions in education, particularly where this applied to children from wealthier homes. Although Locke's writings suggested there need be little difference in the way elite parents educated their sons and daughters, boys and girls were not considered educational equals. That public schools and universities were only open to boys does not mean that all female education was trivial and superficial. In homes where reading material was available through a father's library, many daughters, like the Wesley girls, had access to this valuable learning resource.[24] Others were instructed by tutors or governesses at home, or attended small boarding schools. Indeed, the level of education for girls is easy to underestimate since the schools they attended were generally small private establishments that opened and closed as the need arose. The experiences of Emilia and Kezzia Wesley suggest that teaching in small boarding schools was not always a rewarding or valued occupation.

Wesley encouraged female education. In line with the sentiments of the day, he believed that the family home was the most suitable place for girls to be educated, since only there could their virtue be protected, and their piety nurtured. He published 'A Female Course of Study', but this was only suitable for those who had access to the books he recommended, or could afford to purchase them. Although ostensibly a course of academic learning, Wesley advised young ladies that their study should begin and end with divinity; on completion of his prescribed course, Wesley advised them that they would 'have knowledge enough for any reasonable Christian'.[25] While it was rooted in a restrictive religious perspective, Wesley's course of study gave girls an opportunity to expand their intellect, and advance their learning.

Despite favouring home education, Wesley frequently corresponded with Mistresses who ran their own small boarding schools for girls. It would seem from this correspondence that although he encouraged instruction necessary to fit girls 'for the world to come', some parents were eager for their daughters to gain more 'worldly' accomplishments such as dancing and embroidery. To Mary Bishop's comment that she needed to 'mix instruction with delight' at her school, Wesley warned that he 'would recommend very few novels',[26] and on asking whether her girls should be taught dancing, he responded that this led 'young women to numberless evils'.[27] On learning that Frances Owen was teaching her girls 'to make artificial flowers, network, and little pieces of embroidery' Wesley lamented the fact that her school had consequently lost its 'original simplicity'.[28]

Although a few girls were admitted to Wesley's 'model' school at Kingswood they were not taught alongside boys. That Molly Lloyd's experience was far from satisfactory may not be representative, but it is clear that demand for places was short-lived, and Wesley himself recommended other establishments for daughters of his followers. The decision to allow preachers to receive money towards their daughters' education might appear progressive, but it is unclear whether this was a commitment to support the education of girls or a financial incentive for Wesley's itinerant preachers. Girls were admitted to Wesley's day schools for children of the poor, and to Wesleyan Sunday schools. Silas Told's account of the Foundery day school suggests that not only did boys outnumber girls, but while boys were taught reading, writing and arithmetic, to 'fit them for a trade', girls received instruction in reading, writing and needlework.[29]

These gender distinctions were commonplace in eighteenth-century education. While non-elite boys were to be instructed for trade, the education for sons from wealthier homes was designed primarily to fashion boys into 'gentlemen'. Manliness was built on competition and endurance; boys were expected to mature into men of sterling character and effeminacy was to be avoided at all costs.[30] While distancing himself from the 'immoral' public schools of the day, Wesley not only contended that his boarding school at Kingswood distanced pupils from 'all kinds of vice', but that boys were 'at the utmost distance from softness and effeminacy'.[31] It would seem that although Wesley's regime at Kingswood resonated with Lockean influences regarding fashioning of a gentleman, many of his followers had no such aspirations for their sons.

Wesley was not alone among Evangelicals in believing that a stable home with parents eager and competent to instruct their children was the ideal. He regarded the family as the seat of virtue and piety.[32] Nevertheless, Wesley did not regard piety and learning as mutually exclusive; indeed, he advised parents that they should teach 'the knowledge of God, and the knowledge of letters at the same time'.[33] In regarding education as training for a life of holiness as well as academic attainment, Wesley's educational practice was frequently characterised by tension between piety and learning. At his school in Kingswood, Wesley sought to safeguard the moral and spiritual wellbeing of pupils, while at the same time providing academic learning. He consistently elevated piety over pedagogical qualification when employing Masters and Mistresses, with the result that Masters appear to have been unwilling or unable to enforce the sort of discipline he demanded.

Wesley believed that children, even if they were very young, could have religious experiences. Arguing that they were capable of 'feeling the things of God', Wesley frequently recorded childhood displays of piety in his *Journal*, or published them in *The Arminian Magazine*. He regarded physical self-denial as morally beneficial, and saw frugality, temperance and sobriety as indicators of piety. He was convinced of the importance of introspection, feeling and emotion in religious development. Despite this, Wesley was frequently astonished to discover that displays of religious fervour at Kingswood School were short-lived. He seems to have been unaware that in an introverted and pressurised atmosphere, pupils might imitate the words and behaviour of their Masters in an attempt to please, rather than this being a genuine response to a religious experience.

Although Wesley's preachers were men of piety, many of them came from humble backgrounds, and were poorly educated. Wesley encouraged their advancement in learning by instilling in them a habit of regular reading and study. He also sought to advance their academic learning by offering them tuition at Kingswood School. Ever the Evangelical, Wesley nevertheless advised them that although gaining knowledge was a good thing, 'saving souls was better'.[34] Wesley's preachers' children tended to have more education than the majority of the population since their parents laid more stress on it. The Methodist Connexion supported itinerant preachers by funding schooling for their children, or offering their sons a place at Kingswood School. Although Wesley advised parents that the aim of his school was 'not so much to teach Greek and Latin, as to train up soldiers for Jesus Christ',[35] his ambition appears to have been far from achieved since the records indicate only a small number of pupils went on to become Methodist preachers.[36]

Wesley understood the importance of reading and writing not only as a vehicle for religious instruction, but as an aid to piety. His Arminian thinking argued that all had the promise of salvation through faith, regardless of status or wealth. He had a great deal of sympathy for the poor, and encouraged schooling for their children, but this was often marked by tension between piety and a degree of learning that might give children aspirations. His aim in educating children of the poor was to protect them against the dangerous influences of a non-Christian way of life, not to elevate them 'above their station'. Nevertheless, instructing children gave adult poor within Methodist Societies opportunities to become involved, either within the Society or as teachers or preachers.[37]

Edwards concluded that, inspired by Wesley's example, Methodists became in the century after his death 'the greatest force (apart from the Established Church) in popular education'.[38] Although the notion of 'popular education' belongs to an age beyond Wesley's lifetime, it is clear that his educational legacy is not insignificant. That his thinking was 'of its day', and neither unique nor innovative, does not counter Tranter's assertion that 'what he did was done at great financial, physical and emotional cost, and done in love'.[39]

Joseph Priestley wrote in 1765:

> A man is a friend of his country who observes and endeavours to supply any defects in the methods of educating youth. A well meaning and sensible man may be mistaken, but a good intention, especially if it be not wholly unaccompanied with good sense, ought to be exempt from censure.[40]

Notes

1 Porter (1998) *England in the Eighteenth Century* p. 156–7
2 Plumb (1950) *England in the Eighteenth Century* p. 96
3 Thompson (2013) *The Making of the English Working Class* p. 811
4 Whitehead (1796) *The life of the Rev. John Wesley* p. 502
5 Rosman (2010) *Evangelicals and Culture* p. 151
6 Baker (1984) *BCE* vol. 3 p. 25
7 Ibid. vol. 9 p. 278
8 Ibid. vol. 4 p. 392
9 Wesley (1781) 'A Plain Account of Kingswood School near Bristol' p. 487–92
10 Lynch (2003) 'John Wesley's Editorial Hand' p. 176
11 Baker (1984) *BCE* vol. 3 p. 348
12 Ibid. vol. 3 p. 340–1
13 Wesley (1773) *Thoughts on the Present Scarcity of Provisions* p. 22
14 Ibid. vol. 9 p. 278
15 Heath (1794) *The New History* p. 75
16 Baker (1943) *Richard Terry and Hull Methodism* p. 1–7
17 Rack (2011) *BCE* vol. 10 p. 139
18 Baker (1984) *BCE* vol. 26 p. 32
19 Wesley (1768a) *A Short Account of the School in Kingswood, Near Bristol*
20 Wesley (1781) 'A Plain Account of Kingswood School near Bristol' p. 487–8
21 Fletcher, John (23/8) 'Proposals towards the Sunday Schools', 'Fletcher-Tooth Papers' ref. Box 23, folder 8 p. 15
22 Fletcher, John (17/9) 'A Moral and Evangelical Catechism for the use of Sunday Schools', 'Fletcher-Tooth Papers' ref. Box 17, folder 9
23 Fletcher, John (43/3/8) 'School Questions' for the use of Sunday schools, 'Fletcher-Tooth Papers' ref. Box 43, folder 3, item 8
24 Potter (2013) 'The Influence of Danish Missionaries to India' p. 3–15
25 Wesley (1780) 'A Female Course of Study' in *The Arminian Magazine 1780* p. 602–4

26 Wesley, John (1792) 'Letter from Mary Bishop to John Wesley dated 18 Aug. 1784' in *The Arminian Magazine* p. 51–2
27 Telford (1931) *The Letters of the Rev. John Wesley* vol. 7 p. 228
28 Wesley (1827) *The Works of the Rev. John Wesley* vol. 10 p. 36
29 Sangster (1963) *Pity My Simplicity* p. 97
30 Bailey (2012) *Parenting in England* p. 106
31 Wesley (1749b) *A Short Account of the School in Kingswood* p. 4
32 Baker (1984) *BCE* vol. 3 p. 335–7
33 Wesley (1755) *Instructions for Children, Fourth Edition* p. 6
34 Rack (2011) *BCE* vol. 10 p. 335
35 Baker (1984) *BCE* vol. 26 p. 279
36 Hastling (1898) *The History of Kingswood School* p. 7–127
37 Whyman (2009) *The Pen and the People* p. 14
38 Edwards, Maldwyn (1965) 'John Wesley' in Davies, Rupert & Rupp, Gordon (eds.) *The History of the Methodist Church in Great Britain* vol. 1 Peterborough: Epworth Press p. 67
39 Tranter (1996) 'John Wesley and the Education of Children' p. 33
40 Priestley (1765) *An Essay on a Course of Liberal Education* p. 7–8

Bibliography

Adair, John (1998) *Puritans: Religion and Politics in Seventeenth Century England and America* Stroud: Sutton Publishing
Albisetti, James C. (ed.) et al. (2010) *Girls' Secondary Education in the Western World* New York: Palgrave Macmillan
Andrew, Donna T. (1989) *Philanthropy and Police: London Charity in the Eighteenth Century* Princeton: Princeton University Press
Andrews, Robert M. (2015) 'Women of the Seventeenth- and Eighteenth-century High Church Tradition: A Biographical and Historiographical Exploration of a Forgotten Phenomenon in Anglican History' in *Anglican and Episcopal History* 84. 1 March 2015 p. 49–64
Anon (1704) *The Whole Duty of Man Laid Down in a Plain and Familiar Way for the Life of All, but Especially the Meanest Reader* London: W. Norton
Anon (1706) *An Account of Charity-schools Lately Erected in England, Wales, and Ireland, with the Benefactions Thereto* London: Joseph Downing
Anon (1708) *An Account of Charity-schools Lately Erected in England and Wales, with the Benefactions Thereto* London: Joseph Downing
Anon (1734) *The New Whole Duty of Man, Containing The Faith as Well as Practice of the Present Age, As the Old Whole Duty of Man Was Design'd for Those Unhappy Times in Which It Was Written*, Thirteenth Edition London: Edward Wichsteed
Aries, Philippe (1996) *Centuries of Childhood* London: Pimlico
Armstrong, Anthony (1973) *The Church of England, The Methodists and Society 1700–1800* London: University of London Press
Astell, Mary (1697) *A Serious Proposal to the Ladies, for the Advancement of their True and Greatest Interest* London: Richard Wilkin
Bailey, Joanne (2007) 'Reassessing Parenting' in Berry, Helen & Foyster, Elizabeth (eds.) *The Family in Early Modern England* Cambridge: Cambridge University Press
Bailey, Joanne (2012) *Parenting in England c1760–1830: Emotion, Identity and Generation* Oxford: Oxford University Press
Baker, Frank (1943) *Richard Terry and Hull Methodism: In the Light of a Hitherto Unknown Letter* Wesley Historical Society
Baker, Frank (1948) *Charles Wesley As Revealed by His Letters: The Wesley Historical Society Lectures No.14* London: The Epworth Press
Baker, Frank (ed.-in-chief) (1984–) *Bi-centennial Edition: The Works of John Wesley vol. 1–4 (Sermons), vol. 9 (Methodist Societies), vol. 18–24 (Journals and Diaries), vol. 25–6 (Letters)* Nashville: Abingdon Press

Bibliography

Ball, Hannah (1880) *Memorials of Miss Hannah Ball: The First Sunday School Teacher*, Third Edition London: Wesleyan Conference Office

Barclay, James (1743) *Treatise on Education: or, An Easy Method of Acquiring Language, and Introducing Children to the Knowledge of History, Geography, Mythology, Antiquities, &c. with Reflections on Taste...* Edinburgh: James Cochran and Company

Barker-Benfield, G. J. (1992) *The Culture of Sensibility: Sex and Society in Eighteenth-Century Britain* London: University of Chicago Press

Bayley, Cornelius (attributed to 1790) *An Address to the Public on Sunday Schools, dated 1 August 1784* Manchester: publisher unknown

Bennett, John (1787) *Strictures on Female Education, Chiefly as it Relates to the Culture of the Heart, in Four Essays, By a Clergyman of the Church of England* London: T. Cadell; J. J. G. and J. Robinsons; Rivington; J. Murray; and Dodsley

Benson, Joseph (1766) Letter from Kingswood School to unnamed correspondent, dated 22 Dec. 1766, John Rylands Library 'Joseph Benson Papers' ref. GB 133PLP 7/6/1

Benson, Joseph (c1768a) Letter to Dr Dixon, undated, John Rylands Library 'Joseph Benson Papers' ref. GB 133PLP 7/6/2

Benson, Joseph (c1768b) Letter to John Wesley (attributed), undated, John Rylands Library 'Joseph Benson Papers' ref. GB 133PLP 7/12/28

Bernard, Thomas (1799) *Account of the Foundling Hospital in London for the Maintenance and Education of Exposed and Deserted Young Children*, Second Edition London: Thomas Jones

Berry, Helen & Foyster, Elizabeth (2007) 'Childless Men' in Berry, Helen & Foyster, Elizabeth (eds.) *The Family in Early Modern England* Cambridge: Cambridge University Press

Berry, Helen & Foyster, Elizabeth (2007) *The Family in Early Modern England* Cambridge: Cambridge University Press

Best, Gary Martin (1988) *Wesley and Kingswood: 1738–1988, 250th Conversion Anniversary* Bridgewater: Bigwood and Staple

Best, Gary Martin (1998) *Continuity and Change: A History of Kingswood School 1748–1998* Kingswood: Kingswood School

Best, Gary Martin (2006) *Charles Wesley: A Biography* Peterborough: Epworth

Best, Gary Martin (2012) *Seven Sisters* Weston-Super-Mare: Woodspring Resource Centre

Bett, Henry (1911) 'John Wesley and Charterhouse School', in *Methodist Recorder* 7 December 1911, London

Bishop, A. M. (undated) 'Kingswood School (for Colliers)' Bath: Kingswood School

Bishop, Michael (1977) 'A Detective Story' *The Kingswood School Magazine* vol. 49. no. 467 February 1977 Bath: Kingswood School (unpaginated)

Bishop, Michael (1983) *The Wesley Pulpit and its Background* Bath: Kingswood School

Bishop, Michael (1996) 'Wesley's Four Schools at Kingswood' in Macquiban, Tim (ed.) *Issues in Education: Some Methodist Perspectives* Oxford: Applied Theology Press

Bishop, Michael (2002) 'Wesley and his Kingswood Schools' in Lenton, John (ed.) *Vital Piety and Learning: Methodism and Education* Oxford: Wesley Historical Society

Body, Alfred H. (1936) *John Wesley and Education* London: Epworth Press

Bollmann, Stefan (2008) *Women who Read are Dangerous* London: Merrell

Booth, Frank (1981) 'Robert Raikes: Founder of the Sunday-School Movement' in Ferguson, John (ed.) *Christianity, Society and Education: Robert Raikes Past, Present and Future* London: SPCK

Borsay, Peter (2006) 'Children, Adolescents and Fashionable Urban Society in Eighteenth-Century England' in Muller, Anja (ed.) *Fashioning Childhood in the Eighteenth Century: Age and Identity* Aldershot: Ashgate Press

Boswell, James (1799) *The Life of Samuel Johnson, LL.D. Comprehending an Account of his Studies and Numerous Works* London: Charles Dilly

Bowden, Martha F. (2002) 'Susanna Wesley's Educational Method' in *Journal of the Canadian Church Historical Society* 44. 1 p. 51–62, Toronto: Canadian Church Historical Society

Bowmer, John C. (ed.) (1963–1964) *Proceedings of the Wesley Historical Society* vol. 34 Leicester: Alfred A. Taberer

Bowmer, John C. & Vickers, John A. (eds.) (1995) *The letters of John Pawson: Methodist Itinerant, 1762–1806; vol.3, Closing years (1799–1806)* Peterborough: World Methodist Historical Society

Brantley, Richard E. (1984) *Locke, Wesley, and the Method of English Romanticism* Gainesville: University of Florida

Briggs, Asa (1981) 'Innovation and Adaption: the Eighteenth-Century Setting' in Ferguson, John (ed.) *Christianity, Society and Education: Robert Raikes Past, Present and Future* London: SPCK

Brokesby, Francis (1701) *Of Education with Respect to Grammar Schools and the Universities: Concluding with Directions to Young Students in the Universities* London: John Hartley

Brown-Lawson, Albert (1994) *John Wesley and the Anglican Evangelicals of the Eighteenth Century Bishop* Auckland: The Pentland Press

Buchanan, James (1770) *Plan of an English Grammar School Education; With an Introductory Inquiry…* London: E. & C. Dilly

Burden, Mark (2013) *A Biographical Dictionary of Tutors at the Dissenters' Private Academies, 1660–1729* Dr Williams's Centre for Dissenting Studies, www.english.qmul.ac.uk/drwilliams/pubs/dictionary.html, accessed 1 February 2013

Burton, Vicki Tolar (2008) *Spiritual Literacy in John Wesley's Methodism, Reading, Writing and Speaking to Believe* Waco: Baylor University Press

Butler, Joseph (1745) *A Sermon Preached in the Parish Church of Christ-Church London, on Thursday May 9th 1745, Being the Time of the Yearly Meeting of the Children Educated in the Charity-schools, in and about the Cities of London and Westminster. By … Joseph Lord Bishop of Bristol… . To Which is Annexed, An Account of the Society for Promoting Christian Knowledge* London: J. Oliver

Butler, Melissa A. (2007) 'Early Liberal Roots of Feminism: John Locke's Attack on Patriarchy' in Hirschmann, Nancy J. & McClure, Kirstie M. (eds.) *Feminist Interpretations of John Locke* Pennsylvania: The Pennsylvania State University Press

Bygrave, Stephen (2009) *Uses of Education: Readings in Enlightenment England* Lewisburg: Bucknell University Press

Campbell, Ted A. (1991) *John Wesley and Christian Antiquity: Religious Vision and Cultural Change* Nashville: Kingswood Books

Carter, Philip (2001) *Men and the Emergence of Polite Society, Britain 1600–1800* Harlow: Longman

Church of England (1687) *The ABC with Catechism, That is to Say, An Introduction to be Learned of Every Person Before he be Brought to be Confirmed by the Bishop* London: The Company of Stationers

Clarke, Adam (1832) *Memoirs of the Wesley Family, Collected Principally from Original Documents* New York: J. Collord

Clarke, Adam (1833) *An Account of the Infancy, Religious and Literary Life of Adam Clarke L.L.D., F.A.S.* London: T. S. Clarke

Clarke, John (1720) *An Essay upon the Education of Youth in Grammar-Schools. In Which the Vulgar Method of Teaching is Examined, and a New One Proposed, for the More Easy and Speedy Training up of Youth to the Knowledge of the Learned Languages; Together with History, Chronology, Geography, &c.* London: John Wyat

Cohen, Michele (2000) *Editorial Introduction: Masculinity; Men Defining Men and Gentlemen 1560–1918* Marlborough: Adam Matthew Publicationshttp://www.ampltd.co.uk/digital_guides/masculinity-part-1/editorial-introduction.aspx: accessed 8 April 2013

Cohen, Michelle (2009) 'Familiar Conversation: The Role of the "Familiar Format" in Education in Eighteenth and Nineteenth-Century England' in Hilton, Mary (ed.) & Shefrin, Jill (ed.), *Educating the Child in Enlightenment Britain: Beliefs, Cultures, Practices* Farnham: Ashgate Press

Cox, Nicholas (1978) *Bridging the Gap: A History of the Corporation of the Sons of the Clergy over Three Hundred Years 1655–1978* Oxford: Becket Publications

Cressy, David (1975) *Education in Tudor and Stuart England* London: Edward Arnold

Cunningham, Hugh (2005) *Children and Childhood in Western Society Since 1500* London: Pearson Longman

Curnock, Nehemiah (1909–1916) *The Journal of the Rev. John Wesley, A. M. Sometime Fellow of Lincoln College, Oxford* London: Charles H. Kelly

Dallimore, Arnold (1980) *George Whitefield, The Life and Times of the Great Evangelist of the Eighteenth Century Revival* vol. 1 & 2 Edinburgh: The Banner of Truth Trust

Dallimore, Arnold A. (1992) *Susanna: The Mother of John and Charles Wesley* Darlington: Evangelical Press

Darby, Abiah (1784) Letter to John Fletcher, 22 Jun. 1784, 'Fletcher-Tooth Papers' ref. GB 135MAM/FL/2/7/1

Davis, Rebecca (2014) *Written Maternal Authority and Eighteenth-Century Education in Britain: Educating by the Book* Farnham: Ashgate

Davies, Rupert & Rupp, Gordon (eds.) (1965) *The History of the Methodist Church in Great Britain* vol. 1 Peterborough: Epworth Press

Deacon, Malcolm (1980) *Philip Doddridge of Northampton 1702–1751* Northampton: Northamptonshire Libraries

Doddridge, Philip (1761) *A Plain and Serious Address to the Master of a Family on the Important Subject of Family Religion*, Fourth Edition London: C. Hitch and L. Hawes, J. Buckland, J. Rivington, R. Baldwin, W. Johnston, J. Richardson, S. Crowder and Co. T. Longman, B. Law, T. Field, and H. Payne and W. Cropley

Doddridge, Philip (1790) *Sermons on the Religious Education of Children, Preached at Northampton by Philip Doddridge DD* London: George Jerry Osborne Jun'r

Edwards, Maldwyn (1965) 'John Wesley' in Davies, Rupert & Rupp, Gordon (eds.) *The History of the Methodist Church in Great Britain* vol. 1 Peterborough: Epworth Press

Edwards, Maldwyn (1972) *New Room* Manchester: Penwick (Leeds)

Elliott, Shirley (1981) 'Raikes and Reform' in Ferguson, John (ed.) *Christianity, Society and Education: Robert Raikes Past, Present and Future* London: SPCK

Elliott-Binns, Leonard E. (1953) *The Early Evangelicals: A Religious and Social Study* London: Lutterworth Press

Ezell, Margaret (1983) 'John Locke's Images of Childhood: Early Eighteenth-Century Response to Some Thoughts Concerning Education', *Eighteenth-Century Studies* 17 John Hopkins University Press p. 150–5

Ferguson, John (ed.) (1981) *Christianity, Society and Education: Robert Raikes Past, Present and Future* London: SPCK

Ferguson, John (1981) 'Robert Raikes's First Sunday School' in Ferguson, John (ed.) *Christianity, Society and Education: Robert Raikes Past, Present and Future* London: SPCK

Fisher, Geoffrey & Hurst, Terry (2007) 'The Significance of the Orphan House' in *The Orphan House of John Wesley: Opened 25th March 1743* Newcastle upon Tyne: Wesley Historical Society

Fletcher, Anthony (2008) *Growing up in England: The Experience of Childhood 1600–1914* New Haven: Yale University Press

Fletcher, John (1778) Letter to Vincent Perronet, undated but attributed 1778, 'Wesley Family papers' ref. GB 133 DDWes/2/40

Fletcher, John (17/9) 'A Moral and Evangelical Catechism for the Use of Sunday Schools', 'Fletcher-Tooth Papers' ref. Box 17, folder 9

Fletcher, John (23/8) 'Proposals towards the Sunday Schools', 'Fletcher-Tooth Papers' ref. Box 23, folder 8

Fletcher, John (43/3/4) 'Prayers for the Use of Sunday Schools', 'Fletcher-Tooth Papers' ref. Box 43, folder 3, item 4

Fletcher, John (43/3/8) 'School Questions' for the use of Sunday schools, 'Fletcher-Tooth Papers' ref. Box 43, folder 3, item 8

Forsaith, Peter S. (ed.) (2008) *Unexampled Labours: Letters of the Revd John Fletcher to leaders in the Evangelical Revival* Peterborough: Epworth

Fowler, Simon (2007) *Workhouse; The People: The Places: The Life Behind Doors* Richmond: The National Archives

The Gentleman's Magazine, and Historical Chronicle Volume LIV for the Year MDCCLXXIV (1784) London: John Nichols

The Gentleman's Magazine, and Historical Chronicle, Volume LVII for the Year MDCCLXXXVII – part one (1787) London: John Nichols

Gentry, Peter & Taylor, Paul (2007) *Bold as a Lion: John Cennick – Moravian Evangelist* Leicester: Life Publications

Gibson, Edmund (1727) *Directions Given to the Clergy of the Diocese of London in the Year 1724*, Second Edition London: S. Buckley

Gibson, William (1986) 'Somerset Evangelical Clergy' in *The Proceedings of the Somerset Archaeological and Natural History Society for 1985/6* vol. 130 p. 135–40

Gibson, William (1994) *Church, State and Society, 1760–1850* Basingstoke: MacMillan

Gibson, William (1997) *A Social History of the Domestic Chaplain, 1530–1840* London: Leicester University Press

Gibson, William (2001) *The Church of England 1688–1832, Unity and Accord* London: Routledge

Gibson, William & Ingram, Robert G. (eds.) (2005) *Religious Identities in Britain. 1660–1832* Aldershot: Ashgate

Gibson, William (2007) *Religion and the Enlightenment 1600–1800: Conflict and the Rise of Civic Humanism in Taunton* Oxford: Peter Lang

Gibson, William (2009) 'Samuel Wesley's Conformity Reconsidered', in *Methodist History* 47. 2, January 2009 Madison: The General Commission on Archives and History of the United Methodist Church

Gibson, William, Forsaith, Peter & Wellings, Martin (eds.) (2013) *The Ashgate Research Companion to World Methodism* Farnham: Ashgate

Gill, Sean (1994) *Women and the Church of England: From the Eighteenth Century to the Present* London: SPCK

Giovanopoulos, Anna-Christina (2006) 'The Legal Status of Children in Eighteenth-Century England' in Muller, Anja (ed.) *Fashioning Childhood in the Eighteenth Century: Age and Identity* Aldershot: Ashgate Press

Glaser, Brigitte (2006) 'Gendered Childhoods: on the Discursive Formation of Young Females in the Eighteenth Century' in Muller, Anja (ed.) *Fashioning Childhood in the Eighteenth Century: Age and Identity* Aldershot: Ashgate Press

The Gloucester Journal (12 January 1789) Gloucester: R. Raikes

Goodman, Joyce (2010) 'Class and Religion' in Albisetti, James C. *et al.* (eds) *Girls' Secondary Education in the Western World* New York: Palgrave Macmillan

Gordon, Felicia (2005) 'Filles publiques or Public Women: The Actress as Citizen: Marie Madeleine Jodin (1741–90) and Mary Darby Robinson (1758–1800)' in Knot, Sarah & Taylor, Barbara (eds.) *Women, Gender and Enlightenment* Basingstoke: Palgrave Macmillan

Graham, William T. (1990) *Wesley's Early Experiments in Education* Ilkeston: Moorley's Publishing

Green, Richard (1896) *The Works of John and Charles Wesley: A Bibliography Containing Exact Account of All the Publications Issued by the Brothers Wesley Arranged in Chronological Order, with a List of the Earliest Editions and Descriptive and Illustrative Notes* London: C. H. Kelly

Green, Vivian Hubert Howard (1961) *The Young Mr Wesley* London: Edward Arnold

Gregory, Jeremy (ed.) (2003) *John Wesley: Tercentenary Essays; Bulletin of the John Rylands University Library of Manchester* 85. 2–3 Summer and Autumn 2003 Manchester: The John Rylands University Library

Gregory, Jeremy (2005) 'In the Church I will Live and Die' in Gibson, William & Ingram, Robert G. (eds.) *Religious Identities in Britain. 1660–1832* Aldershot: Ashgate

Gregory, Jeremy (2010) 'The Long Eighteenth Century' in Maddox, Randy L. & Vickers, Jason E. (eds.) *The Cambridge Companion to John Wesley* Cambridge: Cambridge University Press

Gregory, John (1774) *A Father's Legacy to his Daughters; by the Late Dr Gregory of Edinburgh* Edinburgh: W. Creech

Guerrini, Anita (1999) 'A diet for a Sensitive Soul – Vegetarianism in Eighteenth-century Britain' in *Eighteenth-century Life* 23 May 1999 p. 34–42, The John Hopkins University Press

Hanway, Jonas (1766) *An Earnest Appeal for Mercy to the Children of the Poor, Particularly Those Belonging to the Parishes within the Bills of Mortality, Appointed by an Act of Parliament to be Registered* London: J Dodsley, J. Rivington, H. Woodfall and N. Young

Hanway, Jonas (1767) *Letters on the Importance of the Rising Generation of the Labouring Part of Our Fellow-Subjects; Being an Account of the Miserable State of the Infant Parish Poor; … With Political, Moral, and Religious Observations on the Education and Instruction of the Poor, Marriage, and Population, … In Two Volumes* London: A Millar and T. Cadell; and C. March and G. Woodfall

Hanway, Jonas (1786) *A Comprehensive View of Sunday Schools for the Use of the Indigent Inhabitants of Cities, Towns and Villages in England and Wales, with Reflections on the Causes of the Decay of Our Morals and National Piety, and the Means of Removing Them: Also a Copious School Book, for the Use of Sunday Scholars…* London: Dodsley and Sewel

Harding, Alan (2007) *Selina, Countess of Huntingdon* Peterborough: Epworth

Hastling, Arthur Henry Lee (1898) *The History of Kingswood School: Together with Register of Kingswood School and Woodhouse Grove School, and a List of Masters* London: Charles H. Kelly

Hayter, Thomas (1756) *A Sermon Preached in the Parish-Church of Christ-Church, London on Thursday May 1st 1755; Being the Time of the Yearly Meeting of the Children Educated in Charity-schools, in and about the Cities of London and Westminster* London: J. Oliver

Heath, George (1794) *The New History, Survey and Description of the City and Suburbs of Bristol, or Complete Guide…* Bristol: W. Matthews

Heitzenrater, Richard P. (ed.) (1985) *Diary of an Oxford Methodist: Benjamin Ingham, 1733–1734* Durham: Duke University Press

Heitzenrater, Richard P. (1995) *Wesley and the People Called Methodists* Nashville: Abingdon Press

Heitzenrater, Richard P. (2002) *The Poor and the People Called Methodists* Nashville: Kingswood Books

Hempton, David (2003) 'John Wesley and the Rise of Methodism' in Gregory, Jeremy (ed.) *John Wesley: Tercentenary Essays; Bulletin of the John Rylands University Library of Manchester* 85. 2–3 Summer and Autumn 2003 Manchester: The John Rylands University Library

Hilton, Mary (2007) *Women and the Shaping of the Nation's Young: Education and Public Doctrine in Britain 1750–1850* Aldershot: Ashgate Press

Hilton, Mary & Shefrin, Jill (eds.) (2009) *Educating the Child in Enlightenment Britain: Beliefs, Cultures, Practices* Farnham: Ashgate Press

Himmelfarb, Gertrude (2008) *The Roads to Modernity: The British, French and American Enlightenments* London: Vintage Books

Hindmarsh, Bruce D. (2005) *The Evangelical Conversion Narrative: Spiritual Autobiography in Early Modern England* Oxford: Oxford University Press

Hirschmann, Nancy J. (2007) 'Intersectionality Before Intersectionality Was Cool: The Importance of Class to Feminist Interpretations of Locke' in Hirschmann, Nancy J. & McClure, Kirstie M. (eds.) *Feminist Interpretations of John Locke* Pennsylvania: The Pennsylvania State University Press

Hitchcock, Tim (1992) 'Paupers and Preachers: The SPCK and the Parochial Workhouse Movement' in Davidson, Lee, Hitchcock, Tim, Keirn, Tim & Shoemaker, R. B. (eds.) *Stilling the Grumbling Hive: The Responses to Social and Economic Problems in England 1689–1750* New York: Palgrave Macmillan

Holmes, Geoffrey S. (1986) *Politics, Religion, and Society in England, 1672–1742* London: Hambledon Press

Horn, Pamela (1994) *Children's Work and Welfare 1780–1890* Cambridge: Cambridge University Press

Houswitschka, Christophe (2006) 'Locke's Education or Rousseau's Freedom: Alternative Socializations in Modern Societies' in Muller, Anja (ed.) *Fashioning Childhood in the Eighteenth Century* Aldershot: Ashgate Press

Humphreys, John Doddridge (1830) *The Correspondence and Diary of Philip Doddridge, D. D. Illustrative of Various Particulars in His Life Hitherto Unknown: With Notices of Many of His Contemporaries, and a Sketch of the Ecclesiastical History of the Times in Which He Lived* vol. 4 London: Henry Colburn and Richard Bentley

Humphries, Jane (2010) *Childhood and Child Labour in the British Industrial Revolution* Cambridge: Cambridge University Press

Ives, Arthur Glendinning (1970) *Kingswood School in Wesley's Day and Since* London: Epworth Press

Jackson, Thomas (1862) *Memoirs of the Rev. Charles Wesley M.A., Comprising Notices of His Poetry; of the Rise and Progress of Methodism, and of Contemporary Events and Characters…* Third Edition London: Wesleyan Conference Office

Jacob, William M. (2007) *The Clerical Profession in the Long Eighteenth Century, 1680–1840* Oxford: Oxford University Press

Jesse, William (1785) *Rector of Dowles and Chaplain to the Rt. Hon. The Earl of Glasgow The Importance of Education: A Discourse, Preached in Bewdley Chapel, 27 March 1785* Kidderminster: N. Rollason

Jones, M. G. (1964) *The Charity School Movement: A Study of Eighteenth-century Puritanism* London: Frank Cass and Co.
Jones, M. G. (1968) *Hannah More* New York: Greenwood Press
Kamm, Josephine (1965) *Hope Deferred: Girls Education in English History* London: Methuen & Co.
Kennett, White (1706) *The Charity of Schools for Poor Children – Recommended in a Sermon Preach'd in the Parish-church of St. Sepulchres – May 16, 1706* London: Joseph Downing
Kennett, White (1746) *The Christian Scholar: in Rules and Directions for Children and Youth Sent to English Schools. More Especially Design'd for the Poor Boys Taught and Cloathed by Charity in the Parish of St Botolph, Aldgate. Drawn up and Published at the Request of Some of Their Friends and Benefactors*, Ninth Edition London: S. Birt
Kimbrough, ST Jnr & Beckerlegge, Oliver A. (eds.) (1988) *The Unpublished Poetry of Charles Wesley* vol. 1 Nashville: Kingswood Books
Kimbrough, ST Jnr & Newport, Kennett, G. C. (2008) *The Manuscript Journal of the Reverend Charles Wesley M.A.* vol. 1 & 2 Nashville: Abingdon Press
King, Steven (2000) *Poverty and Welfare in England 1700–1850 – A Regional Perspective* Manchester: Manchester University Press
King, Steven & Timmins, Geoffrey (2001) *Making Sense of the Industrial Revolution: English Economy and Society 1700–1850* Manchester: Manchester University Press
Kingswood School archive: Account book, dated 1764–1770
Knott, Sarah & Taylor, Barbara (eds.) (2005) *Women, Gender and Enlightenment* Basingstoke: Palgrave Macmillan
Knox, Vicesimus (1781) *Liberal Education, or, A Practical Treatise on the Methods of Acquiring Useful and Polite Learning* London: Charles Dilly
Langford, Paul (1989) *A Polite and Commercial People: England 1727–1783* Oxford: Clarendon Press
Laqueur, Thomas Walter (1976) *Religion and Respectability: Sunday Schools and Working Class Culture 1780–1850* London: Yale University Press
Laurence, Anne (1994) *Women in England 1500–1760, A Social History* London: Phoenix Press
Lempa, Heikki (2010) 'Moravian Education in an Eighteenth-Century Context' in Lempa, Heikki & Peucker, Paul (eds.) *Self, Community, World: Moravian Education in a Transatlantic World* Cranbury: Associated University Presses
Lenton, John (ed.) (2002) *Vital Piety and Learning: Methodism and Education* Oxford: Wesley Historical Society
Lenton, John (2009) *John Wesley's Preachers: A Social and Statistical Analysis of the British and Irish Preachers Who Entered the Methodist Itinerancy Before 1791* Milton Keynes: Paternoster
Levene, Alysa (2012) *The Childhood of the Poor: Welfare in Eighteenth-century London* Basingstoke: Palgrave Macmillan
Lloyd, Gareth (2007) *Charles Wesley and the Struggle for Methodist Identity* Oxford: Oxford University Press
Locke, John (1690) *An Essay Concerning Human Understanding* London: Tho. Basset
Locke, John (1693) *Some Thoughts Concerning Education* London: A. & J. Churchill
Lynch, Elizabeth (2003) 'John Wesley's Editorial Hand' in Gregory, Jeremy (ed.) *John Wesley: Tercentenary Essays*; *Bulletin of the John Rylands University Library of Manchester* 85. 2–3, Summer and Autumn 2003 Manchester: The John Rylands University Library
MacDonald, James (1822) *Memoirs of the Rev. Joseph Benson* London: T. Cordeux

Mack, Phyllis (2008) *Heart Religion in the British Enlightenment: Gender and Emotion in Early Methodism* Cambridge: Cambridge University Press

Macquiban, Tim (ed.) (1996) *Issues in Education: Some Methodist Perspectives* Oxford: Applied Theology Press

Maddox, Randy L. (2002) 'Kingswood School Library Holdings (ca 1775)' in *Methodist History* 41. 1, October 2002 p. 342–70, The General Commission on Archives and History: Wesley Studies Resource Centre: Duke University, divinity.duke.edu, accessed 24 September 2013

Maddox, Randy L. & Vickers, Jason E. (eds.) (2010) *The Cambridge Companion to John Wesley* Cambridge: Cambridge University Press

Malcolmson, Robert W. (1986) *A Set of Ungovernable People: The Kingswood Colliers in the Eighteenth Century* Bristol: Kingswood District Council

Mandeville, Bernard (1723) 'An Essay on Charity and Charity Schools' in *The Fable of the Bees, or, Private Vices, Public Benefits*, Second Edition London: Edmund Parker

Marquardt, Manfred (1992) *John Wesley's Social Ethics: Praxis and Principles* Nashville: Abingdon Press

Martin, Mary Clare (2009) 'Marketing Religious Identity: Female Educators, Methodist Culture, and Eighteenth-Century Childhood' in Hilton, Mary & Shefrin, Jill (eds.) *Educating the Child in Enlightenment Britain: Beliefs, Cultures, Practices* Farnham: Ashgate Press

Maser, Frederick F. (1990) *The Wesley Sisters* Peterborough: Foundery Press

Mather, Frederick Clare (1992) *High Church Prophet: Bishop Samuel Horsley (1733–1806) and the Caroline Tradition in the Later Georgian Church* Oxford: Clarendon Press

Mathews, Horace Frederick (1949) *Methodism and the Education of the People* London: Epworth Press

Mettele, Gisela (2010) 'Erudition vs. Experience: Gender, Communal Narration, and the Shaping of Eighteenth-Century Moravian Religious Thought' in Lempa, Heikki & Peucker, Paul (eds.), *Self, Community, World: Moravian Education in a Transatlantic World* Cranbury: Associated University Presses

Midgley, Graham (1996) *University Life in Eighteenth-Century Oxford* New Haven: Yale University Press

Milburn, Geoffrey (2007) 'The Significance of the Orphan House' in Fisher, Geoffrey & Hurst, Terry *The Orphan House of John Wesley: Opened 25th March 1743* Newcastle upon Tyne: Wesley Historical Society

Moran, Mary Catherine (2005) 'Between the Savage and the Civil: Dr John Gregory's Natural History of Femininity' in Knott, Sarah & Taylor, Barbara (eds.) *Women, Gender and Enlightenment* Basingstoke: Palgrave Macmillan

More, Hannah (1796a) *The Sunday School* London: Cheap Repository for Moral and Religious Tracts

More, Hannah (1796b) *The History of Hester Wilmot; or, the second part of The Sunday School* London: Cheap Repository for Moral and Religious Tracts

More, Hannah (1796c) *The History of Hester Wilmot; or, the New Gown Part II Being a Continuation of The Sunday School* London: Cheap Repository for Moral and Religious Tracts

More, Hannah, (Attributed to) (1798) *Historical Questions from the Bible, with Answers Written for the Mendip Schools*, Third Edition Bath: S. Hazard

More, Hannah (1799) *Strictures on the Modern System of Female Education with a View to the Principles and Conduct of Women of Rank and Fortune* vol. 1 London: T. Cadell, Jun and W. Davies

Morrow, Thomas M. (1967) *Early Methodist Women* London: Epworth Press
Muller, Anja (ed.) (2006) *Fashioning Childhood in the Eighteenth Century: Age and Identity* Aldershot: Ashgate Press
Muller, Anja (2009) *Framing Childhood in Eighteenth-century Periodicals and Prints 1689–1789* Farnham: Ashgate Press
Naglee, David Ingersoll (1987) *From Font to Faith: John Wesley on Infant Baptism and the Nurture of Children* New York: Peter Lang
Neuburg, Victor E. (1971) *Popular Education in 18th Century England* London: The Woburn Press
Newport, Kenneth G. C. & Campbell, Ted A. (eds.) (2007) *Charles Wesley Life, Literature and Legacy* Peterborough: Epworth Press
Norris, Clive (2013) '*Charles Wesley's Expenditure on Educating his Children*' April 2013, Unpublished research notes for PhD thesis: Oxford Brookes University
Norris, Clive (2014) '*Education, Welfare and Missions*' 15 January 2014, Unpublished research notes for PhD thesis: Oxford Brookes University
Norris, Clive Murray (2015) '*Prophets and Profits: The Financing of Wesleyan Methodism c1740–1800*' PhD: Oxford Brookes University
Ollard, Sidney Leslie (1911) *The Six Students of St. Edmund Hall expelled from the University of Oxford in 1768* Oxford: A. R. Mowbray & Co.
Olleson, Philip (2003) *Samuel Wesley: The Man and his Music* Woodbridge: Boydell Press
Parker, Irene (1914) *Dissenting Academies in England: Their Rise and Progress and their Place among the Educational Systems of the Country* Cambridge: Cambridge University Press
Parr, Samuel (1785) *A Discourse on Education and on the Plans Pursued in Charity-schools* London: T. Cadell and T. Evans
Paxman, David B. (2015) 'Imaging the Child: Bad Parents in the Mid-Eighteenth-Century English Novel' in *Journal for Eighteenth-Century Studies* 38. 1, March 2015 p. 135–151, http://onlinelibrary.wiley.com.oxfordbrookes.idm.oclc.org/enhanced/dui/10.1111/1754-0208.12163/full: accessed June 2015
Payne, Dianne (2006) 'London's Charity School Children: The "Scum of the Parish"?' in *British Journal for Eighteenth-Century Studies*. 29 p. 383–97, Wiley-Blackwell
Percy, Carol (2009) 'Learning and Virtue' in Hilton, Mary & Shefrin, Jill (eds.) *Educating the Child in Enlightenment Britain: Beliefs, Cultures, Practices* Farnham: Ashgate Press
Peters, Michael (2008) *Robert Raikes: The Founder of Sunday School 1780; The Story of How Sunday School Began* Enumclaw: Pleasant Word
Picard, Liza (2000) *Dr Johnson's London: Coffee-Houses and Climbing Boys, Medicine, Toothpaste and Gin, Poverty and Press-Gangs, Freakshows and Female Education* London: Phoenix Press
Pitt, William Morton, MP & FRS (1789) *A Plan for the Extension and Regulation of Sunday Schools, Proposed by William Morton Pitt, ... Approved and Recommended by the Society Instituted in London in the Year 1785* London: The Sunday School Society
Plumb, J. H. (1950) *England in the Eighteenth Century (1714–1818)* Harmondsworth: Penguin Books
Podmore, Colin (1998) *The Moravian Church in England 1728–1760* Oxford: Clarendon Press
Pollock, Linda A. (1983) *Forgotten Children: Parent-child Relations from 1500 to 1900* Cambridge: Cambridge University Press
Porter, Roy (1998) *England in the Eighteenth Century* London: The Folio Society
Porter, Roy (2000) *Enlightenment: Britain and the Creation of the Modern World* London: Penguin Books

Potter, Claire (2013) '*The Influence of Danish Missionaries to India on Susanna Wesley's Methods of Education and Inspiration, and the Subsequent Influence on John Wesley*' Unpublished paper given at the Oxford Institute of Methodist Theological Studies, August 2013

Priestley, Joseph (1765) *An Essay on a Course of Liberal Education for Civil and Active Life.... To Which are Added, Remarks on a Code of Education, Proposed by Dr Brown, in a Late Treatise, Intitled, Thoughts on Civil Liberty, &c.* London: C. Henderson, T. Becket, De Hondt, J. Johnson and Davenport

Priestley, Joseph (1778) *Miscellaneous Observations Relating to Education. More Especially, as It Respects the Conduct of the Mind* Bath: R. Cuttwell

Pugh, Gillian (2007) *London's Forgotten Children: Thomas Coram and the Foundling Hospital* Stroud: Tempus Publishing

Rack, Henry D. (2002) *Reasonable Enthusiast: John Wesley and the Rise of Methodism*, Third Edition London: Epworth Press

Rack, Henry D. (ed.) (2011) *Bi-centennial Edition: The Works of John Wesley vol. 10 (The Methodist Societies, The Minutes of Conference)* Nashville: Abingdon Press

Raikes, Robert (1785) 'An Account of the Sunday-Charity Schools, Lately Begun in Various Parts of England, Gloucester, June 5 1784' in Wesley, John (ed.) *The Arminian Magazine* p. 41–3

Raikes, Robert (1787) Letter to the 'Society Established in London for the Support and Encouragement of Sunday Schools, Gloucester, 7 Oct. 1786' in *The Gentleman's Magazine, and Historical Chronicle, Volume LVII for the Year MDCCLXXXVII – part one* London: John Nichols

Rand, Benjamin (ed.) (1927) *The Correspondence of John Locke and Edward Clarke: Edited, with a Biographical Study* London: Oxford University Press

The Records of Fonmon Castle (1953) Glamorgan: Brown & Sons

Rivers, Isabel & Wykes, David L. (eds.) (2008) *Joseph Priestley, Scientist, Philosopher and Theologian* Oxford: Oxford University Press

Rivers, Isabel (2010) 'John Wesley as Editor and Publisher' in Maddox, Randy L. & Vickers, Jason E. (eds.) *The Cambridge Companion to John Wesley* Cambridge: Cambridge University Press

Rodell, Jonathan (2013) 'Methodism and Social Justice' in Gibson, William, Forsaith, Peter & Wellings, Martin (eds.) *The Ashgate Research Companion to World Methodism* Farnham: Ashgate

Rogal, Samuel J. (1994) 'Ladies Huntingdon, Glenorchy, and Maxwell: Militant Methodist Women' in *Methodist History* 32. 2 January 1994 p. 126–32

Rosman, Doreen (2010) *Evangelicals and Culture, 1790–1833*, Second Edition Oregon: Pickwick Publications

Rousseau, Jean-Jacques (1762) *Emilius and Sophia: or A New System of Education* London: R. Griffiths, T. Becket and P. A. de Hondt

Sackett, A. Barrett (1972) *James Rouquet and his Part in Early Methodism* Chester: Wesley Historical Society

Sangster, Paul (1963) *Pity My Simplicity: The Evangelical Revival and the Religious Education of Children 1738–1800* London: Epworth Press

Schlenther, Boyd Stanley (1997) *Queen of the Methodists: The Countess of Huntingdon and the Eighteenth-century Crisis of Faith and Society* Durham: Durham Academic Press

Schmid, Pia (2010) 'Moravian Memoirs as a Source for the History of Education' in Lempa, Heikki & Peucker, Paul (eds.) *Self, Community, World: Moravian Education in a Transatlantic World* Cranbury: Associated University Presses

Schunka, Alexander (2010) 'A Missing Link: Daniel Ernst Jablonski as the Connection Between Comenius and Zinzendorf' in Lempa, Heikki & Peucker, Paul (eds.) *Self, Community, World: Moravian Education in a Transatlantic World* Cranbury: Associated University Presses

Shefrin, Jill (2009) 'Adapted for and Used in Infants' Schools' in Hilton, Mary & Shefrin, Jill (eds.) *Educating the Child in Enlightenment Britain: Beliefs, Cultures, Practices* Farnham: Ashgate Press

Shenstone, William (1742) *The School-mistress, A Poem. In Imitation of Spenser* London: R. Dodsley

Smith, Adam (1776) *An Inquiry into the Nature and Causes of the Wealth of Nations* vol. 1 Dublin: Messrs. Whitestone, Chamberlaine, W. Watson, Potts, S. Watson and 15 others

Smith, Adam (1790) *The Theory of Moral Sentiments; or, An Essay Towards an Analysis of the Principles by Which Men Naturally Judge Concerning the Conduct and Character, First of Their Neighbours, and Afterwards of Themselves...* vol. 2, Sixth Edition London: A. Strahan; A. Cadell; W. Creech, and J. Bell & Co.

Smith, Timothy Wilson (2004) *Johnson* London: Hans Publishing

Snowden, Rita F. (1963) *Such a Woman: The Story of Susannah Wesley* London: Epworth Press

Soloway, Richard A. (1969) *Prelates and People: Ecclesiastical Social Thought in England 1783–1852* London: Routledge

Speck, W. A. (1977) *Stability and Strife: England 1714–1760* London: Edward Arnold

Stamp, William Wood (1863) *The Orphan-house of Wesley; with Notices of Early Methodism in Newcastle-upon-Tyne, And Its Vicinity* London: John Mason

Stevenson, George John (1872) *City Road Chapel London and Its Associations Historical, Biographical and Memorial* London: George J. Stevenson

Stewart, W. A. Campbell (1953) *Quakers and Education: As Seen in their Schools in England* London: The Epworth Press

Stott, Anne (2003) *Hannah More: The First Victorian* Oxford: Oxford University Press

Stott, Anne (2009) 'Evangelicalism and Enlightenment: The Educational Agenda of Hannah More' in Hilton, Mary & Shefrin, Jill (eds.) *Educating the Child in Enlightenment Britain: Beliefs, Cultures, Practices* Farnham: Ashgate Press

Streiff, Patrick (2001) *Reluctant Saint? A Theological Biography of Fletcher of Madeley* Peterborough: Epworth Press

Tadmor, Naomi (2001) *Family and Friends in Eighteenth-Century England: Household, Kinship and Patronage* Cambridge: Cambridge University Press

Telford, John (ed.) (1931) *The Letters of the Rev. John Wesley*, A.M. (8 volumes) London: The Epworth Press

Thompson, E. P. (2013) *The Making of the English Working Class* London: Penguin Books

Thompson, Edgar W. (1938) *Wesley at Charterhouse* London: Epworth Press

Thompson, H. P. (1954) *Thomas Bray* London: SPCK

Told, Silas (1786) *An Account of the Life, and Dealings of God with Silas Told, Late Preacher of the Gospel: Wherein is Set Forth the Wonderful Display of Divine Providence Towards Him When at Sea, His Many Sufferings Abroad...* London: Gilbert and Plummer, and T. Scollick

Tomkins, Stephen (2010) *The Clapham Sect: How Wilberforce's Circle Transformed Britain* Oxford: Lion Hudson

Tompson, Richard S. (1971) *Classics or Charity? The Dilemma of the Eighteenth-Century Grammar School* Manchester: Manchester University Press

Tranter, Donald (1996) 'John Wesley and the Education of Children' in Macquiban, Tim (ed.) *Issues in Education: Some Methodist Perspectives* Oxford: Applied Theology Press

Trimmer, Sarah (1787) *The Economy of Charity, or, An Address to Ladies Concerning Sunday-schools; the Establishment of Schools of Industry under Female Inspection and the Distribution of Voluntary Benefactions; … To Which is Added an Appendix, Containing an Account of the Sunday-schools in Old Brentford* London: T. Bensley; for T. Longman; G. G. J. and J. Robinson; and J. Johnson

Trimmer, Sarah (1792) *Reflections upon the Education of Children in Charity Schools* London: Longman

Tudur, Geraint (2000) *Howell Harris: From Conversion to Separation 1735–1750* Cardiff: Cardiff University Press

Turberville, Arthur Stanley (ed.) (1952) *Johnson's England: An Account of the Life and Manners of his Age* vol. 1–2 Oxford: Clarendon Press

Turnbull, Richard (2012) *Reviving the Heart: The Story of the Eighteenth Century Revival* Oxford: Lion Hudson

Turner, William (1793) *Sermons on Various Subjects: Published at the Request of a Congregation of Protestant Dissenters in Wakefield* London: Joseph Johnson

Tyacke, Nicolas (2001) *Aspects of English Protestantism c1530–1700* Manchester: Manchester University Press

Tye, Sally (2014) 'Religion, The SPCK and the Westminster Workhouses: Re-enchanting the Eighteenth-Century Workhouse' PhD thesis: Oxford Brookes University

Tyerman, Luke (1870) *The Life and Times of the Rev. John Wesley, M.A. Founder of the Methodists* vol. 1 London: Hodder and Stoughton

Tyson, John R. & Schlenther, B. S. (2006) *In the Midst of Early Methodism: Lady Huntingdon and Her Correspondence* Plymouth: The Scarecrow Press

Vickers, Jason E. (2009) *Wesley: A Guide for the Perplexed* London: T & T Clark

Vogt, Peter (2010) 'Headless and Un-Erudite: Anti-Intellectual Tendencies in Zinzendorf's Approach to Education' Lempa, Heikki & Peucker, Paul (eds.) *Self, Community, World: Moravian Education in a Transatlantic World* Cranbury: Associated University Presses

Wallace, Charles (ed.) (1997) *Susanna Wesley: The Complete Writings* New York: Oxford University Press

Wallace, Charles (2007) 'Charles Wesley and Susanna' in Newport, Kenneth G. C. & Campbell, Ted A. (eds.) *Charles Wesley Life, Literature and Legacy* Peterborough: Epworth Press

Walsh, John, Haydon, Colin & Taylor, Stephen (eds.) (1993) *The Church of England c.1689–c.1833: From Toleration to Tractarianism* Cambridge: Cambridge University Press

Watts, Isaac (1728) *An Essay Towards the Encouragement of Charity Schools Particularly Those Which Are Supported by Protestant Dissenters, for Teaching the Children of the Poor to Read and Work: Together with Some Apology for Those Schools… To Which is Prefix'd, An Address to the Supporters of These Schools* London: John Clark and Richard Hett: Emanuel Matthews, and Richard Ford

Wearmouth, Robert F. (1945) *Methodism and the Common People of the Eighteenth Century* London: The Epworth Press

Welch, Edwin (1995) *Spiritual Pilgrim: A Reassessment of the Life of the Countess of Huntingdon* Cardiff: University of Wales

Wesley, Charles (1749a) Letter to Mrs Mary Jones, dated 30 Oct. 1749, John Rylands Library 'Charles Wesley Papers' [copy] reference GB133 DDCW/1/25 [original at Glamorgan County Records Office]

Wesley, Charles (1749b) Letter to Mrs Mary Jones, dated 7 Nov. 1749, John Rylands Library 'Charles Wesley Papers' [copy] reference GB133 DDCW/1/27 [original at Glamorgan County Records Office]

Wesley, Charles (1750a) Letter to Mrs Mary Jones, dated 11 Jan. 1750, 'Charles Wesley Papers' [copy] reference GB133 DDCW/1/28 [original at Glamorgan County Records Office]

Wesley, Charles (1750b) Letter to Mrs Mary Jones, dated 13 Jan. 1750, 'Charles Wesley Papers' [copy] reference GB133 DDCW/1/30 [original at Glamorgan County Records Office]

Wesley, Charles (1751a) Letter to Mrs Mary Jones, dated 29 Dec. 1751, 'Charles Wesley Papers' [copy] reference GB133 DDCW/1/42A [original at Glamorgan County Records Office]

Wesley, Charles (1751b) letter to Mrs Mary Jones, dated 31 Dec. 1751, 'Charles Wesley Papers' [copy] reference GB133 DDCW/1/42B [original at Glamorgan County Records Office]

Wesley, Charles (c1776) fragment of a letter to Samuel Wesley junior, undated but attributed c1776 'The Wesley Family Papers' ref. GB133 DDWF/27/7

Wesley, Charles (1780) *A Collection of Hymns for the Use of the People Called Methodists* London: J. Paramore

Wesley, John (1746) *Lessons for Children* Bristol: Felix Farley

Wesley, John (1747) *Lessons for Children, Part II* Bristol: Felix Farley

Wesley, John (1748) *Lessons for Children, Part III* Bristol: Felix Farley

Wesley, John (1749a) *A Christian Library, Consisting of Extracts from and Abridgment of the Choicest Pieces of Practical Divinity, Which Have Been Publish'd in the English Tongue* vol. 21 Bristol: Felix Farley

Wesley, John (1749b) *A Short Account of the School in Kingswood, Near Bristol* Bristol: Felix Farley

Wesley, John (1749c) *The Manners of the Antient Christians Extracted from a French Author* Bristol: Felix Farley

Wesley, John (1754a) *Lessons for Children, Part IV* London: Henry Cock

Wesley, John (1754b) Letter to Samuel Furley, dated 30 Mar. 1754 [Kingswood School archive]

Wesley, John (1755) *Instructions for Children*, Fourth Edition London: Henry Cock

Wesley, John (1765) *Thoughts on a Single Life* London: J. Paramore

Wesley, John (1768a) *A Short Account of the School in Kingswood, Near Bristol* Bristol: William Pine

Wesley, John (1768b) Letter from John Wesley to Joseph Benson, dated 7 Nov. 1768 [Kingswood School archive]

Wesley, John (1768?) Letter to Joseph Benson, undated but attributed 1769 [Kingswood School archive] Author's note: the evidence suggests this letter was actually written in 1768

Wesley, John (1769) Letter to Joseph Benson, undated but attributed 1769 [Kingswood School Archive]

Wesley, John (1773) *Thoughts on the Present Scarcity of Provisions* London: R. Hawes

Wesley, John (1778–1797) *The Arminian Magazine: Consisting Chiefly of Extracts and Original Treatises on Universal Redemption* 1–20, London: J. Paramore

Wesley, John (1778) 'Letter to John Wesley dated 9 Aug. 1748' in *The Arminian Magazine for the Year 1778, Consisting Chiefly of Extracts and Original Treatises on Universal Redemption* London: J. Paramore p. 246

Wesley, John (1779) *Minutes of Several Conversations, between the Rev. John Wesley, A.M. and the Preachers in Connection with Him, Containing the Form of Discipline Established Among the Preachers and People in the Methodist Societies* London: G. Whitfield

Wesley, John (1780) 'A Female Course of Study, Only Intended for Those, Who Have a Good Understanding and Much Leisure' in *The Arminian Magazine for the year 1780, Consisting Chiefly of Extracts and Original Treatises on Universal Redemption* 3 p. 602–4, London: J. Paramore

Wesley, John (1781) 'A Plain Account of Kingswood School near Bristol', in *The Arminian Magazine for the Year 1781, Consisting Chiefly of Extracts and Original Treatises on Universal Redemption* 4 p. 381–4, 432–5, 486–7, London: J. Paramore

Wesley, John (1783a) 'A Thought on the Manner of Educating Children' in *The Arminian Magazine, for the Year 1783, Consisting of Extracts and Original Treatises on Universal Redemption* 6 p. 380–3, London: J. Paramore

Wesley, John (1783b) *The Duty and Advantage of Early Rising* London: J. Paramore

Wesley, John (1787a) Letter to Thomas McGeary, dated 15 Feb. 1787 [Kingswood School archive]

Wesley, John (1787b) 'A Short Account of Miss Sarah Butler' in *The Arminian Magazine for the Year 1787, Consisting Chiefly of Extracts and Original Treatises on Universal Redemption* London: J. Paramore p. 246

Wesley, John (1787c) 'Thoughts on Methodism' in *The Arminian Magazine for the Year 1787, Consisting Chiefly of Extracts and Original Treatises on Universal Redemption* 10 p. 100–1, London: J. Paramore

Wesley, John (1788a) 'An Account of a Sunday School' in *The Arminian Magazine for the year 1788, Consisting Chiefly of Extracts and Original Treatises on Universal Redemption* 11 p. 489–90, London: J. Paramore

Wesley, John (1788b) 'An Account of the work of God begun among the Children at Whittlebury' in *The Arminian Magazine for the Year 1788, Consisting Chiefly of Extracts and Original Treatises on Universal Redemption* 11 p. 491–4, London: J. Paramore

Wesley, John (1788c) 'An Extract from a Poem on Slavery by Hannah More' in *The Arminian Magazine for the year 1788, Consisting Chiefly of Extracts and Original Treatises on Universal Redemption* 11 p. 558–60, 612–16, London: J. Paramore

Wesley, John (1788d) 'Letter from Mary Bishop to John Wesley dated 4 March 1777' in *The Arminian Magazine for the Year 1788, Consisting Chiefly of Extracts and Original Treatises on Universal Redemption* 11 p. 101–2, London: J. Paramore

Wesley, John (1788e) 'Letter to John Wesley from William Spencer dated 9 August 1748' in *The Arminian Magazine for the Year 1788, Consisting Chiefly of Extracts and Original Treatises on Universal Redemption* p. 533–4, London: J. Paramore

Wesley, John (1792) 'Letter from Mary Bishop to John Wesley dated 18 Aug 1784' in *The Arminian Magazine for the Year 1792, Consisting Chiefly of Extracts and Original Treatises on Universal Redemption* 4 p. 51–2, London: J. Paramore

Wesley, John (1827) *The Works of the Rev. John Wesley in Ten Volumes, Containing Tracts and Letters on Various Subjects*; First American Edition New York: J. & J. Harper

Wesley, John (1862) *Minutes of The Methodist Conference from the First held in London 1744–1798 and Large Minutes 1753–1789* London: John Mason

Wesley, Samuel (1703) *A Letter from a Country Divine to his Friend in London, Concerning the Education of the Dissenters, in Their Private Academies; … Humbly Offer'd to the Consideration of the Grand Committee of Parliament for Religion, Now Sitting* London: Robert Clavel

Wesley, Samuel (1707) *Reply to Mr Palmer's Vindication of the Learning, Loyalty, Morals and Most Christian Behaviour of the Dissenters towards the Church of England* London: Robert Clavel

Whitefield, George (1738) *The Great Duty of Family Religion – A Sermon Preached at the Parish Church of Saint Vedast, Foster-lane* London: W. Bowyer

Whitehead, John (1796) *The Life of the Rev. John Wesley, M.A. Some Time Fellow of Lincoln-College, Oxford. Collected from his Private Papers and Printed Works* vol. 2 London: Stephen Couchman

Whitehouse, Tessa (ed.) (2011) *Dissenting Education and the Legacy of John Jennings, c.1720–c.1729*, Second edition revised 2011, Dr Williams' Centre for Dissenting Studies, www.english.qmul.ac.uk/drwilliams/pubs, accessed 1 February 2013

Whitehouse, Tessa (2011) 'Introduction to John Jenning's Academy Timetable and Reading Lists' in Whitehouse, Tessa (ed.), *Dissenting Education and the Legacy of John Jennings, c.1720–c.1729*, Second Edition revised 2011, Dr Williams' Centre for Dissenting Studies, www.english.qmul.ac.uk/drwilliams/pubs, accessed 1 February 2013

Whyman, Susan E. (2009) *The Pen and the People: English Letter Writers 1660–1800* Oxford: Oxford University Press

Wilson, David Robert (2010) '*Church and Chapel: Parish Ministry and Methodism in Madeley c1760–1785 – with special reference to the Ministry of John Fletcher*', PhD thesis: University of Manchester

Woodley, Sophia (2009) 'Oh Miserable and Most Ruinous Measure: The Debate between Private and Public Education in Britain, 1760–1800' in Hilton, Mary & Shefrin, Jill (eds.) *Educating the Child in Enlightenment Britain: Beliefs, Cultures, Practices* Farnham: Ashgate Press

Wykes, David L. (2008) 'Joseph Priestley, Minister, and Teacher' in Rivers, Isabel & Wykes, David L. (eds.) *Joseph Priestley, Scientist, Philosopher and Theologian* Oxford: Oxford University Press

Yonan, Jonathan (2010) 'Evangelicalism and Enlightenment: Two Generations in the Okely Family' in Lempa, Heikki & Peucker, Paul (eds.) *Self, Community, World: Moravian Education in a Transatlantic World* Cranbury: Associated University Presses

Index

adolescent boys 46, 71–2, 120
Annesley, Samuel (father of Susanna Wesley) 42
arithmetic 86–7, 92, 115, 153
Arminians 10, 64–6, 117–18; doctrine of free will 3, 36, 97 *see also* Wesley, John
Astell, Mary 18–19, 29, 40

Ball, Hannah 153–4
Barclay, James 63, 115
Bayley, Cornelius 155
Bennett, John 18
Benson, Joseph 96; at Kingswood 66, 69–70, 75 106, 108, 119, 131, 133–4; at Trevecka 137–40
Berridge, John 136, 139
Bishop, Mary 41, 61–2, 138, 177
Book Room, The *see* Foundery, The
Bosanquet, Mary *see* Fletcher, Mary
Brokesby, Francis 6, 21
Buchanan, James 17
Butler, Joseph 26

Calvinists 64–6, 117–18, 136; doctrine of predestination 3, 36, 66, 89, 136, 140–1 *see also* Wesley, John
catechism 6, 44, 62, 85–6, 92, 149–51, 157, 162–4
Cecil, Richard 132
Cennick, John 89–90
Chapone, Hester 19
charity schools *see* schools
Charterhouse School *see* Wesley, John
Cheap Repository Tracts *see* More, Hannah
Cheyne, George 68
childhood, concepts of 5–6, 13–18, 25, 29

Christ Church *see* Wesley, John
Church of England 3, 7–8, 25–8, 46, 49, 64–5, 86, 151–2; Thirty-nine articles 33n93, 64–6, 114 *see also* clergy
Clarke, Adam 37–8, 110, 130, 134–5, 142
Clarke, John 115
class 7, 8, 26, 28, 98, 99n4, 152
clergy (Anglican) 3, 7, 21, 46, 64, 132, 139, 149–52
Coram, Thomas 76–7, 86–7

dancing 14, 19–20, 23, 44, 62, 177
Darby, Abiah 156
daughters *see* family
diary writing 20, 47, 72
diet 44, 67–8, 109, 119
Dissent 7–8, 20, 24–5, 36, 136–7, 139, 154, 164
Dissenting academies and schools *see* education, Dissenting
Doddridge, Phillip 25, 40, 74, 92, 117–20, 128

education: classical 7, 13, 19, 22–4, 29, 115, 120; Dissenting 7, 24, 29, 42, 115–18, 120–1, 176; female 9, 18–20, 41, 61, 85–7, 158–9 *see also* Wesley, John; private 20–3, 29 *see also* tutors; public 7, 18, 21–3, 29, 110, 114–15, 176–7 *see also* schools
effeminacy *see* gender
Emile *see* Rousseau
emotion, displays of 9, 58, 69, 71–2, 76, 178
Epworth *see* Wesley, John
Evangelicals 5, 17, 20, 28, 132, 148, 159, 173

family 18, 29, 108, 127–8, 152–3; daughters 14, 19, 29, 176; sons 13–14, 29, 176 *see also* parents
fasting 47, 67, 70, 109
fathers *see* parents
female educators *see* education, female
Fetter Lane Society 49–50
Fletcher, John 96–8, 143n12; and Kingswood 134; Sunday schools 96, 156–7; at Trevecka 137–41
Fletcher, Mary (nee Bosanquet) 61–2, 96, 157, 166
Fox, George 4, 39
Foundery, The 50, 67, 91–5; Book Room 73, 81n122, 91, 94; Told, Silas 92, 177
Foundling Hospital, The 85–6 *see also* Coram, Thomas
Francke, August Hermann 48 *see also* Halle
French Revolution 8, 10, 28, 163–4, 166

gender 17–23, 29, 40–2, 60, 85–7, 92, 156; effeminacy 7, 23, 107, 177; gentlemen, fashioning of 5, 9, 13–14, 107–8, 116, 177; manliness/masculinity 14, 17–18, 23, 71, 107, 177; girls & young women 9, 18, 20, 41, 61, 85–7, 158–9
governesses 20, 59, 176
Gregory, John 18–19
Grimshaw, William 60, 122n33

Halle 48–9, 88, 93
Hanway, Jonas 6, 151, 153
Hayter, Thomas 6, 85–6
heart religion *see* Moravians
Henderson, John 72
Herrnhut *see* Moravians
Hindmarsh, James 69–71
Holy Club 45–9, 51, 67
Horsley, Samuel 151, 164–5
Huntingdon, Lady Selina (Countess of) 38, 46, 64–5, 128; at Trevecka 136–43

industriousness 8–9, 15–16, 36, 68, 76, 86
introspection 9, 48, 69, 72, 175, 178

Jena *see* Moravians
Jennings, John 81n138, 117
Jesse, William 149
Johnson, Samuel 22–3, 47, 53n46, 65, 83–4
Jones, Mary 38, 69, 77n20, 106, 110–11, 121

Kennett, White 6, 8, 22, 34n114, 63, 92, 103n107
Kingswood: academical course 64–6, 116, 130, 142, 173, 175; account books 66, 117, 119; boarding school 2, 4–5, 60–1, 63, 68–71, 75, 105–11, 129–34; colliers 87–8, 101n48; colliers school 2, 58, 88–90, 145n64; girls at 60–1, 107, 120, 177; parlour boarders 10, 58, 60, 106, 110, 127, 130, 142; water supply 109–10
Knox, Vicesimus 19, 23

Law, William 47, 51, 67, 81n133
literacy 6, 22, 85, 87, 152, 157, 172
Lloyd, Samuel 60–1, 123n62, 177
Locke, John 5, 13–18, 29, 39, 51, 97–8, 117, 176; on the poor 24, 84; working schools 25

Mandeville, Bernard 6, 8, 21, 26–7, 51n1, 83, 128
manliness *see* gender
masculinity *see* gender
Maurice, Thomas 68, 70
Maxwell, Lady Darcy 63, 97
McGeary, Thomas 63, 131, 135, 141
Methodism 2, 51, 71, 84, 97–8, 128, 132, 139
Methodist: Conference 62, 73, 94, 105, 109, 128–34; day schools 41, 87, 90–9; preaching houses 50, 84, 89, 93–6; Societies 89–91, 98, 109, 133, 172; Sunday schools 153–7
Methodists 9, 71, 84, 136, 156
Molther, Philip *see* Moravians
Moravians 36, 50–1, 71; heart religion 48–9, 69, 174 Herrnhut 49, 51; Jena 49, 51; Molther, Philip 50; Spangenberg, August Gottlieb 49–50
More, Hannah 2, 17, 148, 159–66; Cheap Repository Tracts 10, 162, 166; on female education 17–20; Mendip schools 159–66
Morton, Charles 42
mothers *see* parents

needlework/sewing 20, 60, 87, 92, 98, 158
New Room, The (Bristol) 89, 93–5, 102n63
Northampton Academy 74, 93, 117–20, 145n69

original sin 1, 6, 10, 13, 15–17, 161, 176
Orphan House (Newcastle) 67, 93–5, 155–6
Owen, Frances 61, 177
Oxford University 9, 24, 42, 45–8, 51, 64, 118, 132, 173; St. Edmund Hall 58, 64–6, 76, 116, 127, 140, 146n88 *see also* Wesley, John

Paine, Thomas 28, 164
parents 21, 24, 27, 36; fathers 6, 14, 17, 108, 176; mothers 3, 6, 9, 13–14, 17–18, 29, 148, 163; parenting 1, 2, 6, 15–17, 29, 38, 67, 86 *see also* Wesley, John
parlour boarders *see* Kingswood School
Pawson, John 108, 131–2
philanthropy 13, 25, 148, 150–1, 165
piety 4–7, 9, 48–50, 59, 63, 107, 127–8, 132
Pitt, William Morton 151
Port Royal schools 48
predestination *see* Calvinists
Priestley, Joseph 87, 116, 118, 179
Puritan 1, 3, 6, 15, 17, 36–8, 111

Quakers 4, 24, 39, 156

Raikes, Robert 149–52, 154, 156, 161, 166
reading 6–7, 20–1, 40–1, 60, 73, 85–7, 132–3, 152, 157
reason 4, 14, 16, 18–19, 69, 98, 160
religious revivals 68–72, 76, 178
Romaine, William 152
rote learning 14, 19, 22, 161
Rousseau, Jean-Jacques 5–6, 16–18, 39

St. Edmund Hall *see* Oxford
salvation 4, 8, 17, 89, 95, 97, 106
Salzburgers 88 *see also* Halle
schools: charity 8, 25–8, 84–7, 91; dame 22; grammar schools 7, 13–14, 22, 24, 114–16; of industry 158–9; *see also* education
self-denial 9, 45, 58, 67–8, 175
Smith, Adam 6, 8, 18, 78n52, 83–4, 152
Society for Promoting Christian Knowledge (SPCK) 25–7, 42, 91, 151, 164
sons *see* family
Spangenberg, August Gottlieb *see* Moravians
Sunday schools 10, 28, 165–6; Anglican 149–53, 157–65; Methodist 153–7

teachers 22–3, 27, 63, 158–9, 161–2, 165; Masters/ushers 4, 22, 46, 114; pay 21, 63, 155; female educators 18, 20–2, 41–4, 59–62, 90, 93, 97, 107, 157–66
Told, Silas *see* Foundery, The
toys (and games) 16, 44, 107, 113
Trevecka College 10, 72, 127, 136–41, 173 *see also* Benson, Joseph; Fletcher, John; *and* Huntingdon, Lady
Trimmer, Sarah 2, 18, 32n51, 52n24, 78n51, 148, 161, 166; on the poor 28, 84–5, 100n30, 100n32; Sunday schools 157–9
Turner, William 151
tutors 13–14, 16, 19, 21, 24, 46, 176 *see also* education, private

universities 23–4, 29, 36, 41, 51, 55n97, 116, 132, 173–4 *see also* Oxford

Veal, Edward 42

Warburton, William 7, 51
Warrington Academy 116–18
Watts, Isaac 6, 23, 25, 85–7
Wesley, Charles 38, 69, 107, 113–14, 121; children of 60, 73, 112–13, 121; Holy Club 47, 51; Kingswood 90, 105, 108, 110–13, 121; and Trevecka 136, 138
Wesley, Emelia [Emily] (sister of John) 44, 59–60, 176
Wesley, Hetty [Mehetabel or Kitty] (sister of John) 59
Wesley, John: Arminian Magazine 75; Arminian philosophy 1, 9–10, 36, 83, 89–90, 95, 139–41 see also Arminians; at Charterhouse 3, 9, 45, 51, 125n97; on children 5, 37–9, 83, 87, 92, 95, 175; on child-rearing 1, 36–7, 39–40, 59, 127–9; at Christ Church & Lincoln College (Oxford) 3, 45, 47, 133; as editor 3, 9, 72–5, 77; at Epworth 3, 40–5, 50, 128; on female education 4, 9–10, 40–1, 50, 58–62, 76, 129, 176–7; on marriage 129, 142n13; on Oxford 58, 64–6, 76, 116–17, 132, 173, 175; on parenting 4, 36–8, 128–9, 142, 174, 178; on Methodist preachers 69, 95, 99n10, 110, 113, 132–6, 142, 175, 178; on teachers 63–4, 76
Wesley, Kezzia [Kezze or Kez] (sister of John) 59–60, 73, 176

Wesley, Martha [Patty or Pat] (sister of John) 37, 59
Wesley, Samuel (brother of John) 41, 43, 45, 74, 101n48
Wesley, Samuel (father of John) 3, 41–5, 56n116, 59, 74
Wesley, Susanna (mother of John) 3, 9, 36–7, 39, 41–5, 50–1, 67, 92, 174; 'education letter' 2–3, 43, 173–4; education of daughters 40–2, 59

Whitefield, George 56n121 65, 88–90, 128, 136, 139–40, 154, 175
Whole Duty of Man, The 26, 86, 127–8
Wilberforce, William 160–2
writing 6, 20–1, 48, 60, 85–7, 92, 115, 178

Zinzendorf, Count Nikolaus Ludwig von 48–51, 69